BIBLE
MARY

The Mother of Jesus in the Word of God

JOHN R. WAISS

Catholic
Answers
Press

Published by Catholic Answers, Inc.
2020 Gillespie Way
El Cajon, California 92020
1-888-291-8000 orders
619-387-0042 fax
catholic.com

Printed in the United States of America

Cover design by Maria Bowman
Interior design by Russell Graphic Design

978-1-68357-337-1
978-1-68357-338-8 Kindle
978-1-68357-339-5 ePub

Contents

Acknowledgments 7

Introduction: A Portrait of Love 9

Part I: New Insights and Ancient Biblical Keys 19

1   New Insights and Openness for Mary 23

2   Mary Foreshadowed 35

3   Mary According to Luke 47

4   Mary in Typology... 73

5   Keys to Other Marian Types and Figures 101

Part II: Mary's Scriptural Portrait 121

6   Mary's Virginity... 125

7   Mary's Divine and Spiritual Motherhood 157

8   Mary's Immaculate Origen................................. 173

9   Mediating Cooperation..................................... 201

10 A Helper Fit for the Redeemer 217

11 Mary's Rapture 235

12 Blessing and Praying to Mary in Heaven.................. 249

Conclusions 271

About the Author... 285

Ancient Keys to Understanding Mary in Scripture............. 287

Cited References... 289

Index to the Catechism of the Catholic Church............ 297

Scripture Index... 301

Endnotes 302

Acknowledgments

I am grateful to my readers, some of whom must go unmentioned. Yet their feedback and encouragement moved this study forward, including from Steve Miller at Harvest House.

Rev. Bill Tarbell was one of the earliest readers of the initial draft. His positive response and Presbyterian perspectives helped me refine and expand the research to include more Protestant perspectives. Kerry Zuhlke, Anna Migeon, and Edward O'Connor gave me additional insights to help better organize the material. Fr. Barry Cole helped simplify the flow of ideas and identify statements that could be confusing to some.

I appreciate the feedback of each person, making this work a real dialogue between people interested in the subject. I also appreciate the many who have prayed for me and for the fruit of this work: *all the glory to God.*

Introduction:
A Portrait of Love

This book grew out of a dialogue with Evangelical minister James G. McCarthy, published as *Letters Between a Catholic and an Evangelical* (Eugene: Harvest House, 2003). Discussing the topic of the Virgin Mary,* my friend commented, "The first time I read the entire Bible, I was struck by how little it said about Mary."

This caught me by surprise. So—to explain Catholic teaching on Mary—I began seeking out as many Bible references as I could, including ones early Christians used. Jim's challenge kindled new insights—insights too exciting to keep to myself—especially about how early Christians approached Scripture. Those insights led to this book. I am forever indebted to Jim for this; I hope the reader will feel the same.

Let me put my cards on the table: I am a Catholic priest who fully believes all that Christ teaches through the Church. I believe in the Bible as the revealed word of God and see no conflict between it and Catholic teaching. I seek to show that this is true, especially with regard to Mary.

---

* The title *Virgin Mary* is used to refer to Jesus' mother, to contrast her to other Marys (such as Moses' sister, Mary Magdalene, etc.). Christians adopted this title long ago to acknowledge the fulfillment of the prophecy: "'A virgin shall conceive and bear a son, and his name shall be called Immanuel' (which means, God with us)" (Matt. 1:23, quoting Isa. 7:14). Chapter 10 will cover this specific topic.

Catholics do not believe in worshiping angels or saints—not even Mary. The Catholic Church condemns such worship as idolatry, a heretical and excommunicable offense. Although I do not worship her, I do love her. And how could I not love the Virgin Mary? If I love and worship Christ as my Lord, God, and Savior, how could I not love anyone he loves? Or if I love and worship the Holy Spirit, and love the Bible he inspired, how could I not love her whom the Spirit loved and overshadowed?

Early Christian Ways of Reading the Bible

Protestants and Catholics approach Scripture differently, but a love for Scripture and desires for mutual understanding can help us bridge our differences. We both read the same Scripture, but we do so differently, depending on our dispositions. For example, ask an atheist to read the Bible, and it will either bore him or make him sick. A Christian picks up the same book and sees Christ whom he loves, stirring up flames to love him more and to share him with others. Similarly, a young man picks up his girlfriend's love letter, and he is moved to tears of joy; his little brother picks it up and laughs. This is why the topic of Mary can be so difficult, especially for Catholics. When we discuss Mary with a Protestant, we can easily become defensive, like the older brother. I ask the reader to be sensitive to this; it takes humility to put what you read into a context of a personal relationship of love. So, if we acknowledge that we speak different languages—that similar words may mean different things and we read Scripture differently—we can pursue unity by discovering a common way of reading the Bible.

Secularists read the Bible in a supposedly scientific way, seeking the "historical Jesus," which reduces Jesus to a few platitudes foreign to the Jesus of Faith that has been transmitted to us through the ages. Doing the same with Mary, they strive for the "historical Mary," finding little reliable information about her in the Bible. As Fr. Denis Farkasfalvy puts it,

> Those who consider the historical-critical method the one and only ultimately valid method, defining and verifying (or rejecting) all other methods, may find in the Old Testament very few or no texts applicable to Mary, except possibly by analogy, extrapolation, or symbolism, all constituting some sort of *eisegesis.* . . . In fact, the historical-critical approach usually assumes that the meaning of a text must reflect knowledge available for its author at the time he or she is writing. Thus . . . the hagiographer can report only events and persons belonging to his past or his present but not to the future.[1]

Such an approach views the Bible as a mere human composition with no room for God. I beg to differ and to find new ways of reading the Bible that are open to God . . . new ways that are really old.

By rediscovering how early Christians read the Bible, we can discover the Jesus of the Bible and what we can call the *Bible Mary*. This can be a bit jolting, as the ways early Christians employed Scripture are foreign to most modern readers—including Catholics. For example, Gregory of Nyssa (d. 394) applied the text of Moses at the burning bush (Exod. 3:1–3) to Mary.[2] Jerome (d. 419) applied prophecies about the temple (Ezek. 44:1–2) and the earth (Ps. 98) to Mary.[3] These Christians did this in the most natural and logical way, because the Holy Spirit inflamed them with love to read the Old Testament and to write the New—the

Gospel of Love—putting their objective witness through the "subjective" lens of love for Jesus Christ.

New Testament writers quoted the Old in this way—a way that was natural to them but foreign to modern exegetes. For example, Matthew applied Rachel's lament (Jer. 31:15) to the slaughter of the innocents (Matt. 2:16–18). The prophecy's immediate fulfillment concerned the lost tribes of Israel under the king of Ephraim (son of Joseph, who was son of Rachel). But Matthew saw it fulfilled in Christ, using biblical types and prophecies that had multiple fulfillments. Reading Scripture this way permeates the New Testament, as well as the writings of Church Fathers.

Reflecting and pondering on how early Christians applied Scripture to Mary leads to discovering their love for Christ and Mary. This also leads to discovering objective "keys" behind their apparent subjective use of Scripture. We will attempt to make explicit those keys.

Such keys are not new. Some are even familiar to Protestants—for example, the use of typology. Whereas these scholars comfortably apply them to Jesus, many fail to realize the rich consequences these biblical principles have for understanding Mary and other topics, too. I hope the reader will come to appreciate these exciting discoveries that make explicit the scriptural foundation for what Catholics have accepted implicitly for twenty centuries.

I will attempt to present Scripture objectively, yet with religious and cultural convictions—which include a relationship with Jesus and Mary. This cannot but affect our study. I love the person I am describing and her son. Some may be suspicious or even critical of that relationship, but I believe that the Person who inspired Scripture, and the persons who wrote them down, loves her, too. I have "sensed" our Lord asking me to be that "disciple whom he loves" in John 19:25–27. So I have accepted Mary into my home and heart, promising Jesus always to treat his mother as my own.

Mary's Biblical Portrait: a Source of Christian Unity?

Discussing topics dividing Christians is hard, since stubborn pride often gets in the way. I too have used Scripture to corner fellow Christians, winning no conversions in doing so. Yet if we are humble and open, apparent conflict can be resolved into a mutually enriching dialogue. My exchanges with non-Catholic Christians have stirred in me a greater love for God's word, the best basis for honest dialogue.

Researching the topic of Mary has required reading and rereading the Bible, seeking interpretive principles that early Christians found in Scripture. This has pushed me beyond the Catholic *Catechism* to discover the Mary of Scripture, the *Bible Mary*. In addition, a number of Protestant scholars are rediscovering Mary. They speak positively of Mary, overcoming former trepidation with fresh insights and deep perspectives of the Messiah's mother. The goal of this book is to discover the *biblical portrait* that the Holy Spirit painted.

Christ prays that all Christians be one (John 17:21), one body in him (Col. 3:12–15). Love for Scripture should lead to unity, sanctifying us in the truth (John 17:17), a truth that shines throughout God's word. Surprisingly, our study of *Mary*, instead of being an object of contention and division, may help us resolve many of our differences and foster Christian unity on a common admiration for Mary as a woman of faith and blessed by God to bear his Son. God gave us our most precious treasure—his only-begotten Son—through Mary, and Mary continues to bring Jesus to Christians and Christians to Jesus, asking us only to "do whatever he tells you" (John 2:5).

Being Christian means being in fellowship with God and with all who have fellowship with God (1 John 1:3, 6–7)—including Mary. So we cannot treat this topic in a sterile fashion. If you want to get something out of this book, you must open yourself up to get to know Mary—to get to know Mary as a fellow Christian, as a real person who knows and loves Christ, as the Holy Spirit presents her to us in Scripture, so as to love her as Christ did.

> May the reader come to love Mary as Jesus loves her.
> This is my ultimate objective. Please humbly pray
> for this as you read.

And I ask you to be patient. I don't expect us to agree on everything. These are matters of faith and love, a most beautiful love, the fairest of loves. Please, pray over these Scripture passages slowly and ask the Holy Spirit to guide you, as I believe he has me.

Plan for Our Study

If the Spirit loved Mary and inspired the Bible, then why is it so hard to find Mary there? Scripture mentions Moses more than 800 times, including more than eighty times in the New Testament. The same is true with Abraham (300/70), David (900/50), and Elijah (100/30). We would expect the same of Mary. So our goal it to identify all Bible passages relevant to Mary in God's love letters for man.

Part I surveys recent Protestants who seem intrigued by the figure of Mary in the Bible. These authors and scholars give us a good idea of what Scripture passages can validly be applied to Mary. Certainly there are more detailed studies—such as Tim Perry's research in *Mary for Evangelicals*[4]—but I will limit myself to surveying various

Protestant authors for what Scripture passages they find applicable to the Virgin Mary. We then draw out keys used to identify the Old and New Testament passages relevant to Mary, opening our perspectives.

Part II applies this compilation of Scripture to the various doctrinal statements made about Mary over the centuries, connecting each Marian doctrine to the Christological controversy of the era, citing some early Christian writings in this regard, but focusing on what God's word conveys regarding each doctrine.

Just as the gospel cannot be "proved" scientifically but must be believed on faith, we don't expect this way of using Scripture to "prove" Marian doctrines to the satisfaction of all. Yet seeing how early Christians read the Bible and developed traditional Marian teachings from Scripture can strengthen and deepen our faith in all that Scripture teaches.

QUESTIONS AND ANSWERS*

Q: Will not your Catholic beliefs bias your approach to Scripture?

A: There is no doubt that my Catholic faith influences how I read the Bible, yet no one comes to the Bible with a blank slate. A Protestant reads the Bible already influenced and predisposed by how he was taught, and by the family and the culture in which he grew up. This cannot be avoided.

---

* These questions and answers have been added at the end of each chapter to hit issues not fully addressed in the section. This will keep the discussion simple while allowing us to address questions that arise naturally. Most questions are from real people, although some come from common arguments against Catholic teaching.

Early Christian authors read the Bible quite differently from how we do today. The intention of this work is to re-discover how they read Scripture and apply it to Mary.

Q: If we both believe in the same Bible, then why do we believe different doctrines?

A: I find that we often speak different languages using the same words, because we apply different meanings and connotations to those words. For example, many Protestants tend to associate *prayer* exclusively with worship, considering prayer as speaking *only* to God: accessing the Father, through Christ, in the Spirit (Eph. 2:18). Catholics, on the other hand, see prayer as conversation and dialogue, putting prayer on the same plane as talking with family or friends. So Catholics converse ("pray") with angels, saints, and Mary in the same way as we lovingly speak to friends without worshiping them. Were we to address angels and saints as accessing the Father, through Christ, in the Spirit, it would be idolatry. So if we use the Protestant meaning for *prayer*, then Catholics too "pray" to God and to God *alone*, and we would have to develop an appropriate term to describe how we converse with and make requests of family, friends, angels, and saints.

This book seeks to bridge the gap of having different meanings for the same words by turning to ancient Christians.

Q: The early Christians are not alive to tell us how they read Scripture, so how do we know how they read it?

A: We don't have to go to extra-biblical sources (yet we do just to confirm what we discover in the Bible).

First, let's look at how our Lord read and interpreted the Old Testament. Early Christians were keen on following Christ closely. Then we can look at how New Testament writers read and interpreted the Old, such as the Evangelists and apostles, especially Paul. The way they used Scripture is quite revealing—nothing like the modern hermeneutics that Catholics and other Christians are taught today. The results are fascinating.

When we read, we tend to hear what we want to hear, thinking the writer reads Scripture as we do. That simply is not true, nor is it faithful to the text, nor fair to the human writer, nor open to the divine author.

Q: You seem to approach the Bible with your beliefs already set, looking to confirm Catholic dogmas on Mary. Why not just let the Bible establish the Christian faith for us?

A: Most parents don't just read the Bible to their children and expect each child to develop his own beliefs. Rather, parents explain the Bible with their beliefs already set.

Early Church Fathers describe all the Marian dogmas, often taking for granted their authenticity as truths of faith. These early Christians often used Scripture to support those dogmas, yet in very un-modern ways. As the Catholic Church admits,

> often there are theologians and preachers who, following in the footsteps of the holy [Church] Fathers, have been rather free in their use of events and expressions taken from Sacred Scripture to explain their belief . . . [employing] statements and various images and analogies of Sacred Scripture to illustrate and confirm the doctrine of the Assumption (*Munificentissimus Deus* 26, 29).

Protestant theologian Daniel Migliore realizes that we all tend to let our prejudices affect our view of Mary. So, he asks, why not let Mary be what the Bible describes her as being: a woman of humble yet courageous faith from whom we might learn to praise the sovereign grace of God, cry out against injustice, and acknowledge our daily need for repentance and forgiveness?[5]

We all need to strive to let the Bible speak to us about the mother of the Messiah. The Second Vatican Council, and the recent *Catechism of the Catholic Church*,[6] shows an openness to read Scripture in an entirely new way—or rather, to return to the ancient way in which the New Testament was written, read, and interpreted by the most ancient of Christians. That is what we seek.

Part I

NEW INSIGHTS
AND ANCIENT
BIBLICAL KEYS

Before addressing the dogmatic inferences on Mary in
Scripture, we seek to uncover all, or almost all, Bible passages applicable to Mary. We start by surveying some recent
Scripture studies by Christian scholars. Identifying the more
obvious Scripture passages on Mary, without being exhaus-
tive, these scholars use the Bible to bridge doctrinal divides
with Catholics. Some of their insights will be familiar, others new and exciting.

Catholics shouldn't discard insights into Mary simply
because they are from Protestants. Our Lord tells us, "He
that is not against us is for us" (Mark 9:40). We believe that
the Spirit, who inspires Sacred Scripture—which we read
alongside our fellow Christians—guides the Magisterium in
discerning doctrinal truth as it did Peter:

> And we have the prophetic word made more sure. You
> will do well to pay attention to this as to a lamp shining
> in a dark place . . . that no prophecy of Scripture is a

matter of one's own interpretation, because no prophecy ever came by the impulse of man, but men moved by the Holy Spirit spoke from God (2 Pet. 1:19–21).

All authority is from God, who speaks in Scripture and who is at work in any Christian who humbly lets himself be guided by his gentle action. But if some interpretation contradicts what the Spirit reveals in Scripture—such as contradicting that Jesus is true God and true man—then the Spirit moves the Church to discern the truth, as John attests (1 John 4:1–3).

We hope to uncover the keys used by early Christians— whether consciously or unconsciously—what Jaroslav Pelikan calls a "prophecy-fulfillment hermeneutic": principles or patterns of reading Scripture guiding early Christians to identify and apply Scripture to Mary. This should help us go beyond polemics surrounding the most blessed of women, as Scot McKnight suggests:

> A book about Mary for Evangelicals that focuses on the real Mary, so far as I know, has never been written. Other books have engaged in polemics about the Immaculate Conception, her perpetual virginity, devotion to Mary, and other so-called Marian dogmas. But, to my knowledge, no one has written a book about the life and character of Mary helping us develop a positive, Protestant view of Mary. . . . Mary is in the Bible; we need to believe what the Bible says about Mary.[7]

The results are disarmingly elegant, almost too obvious to miss. We will be able to analyze and categorize additional Marian passages, and then assess their dogmatic value in the third part of our study. Let's not shy away from our differences, but discover ways to address them with the full power of our common language: Scripture. As Lutheran Charles Dickson points out, "any attempt at reaching a consensus of belief must begin with common ground shared by all groups, and that ground seems to be the Scriptures."[8]

So let's confidently discern how the Spirit may be leading our fellow Christians through Scripture, as we strive to "follow the pattern of the sound words" so as to "guard the truth that has been entrusted to you by the Holy Spirit who dwells within us" (2 Tim. 1:13–14). I'm sure we will find a *pattern of sound words* that reveal the true *Bible Mary*.

New Insights and Openness for Mary

Catholics and Protestants have much to learn from one another. Catholics can benefit from the extensive experience of Protestants in examining Scripture, just as the Beroean Jews did in responding to Paul's preaching:

> The brethren immediately sent Paul and Silas away by night to Beroea; and when they arrived they went into the Jewish synagogue. Now these Jews were more noble than those in Thessalonica, for they received the word with all eagerness, examining the scriptures daily to see if these things were so. Many of them therefore believed (Acts 17:10–12).

Let's search Scripture for the truth, especially regarding Mary.

In recent years, many Protestants have discovered scriptural insights into Mary previously hidden. *Time* magazine did a feature article on this: "Hail, Mary: Catholics have long revered her, but now Protestants are finding their own reasons to celebrate the mother of Jesus."[9] Earlier, the Protestant journal *Christianity Today* dedicated several positive articles by

Protestant scholars on Mary's role in theology and worship,[10] as did *Christian History & Biography*.[11] Even the Public Broadcasting System (PBS) did a television special on this trend.[12]

Protestant scholars have published significant research on Mary in several recent books, including from renowned Yale historian Jaroslav Pelikan,[13] British theologian of systematic theology John Macquarrie,[14] and Beverly Roberts Gaventa of Princeton Theological Seminary.[15]

Why this new enthusiasm regarding Mary and the Bible? Does this mean that the topic of Mary no longer needs to divide Catholics and Protestants? Pelikan suggests that Mary's role in Christian teaching is necessary to battle the secularist trends of our age:

> Within the history of Christianity, it is difficult to think of a more fitting theme to explore for its bearing on these issues than the Virgin Mary . . . [who has] maintained her hold on most of the Western world even in a secular age and even in the face of anti-religious propaganda and downright persecution during the Communist era in Eastern and Central Europe.[16]

Tim Perry links this new fascination with Mary to a deepening fascination with Christ:

> I have come to learn, gladly, that . . . Christians East and West, Roman Catholic and Protestant, are fascinated with Mary because we are fascinated with Jesus. She directs the faithful away from herself, always to her son.[17]

A Humble Openness to Mary

This new trend among Protestants is refreshing, Daniel Migliore suggests:

Reformed theology has never given much attention to Mary; the mother of Jesus. . . . Despite the respect and honor the Reformers gave to Mary, she virtually dropped out of Protestant theology and piety in the increasingly polemical post-Reformation period.[18]

Professor Gaventa identifies a "Protestant anxiety about overemphasizing Mary's role,"[19] leading them to reject and dismiss "even the biblical Mary . . . to differentiate themselves from the Catholic Church . . . simply by ignoring her," as Nora Lozano-Diaz concludes.[20] Yet Jeanne Stevenson-Moessner suggests,

As we seek to understand more deeply Jesus' person, his teachings, and his spiritual family the Church, we may need to find again this woman who is sometimes hidden from us. We do not have to elevate Mary to the Trinity. We do need to remember and enunciate that she is blessed among women.[21]

Though feeling that Catholics went too far, Dick McClain realizes that he and his fellow Protestants did, too.[22] Scot McKnight also decries the under-emphasis on Mary in Protestant theology.[23] Perhaps Protestants did this so as to maintain the biblical foundation of their dogmas. Even so, the Holy Spirit seems to be moving both Protestants and Catholics to uncover the biblical richness of this wonderful topic.

As Protestant scholars humbly put aside their tendencies to react to Catholicism, Catholics should humbly drop our defensiveness so as to open ourselves to the full biblical truth about Mary. Let us strive to explain our beliefs about Mary using Scripture, as did Christ, who, "beginning with Moses and all the prophets . . . [interpreted] all the Scriptures the things concerning himself" (Luke 24:27).

Timothy George calls "Evangelicals to recover a fully biblical appreciation of the Blessed Virgin Mary and her role in the history of salvation, and to do so precisely as Evangelicals":

> Honoring Mary certainly doesn't come naturally to Protestants. For complex historical reasons, to be a Protestant has meant not to be a Roman Catholic. To worship Jesus means not to honor Mary, even if such honor is biblically grounded and theologically sound.[24]

Luther preached, "The holy mother of God did not become good, was not saved, by her virginity or her motherhood, but rather by the will of faith and the works of God." Heinrich Bullinger, Zwingli's successor, also extolled her: "In Mary, then, everything is extraordinary and even more majestic, because it has sprung from the purest faith and burning love for God."[25]

Gaventa calls on Protestants to face their fear of the unknown and to join Catholics and the Reformers in "blessing" Mary.[26] Fear not, for God will guide us. Scripture is rich, and Catholics and Protestants can learn from each other if we dare to follow our Lord, who is meek and humble of heart. It is time for both Catholics and non-Catholics to discover the *Bible Mary*.

INSIGHT 1:
Fascination with Mary arises from a fascination with Christ and with what the Bible teaches about them.

Maternal and Feminine Insights

Bonnie Miller-McLemore writes,

> Perhaps it is time that Protestants, who generally do not think all that much about Jesus even having a mother, also find inspiration, consolation, and liberation in Mary as mother.[27]

Reflecting on this, Beverly Gaventa explains how the Holy Spirit helped her find new insights into the mother of the Redeemer:

> I . . . write as a mother. My profound connection with my child makes it impossible for me to do otherwise, and I cannot pretend to distance myself from certain aspects of these texts. When Matthew's Gospel depicts the bloody Roman sword in Bethlehem and the threat to Jesus, a cold fear grabs me. When Luke describes Mary's puzzlement over the son who is both hers and not hers, I worry with her and for her. Some may find this lamentably sentimental. For me it is simply a fact of life.[28]

Mary's motherhood helped Gaventa to relate to Mary's joys, fears, and sorrows. For Miller-McLemore, such "maternal thinking . . . reinforces the scandal of the gospel, that is, the scandal of God's Son enduring humiliation, rejection, and death at human hands."[29] It gives her new insights into Mary and into the plight of women in the Church and in society:

> For many Protestants—and not just hypersensitive feminist mothers—Mary is almost completely invisible. She seldom appears.

27

With Mary, the silence around maternal thinking is compounded . . . [and] the theological void is further deepened. We do not think of Mary as a maternal subject with religious or theological knowledge. And we do not think of using maternal wisdom as a way to understand Mary's theologizing.[30]

This "maternal thinking" can lead to new appreciation for Mary, to a renewed awareness of the value of motherhood, and to a truly Christian feminism. But it is not necessary to be be a woman to read the Bible this way, as Protestant Timothy George relates:

Evangelicals have frequently been more concerned with Mary's virginity than with her maternity. But Mary was not merely the point of Christ's entrance into the world—the channel through which he passed as water flows through a pipe. She was the mother who cared for the physical needs of Jesus the boy. She nursed him at her breast and nurtured and taught him the ways of the Lord. Doubtless she was the one who taught him to memorize the Psalms and to pray, even as he grew in wisdom and stature and in favor with God and others (Luke 2:52).[31]

All of us—with the experience of our own mothers—can glean theological and biblical insights into Mary, such as viewing her as their spiritual mother, as early Christians did. Lutheran Jon M. Sweeney says,

These ideas have taken their inspiration, in part, from Jesus' teaching that we must have the faith of children in order to enter the kingdom of heaven. How can we learn to have the faith of children without a good mother? All children benefit from a good mother, and Mary can be our spiritual mother, an example and guide.[32]

Indeed, the early Church quite naturally viewed Mary as a spiritual guide, mentor, and loving mother, who cares for us as her children.

As a childless wife, Kathleen Norris related to Mary differently, seeing the profound contradictions of Mary in Scripture through her own childlessness:

> The point about Mary is that she is . . . poor yet gloriously rich. She is blessed among women yet condemned to witness her son's execution. She is human yet God-bearer, and the Word that she willingly bears is destined to pierce her soul.[33]

Shannon Kubiak—trying to inspire teenage girls to give their lives to Christ in a world hostile to Christianity— found that young women can relate to the experiences and ways of thinking of Mary as a young woman, uncovering new details about Mary in Scripture:

> When presented with choices, Mary made the right ones. Hers is a story many of us know all too well. But often we overlook the details hidden in the pages of her life because we are busy seeing what we have always been taught to see. We overlook the fact that before Mary was a mother . . . she was just a girl.[34]

In her interview on PBS, Kubiak explains: "So many of us girls think . . . *I'm no one.* And that's the type of life Mary lived. She was a nobody from the middle of nowhere. And that's what I felt like in my own life, and it's what countless teenage girls across the nation feel like, and God chose to use her for the most incredible task of a lifetime."

Still others—educators—get "a fresh approach to Scripture"[35] viewing Mary as Jesus' first teacher.[36] In particular, Mary can teach us, as she did Jesus, how to approach Scripture, training our ear and our heart to really hear God's word and pray with Scripture.[37]

INSIGHT 2:
"Maternal" and "feminine" insights can lead to a new biblical understanding of Mary.

QUESTIONS AND ANSWERS

Q: The Beroeans verified questionable teachings with Scripture (Acts 17:10–12), avoiding reading more into Scripture than is clearly and explicitly there. Are you proposing this?

A: Let's commend anyone who sincerely tries to use Scripture to discern the truth. Yet what a person gets out of Scripture depends on his knowledge and sensitivity. Remember that when the Sadducees challenged Christ on the resurrection of the dead (Matt. 22:23–33), our Lord quoted Exodus 3:6:

> And as for the resurrection of the dead, have you not read what was said to you by God, "I am the God of Abraham, and the God of Isaac, and the God of Jacob"? He is not God of the dead, but of the living.

I'm sure the Sadducees had read that passage hundreds of times yet never concluded what Jesus and his listeners did.

The Sadducees' prejudice against an afterlife prevented them from seeing the obvious. We need to learn from Jesus to be open to all that Scripture teaches.

Regarding the Beroeans, they verified Paul's preaching by searching the Old Testament—since the New Testament had not been written yet. If it had, they would have rejected it as lacking authority. Certainly Paul preached more than what was clear and explicit in the Old Testament: that Jesus was God and Son of the Most High. The manner of reading Scripture that our Lord, Paul, and the Evangelists used is what we propose.

Q: You suggest that Protestants have a campaign against Mary. I have never seen one in all my years as a Protestant. Although we mention Mary less than Catholics, I remember some moving sermons on Christmas and Good Friday that mention her, and ones on the wedding feast of Cana. Do you really think there is such an anti-Mary campaign?

A: Many Protestants tend to reject anything not found immediately and literally in Scripture.

We could say that there has been a reaction—even an overreaction—to Mary: many Protestants lament losing so much gospel richness by avoiding Mary, as we have seen. It is simply easier to avoid the subject if there is the remotest danger that their preaching and teaching about Mary, or in blessing and honoring her, may in any way be offensive to Christ or to Protestant sensibilities.

Q: Perhaps some Protestants have a growing interest in Mary, but that doesn't mean we are willing to go beyond what is written in the Bible. Are Catholics willing to do the same—ready to abandon exaggerated piety and unbiblical dogmas?

A: Mary's place in salvation history is unique—no one else was mother of the incarnate Word of God—and thus, she holds a unique place in Christian theology, which attempts to make sense of *all* that is written in the Bible. This is not an easy task.

Before we propose abandoning any Christian doctrines—Catholic or not—let's explore *all* that Scripture actually says about Mary. Certainly we should reject teachings or forms of piety that are contrary to God's revealed Word—such as worshiping ancestors—but let's finish our study before evaluating them.

Q: You mention "maternal" and "feminine" insights that we can get from reflecting on Mary. Can such fuzzy and subjective approaches really help us understand Scripture better?

A: Reading the Bible "scientifically" for "objective" content is not the only way. We should also read it to discern God's will for us. As we have seen, several Protestant writers have discovered some powerful insights this way.

For example, you may read Christ's command, "If any man would come after me, let him deny himself and take up his cross and follow me" (Mark 8:34), but not understand what it really means to "take up your cross" until you experience for yourself unjust persecution, suffering, or a life-threatening illness. Many have discovered in Mary the way to carry the cross. They can relate to her pain and her heroic response to the unjust killing of her son.

Upon reflecting on Mary's reaction to the child Jesus remaining in the Temple (Luke 2:41–50), parents, who have experienced the helplessness of losing a child in a crowd, find comfort and consolation knowing that they may not be to blame. Like Mary, we don't always "understand," but it's not necessary that we do, either. Let's learn from her to ponder in our hearts what we fail to understand until God enlightens us.

Q: Okay, this way of reading Scripture may be valid: Mary reminds us how we ought to respond to Christ. But some Catholics focus on dogmas that ignore Scripture, such as that she was sinless and co-redeemer. Will you return to just what Scripture says about her?

A: Her role in doctrine is always secondary and supportive of Christ. If Christ were not fully human and fully divine, then Mary would never be called Mother of God. All Marian doctrines are secondary and supportive of the truly essential doctrines on her son. For this reason, St. Cyril of Alexandria (d. 444) called Mary "the scepter of orthodoxy" for Church teaching on Christ.

If any belief or scriptural interpretation seems to run contrary to God's revelation, there are three possible causes and resolutions (see *Dei Verbum* 11–12):

1. a belief or interpretation is incompatible with God's revelation, so we need to abandon that belief (e.g., using Romans 3:30 to say there is only one God, and so the Holy Spirit is not God);

2. or we don't fully understand the Scripture, so we ought to further explore it (e.g., God is one, but the Father is God, the Word is God—John 1:1—and the Spirit is God—Matt. 28:19);

3. or there was a manuscript error that needs to be corrected.

Let's explore all of Scripture before jumping to conclusions.

Yes, Mary reminds us of how to respond to God. She is awestruck when invited to become his mother. We too should be awestruck when God chooses to use us to evangelize others. Let's also learn to respond to God's grace as Mary did: with faith—blessed is she who believed (Luke 1:45)—and by magnifying God (v. 46).

2

Mary Foreshadowed

Becoming one in Christ is hard if we focus on what divides us. Even early Christians found it difficult to transcend their differences and focus on what united them—Jesus Christ:

> Here there cannot be Greek and Jew, circumcised and uncircumcised, barbarian, Scythian, slave, free man, but Christ is all, and in all. Put on then, as God's chosen ones, holy and beloved, compassion, kindness, lowliness, meekness, and patience, forbearing one another and . . . forgiving each other; as the Lord has forgiven you, so you also must forgive. And above all these put on love, which binds everything together in perfect harmony. And let the peace of Christ rule in your hearts, to which indeed you were called in the one body (Col. 3:11–15).

In Christ's body there cannot be Catholic and Protestant, Evangelical and Calvinist, but only Christ—forgiving and loving each other as one body in perfect harmony.

Let's listen to one another with openness and respect. Though our goal is to identify all relevant texts about Mary, we begin with passages all Christians use. Later we will explore passages early Christians applied to Mary and the keys used to unlock Scripture. Finally, we will piece together the full gospel message concerning the mother of the Messiah.

The most obvious references to the Virgin Mary are those that mention her explicitly. These may be few, but they are the most important. Literal references take priority in any doctrinal discussion and are the basis for all other ways of reading Scripture.

> **KEY 1:**
> *Literal references to Mary take priority.*

Yet the Protestant theologian Daniel Migliore reminds us to keep in mind:

> The Gospel writers were not interested in supplying us with material for a biography of Mary any more than they were in giving us material to write a life of Jesus. Yet Mary stands before us in the Gospels as a woman of faith. The faith of Mary is portrayed—with economy, beauty, and stunning realism—in several clusters of Gospel stories.[38]

Some Scripture passages reference Mary directly, mentioning her by name. Yet the whole Old Testament—God's word—prophetically anticipates the Messiah's coming and his incarnate Word. Due to Mary's intimate relationship to the historical Christ, Old Testament prophecies foreshadowing Christ may also foreshadow her. And so, before exploring the literal references to the Virgin Mary, let us look at some of the Old Testament prophecies that foreshadow her.

Old Testament Foreshadowing as Fulfilled in Christ

Scripture gives us *interpretive keys* to identify these passages. The early Christians may not have developed these keys explicitly, but as we read the New Testament and the Church Fathers, we will discern certain patterns of how the Holy Spirit moved them to apply Scripture to Mary. These Spirit-led patterns are interpretive keys.

Mark Roberts identifies three of these Marian prophecies:

Christians see Mary in three Old Testament passages. Two are obvious prophecies. The first is a little more obscure. After the man and woman sin in Genesis 3, God promised that the "seed" of the woman will "strike the head" of the serpent. If the seed is Christ, then the woman is, in a sense, Mary. Isaiah 7:14 refers to a virgin or young woman (same Hebrew word) who bears a child named Immanuel. Micah 5:2–5 refers to a woman who gives birth to a messianic ruler.[39]

Genesis 3 relays God's prophetic curse of the serpent who tempted Eve: "I will put enmity between you and the woman, and between your seed and her seed; he shall bruise your head, and you shall bruise his heel." This foretells a special enmity or war between Mary's seed (Jesus) and Satan. Using this passage, early Christians, such as Justin Martyr (d. 165), began calling Mary the *New Eve*:[40]

[God] became man by the Virgin so that the course which was taken by disobedience in the beginning through the agency of the serpent, might be also the very course by which it would be put down. For Eve, a virgin and undefiled, conceived the word of the serpent, and bore disobedience and death. But the Virgin Mary received faith

37

and joy when the angel Gabriel announced to her the glad tiding that the Spirit of the Lord would come upon her and the power of the Most High would overshadow her, for which reason the Holy One being born of her is the Son of God.[41]

In Isaiah 7:14, God gives King Ahaz and all of Judah a reassuring sign of his protection against the evil surrounding them: "Therefore the Lord himself will give you a sign. Behold, a young woman shall conceive and bear a son, and shall call his name Immanuel." The reassuring *sign* of God's protection in our war against Satan is the young virgin who conceives Immanuel, *God with us.*

Finally, Micah 5:2–4 prophesies of the town of the Messiah's birth and his mother's "travail" as the Messiah brings back his people to God and feeds them.

But you, O Bethlehem Ephrathah, who are little to be among the clans of Judah, from you shall come forth for me one who is to be ruler in Israel, whose origin is from of old, from ancient days. Therefore he shall give them up until the time when she who is in travail has brought forth; then the rest of his brethren shall return to the people of Israel. And he shall stand and feed his flock in the strength of the Lord . . . for now he shall be great to the ends of the earth.

Sarah Hinlicky Wilson notes many New Testament passages reflect customs, rituals, and laws laid out in the Old, reflecting Mary's religious world:

At the time of Mary's son's presentation . . . Mary's devotion is evident. . . . [She keeps] the law: "And when the days of her purifying are completed, whether for a son or for a daughter, she shall bring to the priest . . . a burnt offering and . . . a sin offering, and he shall offer it before the Lord and make atonement for her. Then she shall be clean from the flow of her blood" (Lev. 12:6–7). The offering, "a pair of turtledoves, or two young pigeons," betrays her poverty, for she cannot afford a year-old lamb.

Out of the nine times in the whole Gospel that Luke uses the expression "the law of the Lord" or the "Law of Moses," five of them appear in this report of Jesus' presentation and early childhood.[42]

Descriptions of Old Testament customs, rituals, and faithful Jewish women were the context of Mary's motherly relationship with Christ. Pope John Paul II concurs.[43]

Although all Scripture finds fulfillment in God's incarnate Word (Matt. 5:17), truths about Mary will be mirrored in truths about Christ, as the Second Vatican Council says:

For Mary, who since her entry into salvation history unites in herself and re-echoes the greatest teachings of the Faith as she is proclaimed and venerated, calls the faithful to her son and his sacrifice and to the love of the Father (*Lumen Gentium* 65).

John Paul II adds,

The council further says that "Mary figured profoundly in the history of salvation and in a certain way unites and mirrors within herself the central truths of the faith." Among all believers she is *like a "mirror"* in which are reflected in the most profound and limpid way "the mighty works of God" (Acts 2:11) (*Redemptoris Mater* 25).

The *Catechism of the Catholic Church* (CCC) says, "What the Catholic faith believes about Mary is based on what it believes about Christ, and what it teaches about Mary illumines in turn its faith in Christ" (487). Applying this to the Bible, we derive another key for identifying Marian Scripture passages:

KEY 2:
Christ, our true model, fulfills all Scripture.
We identify prophecies, laws, customs, and dogmas
describing Mary based on prophecies, laws, customs,
and dogmas describing Christ.

Christians are called "to be conformed to the image of his Son" (Rom. 8:29) by imitating God (Eph. 5:1–2). We can also imitate Paul or any Christian to the extent they imitate Christ: "Be imitators of me, as I am of Christ" (1 Cor. 11:1). This makes Christ's life the interpretive key to our lives and to all Scripture. Mary too would have imitated him, filling her life by identifying herself with him who was God's Son and hers, too. This happens quite naturally in any family: as one person draws closer to God, then others follow. Mary loved Christ and followed him who is the firstborn among many brethren (Rom. 8:29).

The Old Testament preparation for Christ takes up two-thirds of the Bible. So we would hope to find many references to Mary.

Mark and Matthew

Mark makes little reference to Mary or to Jesus' virginal conception of the Holy Spirit, but he does call Jesus "the carpenter, the son of Mary" (6:3) and describes Mary, with some of Jesus' "brothers," seeking him as he preached. Jesus responds to them with his teaching on spiritual brother-, sister-, and motherhood: "Who are my mother and my brethren? . . . Whoever does the will of God is my brother, and sister, and mother" (3:31–35; see also Matt. 12:46–50, Luke 8:19–21).

To Jews trying to understand Jesus, Mary is a "scandal" or stumbling block because had he originated in her, it would imply that he and his message are not divine (Matt. 13:55; Mark 6:3; John 6:42), just as his Galilean origin ostensibly rules out his being a prophet (John 7:50–52).

Tim Perry suggests that Mark was unaware of Jesus' virginal conception and so limited Mary's role.[44] Though this may be true, we can also interpret Mark's omission as a concession to his Jewish listeners, who would understand Jesus' divinity only if they could show how Jesus fulfilled Old Testament prophecies. Were Mark to begin with God becoming man in a virgin's womb, he would risk losing his listeners before conveying his full message. So Mark may well have chosen to focus on Jesus' preaching and miracles instead of on his divine origin.

Matthew tells us how Mary, betrothed to Joseph but before living together, conceives Jesus by the Holy Spirit. Mary fulfills Isaiah's prophecy: remaining a virgin after conceiving and bearing Jesus. Matthew also describes Jesus' birth to Mary in Bethlehem and how they escape Herod's persecution by fleeing to Egypt. They return to Nazareth after Herod's death.

Gaventa has a maternal perspective on these passages, imagining herself in Mary's shoes:

> With his consistent use of the phrase "the child and his mother" Matthew reflects a powerful connection between the two. When the Magi finally arrive at the place of the star, they see both the child and Mary. The flight

to Egypt involves not two parents and the child they protect but Joseph who is instructed to protect "the child
and his mother." If Jesus is threatened, so is his mother.
In Matthew's story, the two belong together. . . . Mary's
exclusive role in Matthew is that of mother. Matthew interprets that maternity, however, not in terms of an emotional attachment or anxiety or grief, but in terms of the
possibilities for destruction that threaten Mary.[45]

So Jesus and Mary are inseparable: Jesus is worshiped as
he resides with his mother; both are threatened together;
both flee to Egypt under Joseph's protection. Thus, Mary
is linked to Christ and Christ to Mary, all the way to Calvary. Her existence has no meaning apart from Christ. Such
observations go beyond enunciating facts to uncover deeper
gospel insights by getting into Mary's shoes.

Paul's Version of Mary

Few of Paul's writings deal with Mary directly. Galatians
4:4 mentions Mary's role in the Incarnation, although almost as in passing, as Byassee mentions:

When Paul makes his one oblique mention of Jesus'
mother it is to point to her as a sign that he was indeed
born ["born of woman"], and so was genuinely human.[46]

Macquarrie draws out some of the significance of Paul's
sparse statements:

He must then also have purposed to bring the human race
to that moment in its history when it had been so cleared
of sin, and sanctified by grace that it would be ready to
receive the gift of the incarnate divine life. That moment

42

in the history of mankind was Mary. Even if we did not know Mary's name or anything about her history and background, we would have to posit this moment in the history of humanity, as indeed Paul does when he says of Jesus that he was "born of a woman" and this happened in "the fullness of the time."[47]

Paul says little about Mary because he says little about the Incarnation—an essential truth of the Faith! Perry concludes,

It is highly probable that the earliest followers of Jesus believed in Christ's preincarnate existence . . . [and] that a preincarnate Christ became a human being. . . . He was "born of a woman, born under the law," and . . . [therefore was] a human male who entered the world in the most natural way—birth. . . . Paul indirectly mentions Mary only with respect to her role as Christ's mother[, saying] nothing regarding Christ's miraculous conception.[48]

Was Paul aware of Mary conceiving Christ virginally and its significance? Perry finds it odd "that a series of texts acknowledging both the preincarnate existence of Christ and his complete humanity would say absolutely nothing about his virginal conception," suggesting that Paul was ignorant of Christ's virginal conception or Mary's role in redemption.[49] More likely, Mary and Christ's *incarnation*—foundational and inseparable from Christ's divinity—were just indisputable for Paul. As he writes,

[Christ] is the image of the invisible God, the firstborn of all creation; for in him all things were created, in heaven and on earth, visible and invisible, whether thrones or dominions or principalities or authorities—all things were created through him and for him. He is before all things, and in him all things hold together (Col. 1:15–17).

John, a profound mystical writer, also only alludes to Christ's birth and Mary as the mother of the eternal Word of God (John 1:1–3), who became flesh and dwelt among us (v. 14) without being born "of bloods" (vv. 12-13).

> **INSIGHT 3:**
> *Paul and John say little about Christ's incarnation or Mary's role, even though these are inseparable teachings key to their theology.*

Next we will explore Paul's great companion and collaborator, Luke, and his insights on the Virgin Mary.

QUESTIONS AND ANSWERS

Q: Both Old and New Testaments say little about Mary. To try to extract something from nothing is not fair to God's word. Shouldn't we restrict ourselves to literal references, as the others are too subjective and difficult to reach agreement on?

A: As we try to identify all Scripture referring to Mary, we are fulfilling Christ's Sermon on the Mount, to fulfill *all* of Scripture:

Think not that I have come to abolish the law and the prophets; I have come not to abolish them but to fulfill them. For truly, I say to you, till heaven and earth pass away, not an iota, not a dot, will pass from the law until all is accomplished. Whoever then relaxes one of the least of these commandments and teaches men so, shall be called least in the kingdom of heaven; but he who does them and teaches them shall be called great in the kingdom of heaven (Matt. 5:17–19).

Would we be "fair to God's word" by reducing what the Bible says to a handful of literal statements? God's word includes *all* that we find in the Bible. Identifying *all* that Scripture says about Mary is to be truly "fair." To fulfill *all* of Scripture means fulfilling not only the literal references, but also the "subjective" ones, or the ones that make us uncomfortable. God gives the Spirit to the apostles and their successors to teach us *all* things (John 14:26). That is why we are interested in *all* Bible passages that may refer to the Virgin Mary.

Q: Not even Catholics practice Old Testament rituals and customs. In fact, Paul tells us they are no longer valid for worship. How is it that they are useful for describing New Testament religious truths?

A: The Old Testament was written not to be discarded. It was written in anticipation of Christ and his Church. Even Protestants use the ancient dictum: *The New Testament lies hidden in the Old and the Old Testament is unveiled in the New* (CCC 129).

Mary expresses her faith and fidelity to God's word by fulfilling Old Testament rituals and customs. She doesn't try to exempt herself due to any privileged position. With trusting obedience, she humbly submits to God's word.

3

Mary According to Luke

The possibility that another religious tradition can offer us insights can seem threatening, as if somehow we don't have all the answers. But John encourages us to put aside such fears, since all truth and love come from God:

> So we know and believe the love God has for us. God is love, and he who abides in love abides in God, and God abides in him. In this is love perfected with us. . . . There is no fear in love, but perfect love casts out fear . . . and he who fears is not perfected in love (1 John 4:16–18).

Loving God and one another overcomes all fears by opening ourselves to the truth, including truths many Protestant scholars now find regarding Mary. Now let's explore their insights taken from Luke's Gospel.*

---

* Many have noted the different style found in chapers one and two of Luke—especially the high frequency of Hebraisms, suggesting that the "eyewitness" source (Luke 1:2) was none other than the Virgin Mary.

God's Amazing Grace

Luke's first two chapters give more details about Jesus' conception and birth than Matthew or John. God sends the angel Gabriel to convey his mission for Mary to be mother of the Messiah. He renames her *Kécharitôméne*, Greek for "full of grace"* or "highly favored one." David Jeffrey links this expression to similar Old Testament commendations, concluding:

> Mary recognized that she had become, like Enoch (Gen. 5:22) and Noah (who "found grace in the eyes of the Lord" [6:8]), one "highly favored" by God (Luke 1:28, 30). She saw that she would forever after be recognized as one "blessed . . . among women" (28, 42). . . . She was the one woman, out of all women, through whom God would fulfill his covenant love and promise.[50]

God's love for Mary is singular, fulfilling his covenant promise in her, linking her to other Old Testament figures and passages. Daniel Migliore sees how Protestants often miss the importance of this and of God showering her with unmerited, electing grace:

> The story of the Annunciation is told not in praise of Mary but in praise of the surprising, unmerited, electing grace of God. Mary is favored and chosen by God (Luke 1:28). It is curious that Reformed theologians have not given more attention to the place of Mary in the doctrine of election.
>
> Her election, of course, is not to be seen as competing with the election of Jesus Christ . . . [but] as a daughter of

---

* The Latin translation of *Kécharitôméne* as *full of grace* dates back to at least the second century and was preserved by Jerome in his Latin Vulgate.

the elect people of Israel, Mary is herself elected and called to a special vocation. This is the meaning of the announcement of the angel that Mary has found favor with God and that she will give birth to the Son of the Most High.[51]

Shannon Kubiak tries to imagine herself in Mary's shoes, to discover what it would be like to be full of grace, to be favored and blessed by God, and to be called to a special mission:

Mary lived a full life by accepting what it meant to be favored and blessed, and by rising to the task of a lifetime— one that wasn't always easy, but certainly proved to be worth it in the end. She signed up for a lifelong adventure when she was just a girl. Are you willing to do the same?[52]

God loved Mary and put such confidence in her, and Mary's response to God's call was to follow him on an adventure of love, not knowing how it would play out.[53]

KEY 3:
God graced (favored) Mary by loving, electing, and choosing her for a special vocation. This links her to others so graced.

Blessed Among Women in Christ

Elizabeth was filled with the Holy Spirit and she exclaimed . . . "*Blessed* are you among women . . . *blessed is she who believed* that there would be a fulfillment of what was spoken to her from the Lord" (Luke 1:41–45*).

---

* The Greek preposition *en* is translated *among* or *in*; when denoting the greatest in a category, it is usually translated *among*. Thus, "among [*en*] those born of women

As Mary was visiting her cousin, the Holy Spirit filled Elizabeth, moving her to call Mary *blessed among women*, *mother of the Lord*, and *blessed is she who believed*, giving early Christians a pattern on how to bless Mary and to link her to others whom God has blessed. By this, the Holy Spirit tells us that Mary is more blessed than any woman (and likely, more than anyone besides Jesus). Scripture blesses holy women such as "Sarah, Rebecca, Rachel, Miriam, Deborah, Hannah, Judith and Esther," but "the purest figure among them is Mary" (CCC 64, 489). Thus whenever the Bible praises a woman, it praises Mary, since she is more blessed and worthy of praise.

Mary's blessedness is based in Christ: "Blessed be the God and Father of our Lord Jesus Christ, who has blessed us in Christ with every spiritual blessing in the heavenly places" (Eph. 1:3–4). Everyone—including Mary—is blessed in Christ.

The Holy Spirit says all generations will call Mary blessed for the "great things" God does in her. Those "great things" magnify God (Luke 1:46–55). If we recognize the source of her blessing—the incarnation of the Second Person of the Trinity—then blessing Mary will not offend God, since Mary's whole being is oriented toward Jesus.

Moved by the Holy Spirit, Elizabeth says, "Blessed are you among women, and blessed is the fruit of your womb!" (Luke 1:42). The Holy Spirit blesses Mary *before* blessing her divine Son. We do not offend God by honoring and blessing Mary, as long as it is in reference to God.

---

there has risen no one greater than John the Baptist" (Matt. 11:11). Likewise, our Lord tells the disciples arguing about who is the greatest: "Let the greatest among [*en*] you become as the youngest" (Luke 22:26; cf. Matt. 18:1; 20:27). Paul condemns the Corinthians for immorality worse than "among [*en*] pagans" (1 Cor. 5:1). By the same token, Mary's blessedness "among [*en*] women" signifies that she is more blessed than any woman.

Elizabeth also says, "And why is this granted me, that
the mother of my Lord should come to me?" (Luke 1:43).
She honors God by recognizing how Mary's visit honors
her. There is no competition here. Indeed, we praise God
for the good things he does in Mary as we praise God in
his marvels. We honor and remember Mary because, as
Scripture says, we remember our leaders, imitate their
faith, and honor all men.[54] This is what Catholics mean
by *venerate*: to acknowledge, honor, and praise a creature's
greatness as a gift from God, magnifying and praising
God as the source of their greatness. This can help us
shed any prior biases, letting the Holy Spirit guide us to
see Scripture in a new light and to identify other passages
about Mary.

Jon Sweeney uses this to find other Marian passages:

> She was pronounced "blessed" by her cousin, Elizabeth
> . . . and there is perhaps no word that has come to define
> her more. . . . "Blessed" links Mary to her Jewish fore-
> bears. Moses said to the people Israel, "If you will only
> obey the Lord your God. . . . Blessed shall be the fruit
> of your womb, the fruit of your ground, and the fruit
> of your livestock," in Deuteronomy 28:1 and 4. "Most
> blessed of women be Jael, the wife of Heber the Kenite,
> of tent-dwelling women most blessed," says Judges 5:24.
> And Uzziah praised Judith for cutting off the head of
> Nebuchadnezzar's top general, saying, "O daughter,
> you are blessed by the Most High God above all other
> women on earth" (Jth. 13:18). . . . Mary is one of these
> great women of Israel . . . but she is clearly more than
> that, too. She is a culmination of the adjective of God's
> action, "blessed."[55]

> **KEY 4:**
> *Mary is blessed in Christ as more blessed than any woman. Thus, when any woman or feminine attribute is praised, Mary is, too.*

For example, we can infer from Scripture that Mary was beautiful—the "fairest among women" (Song of Sol. 5:9; 6:1)—through references such as "the sons of God saw that the daughters of men were fair" (Gen. 6:1–2), or God rewarding Job's steadfastness with three beautiful daughters: "And in all the land there were no women so fair as Job's daughters" (Job 42:15). As "blessed among women," Mary is more blessed and thus more beautiful.

Mary's beauty may carry little theological significance, but it shows us how a simple interpretive key identifies other Marian Scripture passages for consideration. When Scripture praises physical and social feminine traits, such as beauty, gracefulness, and temperance, it indicates that Mary, being more blessed, had all these qualities.[56] The Bible compliments women (and thus Mary) for moral and intellectual virtues as well, mentioning those who are wise, kind, trustworthy, reverent, respectful, and full of good works. Blessed women are modest, pure, clear, spotless, and undefiled—that is, preserved from violation, as were Sarah and Rebekah. A woman's purity and virginity are honored, especially a virgin daughter or a pure bride, or when it frees her from worldly pursuits to follow the Lamb wherever he goes to serve his kingdom.[57]

Being blessed includes spiritual qualities: being holy, good, humble—calling herself lowly—or putting her hope in God.[58] As we saw, Mary's great faith, like the woman healed for touching the fringe of Christ's garment—he told her, "your faith has made you well" (Matt. 9:20–22)—or like the sinful woman who anointed our Lord's feet and wiped them dry with her hair—he praised her for her great love, saying that her faith had saved her (Luke 7:36–50). Yet Mary is more blessed than these women, because she has greater faith, having touched much more than our Lord's tassel or feet—she kissed and bathed the divine infant's whole body.

So biblical women with outstanding feminine qualities prefigure Mary, the ultimate woman of worth (Ruth 3:11).

David Jeffrey links Mary to the Psalms with this key: "Elizabeth's words of greeting to her, 'Blessed are you among women,' echo Psalm 1: 'Blessed is the man who walks not in the counsel of the ungodly.'"[59]

Blessed Is She Who Believed

The principal reason for Mary's greatness—for all generations of Christians to venerate her by calling her blessed—is her faith, which shows up throughout the Bible. As Jesus declares to Thomas: "*Blessed are those who* have not seen and yet *believe*" (John 20:29).

Being Christian means having a relationship with Christ. Jesus himself points this out when he asks the rhetorical question, "Who are my mother and my brothers?" and responds, "Whoever does the will of God is my brother, and sister, and mother" (Mark 3:33–35). By these words Jesus compliments Mary as a person of faith who fulfills God's will, making her Jesus' *spiritual mother and sister.* So when the woman praises Jesus' mother for "the womb that bore you, and the breasts that nursed you!", Jesus tells us the real reason we should bless and praise Mary: "Blessed rather are those who hear the word of God and keep it!" (Luke 11:27–28). Mary keeps God's word in her heart and lives it out her entire life, even to the cross (John 19:25–34). She is more blessed for her *spiritual maternity*—for keeping God's word—than for her physical maternity.*

Mary's faith is remarkable because she trusted completely in God's word. Mary's "yes" to God, "let it be done unto me," is an act of humble faith, of total submission to God, Timothy George notes.[60] Mark Roberts calls her response of faith extraordinary, one all Christians should emulate.[61]

Mary admired Jesus' work with reverential awe and amazement, but not everyone else did: some scoffed and chose not to believe his miracles. How this must have pained her. All faithful Christians experience this when people see God's marvelous works but scoff, discarding them as chance coincidences of some inexplicable scientific cause, or when they scoff at us for refusing to compromise our moral convictions. Mary remained faithful to the Master. Do we?

We see Mary's faith throughout her life. It took great faith to

- commit herself to virginity,** even after marrying Joseph (Luke 1:26–38), then accept that she could conceive and give birth without losing her virginity (CCC 148);[62]

- willingly say yes to God's word—*be it done unto me according to your word* (Luke 1:38)—agreeing to bear God's Son, knowing he would be the sacrificial lamb and suffering servant of Isaiah;

---

* Pope John Paul II's *Redemptoris Mater* develops this theme much more extensively.

** When the angel reveals God's call for her to be his mother (Luke 1:31–38), Mary replies firmly that she does not and will not *know man* (the Greek phrase *andra ou ginosko* is akin to *I don't eat meat*—i.e., *I have no sexual relations with men*. Jaroslav Pelikan notes that the Hebrew scriptures use *to know man* to indicate *marital relations*—Pelikan (1996) 72-73, contrasting Mary, who "knew not man," to Eve, who "knew" Adam to conceive Cain and Seth (Gen. 4:1,25). We will analyze Mary's virginity more fully in Chapter 6 to determine the true scriptural basis of this belief.

- embark on a long trip to Bethlehem while nine months pregnant, not knowing where or when the child would be born (Luke 2:1–7);

- carry him nine months in her womb, nurse him, and take care of him, while worshiping him as God!;

- ask Jesus for a miracle at the wedding feast of Cana (John 2:1–12); it really takes faith, asking a person who had never worked a miracle before!;

- remain faithful to Christ when he is severely persecuted, standing beside him at the foot of his cross (John 19:25–34), unwaveringly enduring the sight of her son suffering horribly (CCC 149); and

- remain with the apostles (Acts 1:14), believing that Christ could build his Church on this group of cowards.

Mary sought God with her whole heart and walked in his ways, as prefigured by men and women of faith (Gen. 5:22–24, Mic. 6:8–9, Hab. 2:4, Rom. 1:17, etc., particularly Elizabeth in Luke 1:5–6). Timothy George sees how her discipleship anticipated her divine motherhood.[63] Jon Sweeney concludes, calling Mary Christ's "first disciple,"

> She believed, and in so believing, became the first true disciple of her as yet unborn son. . . . Mary is the chief disciple because she shows us how to wait on God, expect God, have awe for God, and hope for God, but not with an easy credulity. Hers was not an unquestioning belief; these qualities are, instead, the qualities of a mature disciple. And for Mary, these expectations of awe and hope began at about the age of thirteen![64]

As a disciple of Christ, Mary fulfilled Psalm 119:

> Blessed are those whose way is blameless, who walk in the law of the Lord! Blessed are those who keep his testimonies, who seek him with their whole heart, who also do no wrong, but walk in his ways! (vv. 1–3).

Many women are praised for their faith, prefiguring Mary, such as Sarah (Heb. 11:11–12) and the Canaanite woman (Matt. 15:22–28). Pelikan notices how early Christians linked Mary to many women of faith in the Bible:

> For without invoking the word "faith" explicitly, these words put into action the identification of faith with obedience, and by describing her obedience to the word of God made of her the model of faith. Indeed, beginning with Mary and moving backward through the history of Israel, it would be possible to devise a roll call of female saints—Eve and Sarah, Esther and Ruth, and many more—of whom [Mary] was an exemplar, just as it would be possible to . . . construct a similar roster of female saints since the New Testament era. And by its emphasis on faith such a roster could commend itself even to those heirs of the Protestant Reformation who have traditionally regarded with profound suspicion any such elitism among believers.[65]

Shannon Kubiak even links Mary to great men of faith—such as Abraham—especially insofar as their example influenced her faithful response.[66] The New Testament blesses and honors Abraham as a great paradigm of faith:[67]

> By faith Abraham, when he was tested, offered up Isaac, and he who had received the promises was ready to offer

up his only son . . . He considered that God was able to raise men even from the dead; hence, figuratively speaking, he did receive him back (Heb. 11:17–19).

Mary too should be so honored, having even greater faith (CCC 144), being tested with the sacrifice of her son (CCC 165), believing that God could raise him from the dead; indeed, she did receive him back. All generations call her blessed—as they do Abraham—because she, too, believed, and her faith is accounted to her as righteousness.

Other faith-filled individuals can be identified and related to Mary, such as Abel, Enoch, Noah, Isaac, Jacob, Joseph, Moses' mother, Moses, Joshua, Rahab, and many who ask our Lord for miracles. Scripture enlightens our understanding of Mary through such figures.*

Augustine[68] (and John Paul II[69]) saw Mary's faith as key to understanding Mary as a true disciple. God calls us, as he called Mary, to believe, trust, and surrender to him, freely assenting to, obeying, and cooperating with his word (CCC 148, 488, 490). Mary's faith is free, strong, and courageous, as Scot McKnight points out:

Mary, in faith, consented to God's plan. Mary, in faith, began to carry a cross before Jesus was born. Mary began to suffer for the Messiah before the Messiah suffered.[70]

KEY 5:
Mary, Christ's first disciple, is blessed for her faith.
Persons of faith may prefigure her.

---

*   We could identify more persons of faith in Scripture but have limited ourselves to those passages that explicitly refer to faith, belief, and unbelief. Many other passage make implicit references to faith and persons of faith.

Blessed for Her Love

Every Christian develops a spiritual relationship with Christ, beginning with faith, then growing with charity. Jesus says,

> "Come, O blessed of my Father, inherit the kingdom prepared for you from the foundation of the world; for I was hungry and you gave me food, I was thirsty . . . a stranger . . . naked . . . sick . . . in prison and you came to me."
>
> Then the righteous will answer him, "Lord, when did we see thee hungry . . . thirsty . . . a stranger . . . naked . . . sick or in prison?"
>
> And the King will answer them, "Truly, I say to you, as you did it to one of the least of these my brethren, you did it to me" (Matt. 25:34–40).

Paul writes, "Earnestly desire the higher gifts . . . a still more excellent way. . . . If I have all faith, so as to remove mountains, but have not love, I am nothing. . . . So faith, hope, love . . . but the greatest of these is love" (1 Cor. 12:31–13:2, 13). Though blessed due to her faith, without love, Mary would be nothing. But she loved Christ in a myriad of details of service. This helps us understand how these passages and those praises of others for their charity refer especially to Mary.

For example, we can apply this key to the sinful woman who anointed our Lord:

> Then turning toward the woman he said to Simon, "Do you see this woman? I entered your house, you gave me no water for my feet, but she has wet my feet with her tears and wiped them with her hair. You gave me no kiss, but from the time I came in she has not ceased to kiss my feet. You did not anoint my head

with oil, but she has anointed my feet with ointment. Therefore I tell you, her sins, which are many, are forgiven, for she loved much . . ." And he said to her, "Your sins are forgiven . . . Your faith has saved you; go in peace" (Luke 7:44–50).

Jesus blesses this woman because of her faith and great love; Mary is more blessed, because her faith moved her to love him even more. Another Mary also anointed our Lord shortly before his passion, making Judas indignant over the ointment's value. But Jesus said,

> "Let her alone; why do you trouble her? She has done a beautiful thing to me. For you always have the poor with you, and whenever you will, you can do good to them; but you will not always have me. She has done what she could; she has anointed my body beforehand for burying. And truly, I say to you, wherever the gospel is preached in the whole world, what she has done will be told in memory of her" (Mark 14:6–9; see also Matt. 26:6–13 and John 12:1–8).

The Virgin Mary did even more for Jesus, carrying him in her womb, holding him in her arms, bathing him, etc. Mary would have responded to Jesus when he was hungry and thirsty, when he was cold and naked. She changed his diapers, laundered his clothes, kept a welcoming and clean home, and prepared his meals; she would have taught him Scripture, told him family stories, and more. She did much more than anoint his body, and all with faith and great love. Certainly, everything that she "has done will be told in memory of her," for she is to be blessed for all generations, "wherever the gospel is preached in the whole world."

KEY 6:
*Persons of charity or service may reflect
Mary's faith-filled response of love.*

"Magnifying" God with Scripture

Mary's *Magnificat* (Luke 1:46–55) is a marvelous hymn of praise that recognizes God's work in her. All generations will call her blessed because of the great things God has done in her. Jason Byassee sees how the Magnificat reveals Mary's mastery of Scripture.[71] Beverly Gaventa marvels at Mary's great act of praise and thanksgiving to God, as she considers it an honor and grace to serve as a good disciple. She prophesies to us:

> In the powerful words of the Magnificat, she becomes not only a disciple but also a prophet. With imagery of God exalting the lowly and humbling the mighty, Mary's words recall prominent prophetic themes and anticipate the presence of those same themes in Jesus' sermon at Nazareth.[72]

David Jeffrey links the canticle to divinely inspired poets, Miriam and Hannah.[73] Scot McKnight calls the Magnificat the *"Magna Carta* of early Christian songs," showing its connection to many Old Testament passages,[74] as do Perry[75] and Jeffrey.[76] We can weave these discoveries into the text itself:

> *My soul magnifies the Lord, and my spirit rejoices in God my Savior* (1 Sam. 2:1–2; Ps. 34:2–3, 35:9; Isa. 61:10; Hab. 3:18),
>
> *for he has regarded the low estate of his handmaiden* (Gen. 29:32, 1 Sam. 1:11, Ps. 86:16).
>
> *For behold, henceforth all generations will call me blessed* (Gen. 30:13, Jth. 13:15–20, Ps. 45:13–17, Mal. 3:12);

for he who is mighty has done great things for me (Deut. 10:21, Ps. 71:19b), *and holy is his name* (Ps. 111:9).

And his mercy is on those who fear him from generation to generation (Ps. 103:11,17; 100:5).

He has shown strength with his arm, he has scattered the proud in the imagination of their hearts, he has put down the mighty from their thrones, and exalted those of low degree; he has filled the hungry with good things, and the rich he has sent empty away (1 Sam. 2:7–9; Job 12:19; Ps. 89:10, 107:9, 113:7–9; Prov. 3:34; Ezek. 21:26).

He has helped his servant Israel, in remembrance of his mercy, as he spoke to our fathers, to Abraham and to his posterity forever (2 Sam. 22:51, Ps. 98:3, Isa. 41:8–9, Mic. 7:20).

Sweeney parallels Mary's Magnificat with Psalms 8 and 90,[77] similar to the messianic prophecy of Zephaniah. As the daughter of Jerusalem, Mary seems to sing out the Lord's praises for fulfilling his prophecy to redeem Israel and the whole world, because she sees that in her womb, "the King of Israel, the Lord, is in your midst," who is the Immanuel: *God with us.*

Such parallels were common in how early Christians read the Old Testament. In this way, they discovered passages applicable to the Virgin Mary, reaching new insights into her.

Pondering Christ's Childhood

After Mary and Joseph return from the hill country, God unexpectedly uproots them, directing them to go to Bethlehem, where Jesus will be born. Kubiak ponders how hard God's plans can be:

Think of Mary and how she must have felt on the night she and Joseph rode into Bethlehem. . . . How miserable

Mary must have been on that long ride—and then to find out there was no room for her at the inn. . . . Hadn't she already suffered enough? Don't you think she had already paid more than her fair share of dues? . . .

But I can imagine all of Mary's loneliness faded away the second she heard the first cry of the baby Jesus.

Holding him in her arms was probably all it took to make Mary forget about how hard the ground was.[78]

Obviously, none of us would have planned it this way. When Mary said *yes* to God, she didn't imagine this. But she obeys. She lets God *call the shots*. What a great example of faith.

When the shepherds come to the cave, Mary welcomes them, shows them the child Jesus, and then listens to their story of the angels. Mary marvels and ponders their words in her heart, as Byassee marvels.[79] Bonnie Miller-McLemore includes the Annunciation in Mary's pondering:

[Luke] uses similar phrasing earlier in characterizing Mary's response to her angelic visitation, where Mary pondered or "considered in her mind what sort of greeting this might be" (Luke 1:29b).[80]

Tim Perry links Mary's pondering and her *keeping all these things* to Jacob (Gen. 37:11), who kept the things of Joseph's dreams in his mind, and to Daniel, who pondered the matters of his dream of the four living beasts (Dan. 7:28).[81] Mary's pondering is a notable characteristic of her faith for Macquarrie[82] and Sweeney.[83] And Mary's pondering came to mean more to Miller-McLemore when she became a mother, since this is a natural feminine way of responding to a child, with constant amazement.[84]

After the presentation of the child Jesus in the temple, Mary ponders Simeon's prophetic words:

And Simeon blessed them and said to Mary his mother, "Behold, this child is set for the fall and rising of many in Israel, and for a sign that is spoken against (and a sword will pierce through your own soul also), that thoughts out of many hearts may be revealed" (Luke 2:34–35).

A soul-piercing sword inseparably links Mary to Jesus—the sign to be crossed, contradicted. This prophecy is ominous and threatening for a new mother, as Gaventa describes:

The foreboding element that enters the birth narrative in Simeon's oracle concerns both the resistance to Jesus that will eventually lead to his death and the implications of that death for "Mary, his mother."[85]

Perry links Mary's sword to Old Testament passages,[86] such as "Deliver my soul from the sword" (Ps. 22:20). He also includes:

And I will pour out on the house of David . . . a spirit of compassion . . . so that, when they look on him whom they have pierced, they shall mourn for him, as one mourns for an only child, and weep bitterly over him, as one weeps over a firstborn (Zech. 12:10).

If I bring a sword upon that land, and say, Let a sword go through the land; and I cut off from it man and beast; though these three men were in it, as I live, says the Lord God, they would deliver neither sons nor daughters, but they alone would be delivered (Ezek. 14:17–18).

Jesus goes up to Jerusalem with his mother and father to worship God in the Temple. For McClain, this event shows Mary to be a faithful worshiper.[87] Leaving the Temple, Mary and Joseph lose track of Jesus for three days. Simeon's foreboding words must have echoed in Mary's ears. As Sarah Hinlicky Wilson describes it,

> in Luke's telling, the sword piercing Mary's soul arrives far sooner than the Crucifixion. . . . It occurs in the very next scene, the single account of Jesus' boyhood in the New Testament. If the Presentation foreshadows Jesus' sacrifice on the cross, his loss and re-discovery in the Temple mirrors the Resurrection.[88]

Kubiak also helps us appreciate how much Mary must have suffered in missing Christ:

> She took advantage of every moment she had with her Lord. She loved him—and when she was worried and confused we see her frantically searching for Jesus. As long as she had Jesus, everything was okay.[89]

Mary treasures each moment with Christ, yet she does not understand: how could he allow her such pain (Luke 2:50)? Only after our Lord's death and resurrection, the pain of losing her son for three days will find its full meaning. Byassee sees how Mary continues to be blessed and active through all generations, due to her link to Christ's salvific cross.[90]

> **KEY 7:**
> *Mary magnifies God through Old Testament Scripture,*
> *which she knew and pondered, as she did Christ. Her*
> *faith-filled pondering links her to other Old Testament*
> *figures and anticipates losing Christ at the cross.*

Jesus then returns to subject himself, actively and freely, to his mother and father. He obeys them as his parents, an image of his obedience to his heavenly Father (CCC 532).

Accompanying the Church

In the Acts of the Apostles, Luke continues his account of Mary. Reading between the lines, Kubiak considers what experiencing Christ's resurrection would have meant to Mary—seeing her son, who had suffered so much, alive again! "Imagine Mary's joy when God revealed his eternal plans for her. There was to be life after death—it doesn't get any sweeter than that!"[91]

Luke also describes Mary in the Upper Room with the Lord's disciples at Pentecost. As Byassee explains,

> it is striking that Mary is in the Upper Room at Pente-cost—the only woman present there who is named—to receive the outpouring of God's Spirit at the birth of the Church (Acts 1:14).[92]

Being with our Lord's disciples after the Resurrection has deep theological implications. Mary actively accompanies the Church with her prayerful presence, as Migliore notes:

> We read that all of the followers of Jesus came together after his resurrection and ascension and devoted them-selves constantly to prayer for the coming of God's enliv-ening and empowering Spirit. . . .

Mary prays and waits for the coming of the life-giving Spirit of God. Mary's spirituality is a spirituality of common prayer, of sharing with others in the disciplines and practices of Christian life. The commission that she and the other disciples had received from the crucified and risen Jesus could be acted on only in a context of common, prayerful waiting on God. This waiting is not quietist; it is not mere passivity. It is a persistent, hopeful, and active waiting for the coming of God's Word and Spirit.[93]

Mary's presence in the early Church is essential, as the Holy Spirit attests. It shows the importance of prayer in the Church's efforts to evangelize the world, as Pope Benedict XVI affirms.[94] John Paul II even sees Mary keeping the presence of the risen Jesus among them.[95]

> **INSIGHT 4:**
> *Mary's joy in the risen Jesus was immense.*
> *Her presence at Pentecost highlights her*
> *prayerful role in the Church.*

Early Christians discovered even more Scripture passages shedding light on the mystery of Mary, as we will see.

QUESTIONS AND ANSWERS

Q: Why make such a big deal of a passive, humble, and servile housewife—handmaid, slave—who just took care of her brood of kids and met her husband's desires? Why not focus on women who did something outstanding, like Judith?

A: Mary was not passive, but a strong, resilient woman who offered her whole life to God. Mary's faith exemplifies complete abandonment to God's will, risking everything, including her own life. Kubiak considers this a model for all Christians:

> The penalty in those days for premarital pregnancy was to be stoned to death. Mary knew that when she agreed to be part of God's plan. What we most often fail to realize is that Mary had a choice in this whole matter. Gabriel's words to Mary did not come in the form of a command; she had to agree to the divine offer. Mary submitted to the will of God out of obedience and out of her own free will. . . .
>
> Mary was asked to relinquish her reputation, her honor, and her very life if she needed to in order to answer God's call. Think about that for a second. Mary—who was a virgin—was asked to take on a role that would cause many to think of her as loose in her morals and worthy of death. . . .
>
> What do you know of Calvary love? Calvary (Jesus' crucifixion) had not even happened yet, and Mary held nothing back when it came to what she was willing to give her Lord. Should any less be expected of us?[96]

Migliore compares Mary to the great men of faith of the Old Testament:

> Mary's response—"Here am I, the servant of the Lord, Let it be with me according to your word"—is reminiscent of the replies of Abraham, Moses, Samuel, and Isaiah to the summons of God. It is a free, strong, and courageous response to the sovereign, electing grace of

God addressed to her and has nothing to do with what is commonly understood by words like passivity and servility.[97]

Amazingly, the Spirit calls Mary "blessed among women" (Luke 1:42), just as he did Judith (Jth. 13:15–20). So let's open ourselves to the full scriptural truth about Mary before judging whether Mary was passive and servile or a strong, bold disciple of Jesus Christ.

Q: If God wanted us to know more details about how he took flesh in the womb of the Virgin Mary, then he would have told us so directly, without expecting us to make things up through Old Testament musings. Aren't we "adding" to Scripture by such musings?

A: This simply is the way early Christians read Scripture. In fact, it was the only way they could "prove" that Jesus Christ was God, the Second Person of the Blessed Trinity. Nowhere does Scripture explicitly mention that God is a unity of three divine persons and that the Second Person would be our Messiah.

Consider how the letter to the Hebrews—an early Christian canonical text—uses the Old Testament to "prove" to the Jews that Jesus Christ is God, the fulfillment of the high priesthood, the sacrifice that expiates our sins. Hebrews 1:1–2:9 shows that Jesus is God through Scripture, by quoting

• Psalm 2:7, 97:7, 104:4; 2 Samuel 7:14; Deuteronomy 32:43 (Septuagint) to show that God calls the Messiah his son and thus is greater than the angels, since he never calls an angel his son;

- Psalm 45:6–7 to show that God anoints him and gives him his scepter;

- Psalm 102:25–7 to show that the Messiah was present at creation;

- Psalm 110:1 to show that he is greater than the angels because he sits at God's right hand; and

- Psalm 8:4–6 to show that, as man, the Messiah is lower than the angels, but as lord over everything, he is greater than the angels.

Hebrews uses Scripture in this way to "prove" that Jesus is God, although no passage conveys that teaching literally. In fact, some of its logic could even be disputed. Yet, taken as a whole, Hebrews shows how the Old Testament prepared for Christ; as the second person of the Blessed Trinity, Christ is the best fulfillment of Old Testament Scripture.

The letter does the same regarding the high priesthood and the true expiatory sacrifice, which are connected with Christ's divinity.

Q: You emphasize Mary's maternal relationship with Christ. But Christ belongs to his heavenly Father and came to the earth to be about his Father's business (Luke 2:49). Didn't Christ just use Mary as the vessel to bring him into this world, such that once he grew and matured, he left his earthly father and mother to fulfill his divine mission?

A: It is appalling to think God would "use" Mary just to bear him in her womb and then deny his special relationship with his mother. That would mean God would be treating Mary as an object and not as a person. What would that teach our young people about how to treat their mothers? What would that teach us about how to treat our elderly parents?

Although we are all called to leave our father and mother, and our brothers and sisters—some in order to cling to a spouse (Gen. 2:24), others for the kingdom of God (Matt. 19:10–12) or for the sake of his name (v. 29)—we still must honor our parents (Exod. 20:12; Matt. 19:19; etc.). I find it hard to imagine that Jesus—who had such a big heart for children, for the sick and lame, for Lazarus, Martha, and Mary—would just disregard his relationship with his mother. In fact, Scripture reproves such a person: "He who . . . chases away his mother is a son who causes shame and brings reproach" (Prov. 19:26). Jesus reproves the Pharisees for permitting a person to treat his parents as mere "vessels," dedicating all their income to God as "corban." Could you imagine him then saying to his mother, "All that you have done for me is corban—that is, given to God" (Mark 7:11–12)?

Yet Jesus had to apply to himself what he required of his disciples: "He who loves father or mother more than me is not worthy of me; and he who loves son or daughter more than me is not worthy of me" (Matt. 10:37). Being available to do God's will is more important than physical bonds of blood. If we don't put God first, we are not worthy of him; if Christ didn't put his heavenly Father first, then he would not be worthy of being the Son of God.

Q: Does Mary's pondering define her?

A: Several Protestant scholars arrive at that conclusion, such as Miller-McLemore:

> "Ponder" involves a certain acceptance of realities that go beyond our understanding. At such a point, the only response

is appreciation and perhaps amazement. This play on the text's vocabulary hints at three aspects of mothering that deserve elaboration as powerful activities of mothering implied by Luke's words: attention, anguish, and amazement. . . .

In her attentive pondering, Mary models a certain kind of Christian spirituality of presence, what I have attempted to describe elsewhere as "contemplation in the midst of chaos." Contemplation is not simply something monks do in solitary settings.[98]

Kubiak emphasizes the faith implied in Mary's pondering the word of God:

To treasure the things God told you and keep them in your heart . . . means no matter what—just like Mary—you can see God is telling you the exact words you need to hear for whatever comes next. It means you have learned from the journey you have been on thus far, and your ears and heart are tuned to hear what God is going to say next.[99]

Q: Mary didn't know that Jesus would die on the cross, so how could Jesus' stay in the Temple foreshadow that event?

A: Mary didn't know the time or the manner in which Jesus would die, but she must have read Isaiah's suffering servant prophecies:

From the soles of his feet to the top of his head, there is nothing healthy in him: wounds and bruises and swelling sores. They are not bound up, nor dressed, nor anointed with oil.

There is no beauty in him, nor comeliness: and we have seen him, and there was no sightliness, that we should be attracted to him. Despised and the most abject of men, a man of sorrows and acquainted with infirmity; and his look was as it were hidden and despised. Whereupon we esteemed him not.

He has borne our infirmities and carried our sorrows, and we have taken him for a leper, and as one struck by God and afflicted. But he was wounded for our iniquities and bruised for our sins. On him fell the punishment that brought us salvation, and by his wounds we have been healed. . . .

He offered himself up because it was his will; abused and ill-treated, he opened not his mouth, as a sheep led to the slaughter, dumb as a lamb before its shearers (Isa. 1:6; 53:2–5, 7).

Psalm 21:17–18 also would have warned her: "They have pierced my hands and feet. I can count all my bones, and they stare and gloat over me." Reflecting on these and other passages must have caused Mary anguish enough to ask: When? How? By whom? Then the sorrow, grief, and questioning must have intensified when Jesus suddenly was no longer there. How this would painfully pierce her heart. Finding him would have brought relief, only to repeat the questioning: When? How? By whom?

4

Mary in Typology

The Holy Spirit guided an Ethiopian eunuch as he tried to understand Scripture:

> An angel of the Lord said to Philip, "Rise and go toward the south to the road that goes down from Jerusalem to Gaza." . . . And he rose and went. And behold, an Ethiopian, a eunuch . . . was returning [from Jerusalem]; seated in his chariot, he was reading the prophet Isaiah. And the Spirit said to Philip, "Go up and join this chariot." So Philip ran to him, and heard him reading Isaiah the prophet, and asked, "Do you understand what you are reading?" And he said, "How can I, unless someone guides me?" And he invited Philip to . . . sit with him (Acts 8:26–31).

The eunuch sought to penetrate the message hidden in Isaiah's use of biblical types:

> As a sheep led to the slaughter or a lamb before its shearer is dumb, so he opens not his mouth. In his humiliation justice was denied him. Who can describe his generation? For his life is taken up from the earth (Isa. 53:7–8, Septuagint).

By humbly accepting Philip's help, the eunuch came to see the truth that the "sheep led to the slaughter" was fulfilled in Christ. May the Spirit guide us as we try to do the same for biblical types of Mary.

Many Protestants emphasize a literal reading of Scripture, yet some do turn to early Christian writers for inspiring insights and interpretations of the Bible. As William J. Abraham notes:

> [Evangelicals'] first move will be to explore the full range of biblical texts. However, it is obvious that the theological work cannot stop there. On the one hand, there is a rich tradition of interpretation of the relevant texts that become pertinent if the full meaning of the text is to be mined. . . . Evangelicals have rightly turned to the whole history of exegesis as a source of insight. . . . Thus, the study of Mary in Scripture cannot in the end be confined to Scripture.[100]

Exploring the art, music, and literature of the last twenty centuries, Jaroslav Pelikan discovered that ancient Christians went well beyond Scripture passages that reference Mary literally. They dug deep into the Old Testament to make sense of the New:

> For with their belief in the unity of the Bible, where "the New Testament is hidden in the Old and the Old becomes visible in the New [*Novum in Vetere latet, Vetus in Novo patet*]," and with the consequent ability to toggle effortlessly from one Testament to the other and from fulfillment to prophecy and back again, biblical interpreters throughout most of Christian history have had available to them a vast body of supplementary material. . . .

Indeed, before there were the four Gospels, much less the entire New Testament, there was a Scripture, which Christians eventually came to call "Old Testament" and which, because of the centrality of typology and allegory, and because of the concept of prophecy and fulfillment, we are obliged to call a "Christian Scripture." . . .

As the history of the development of biblical interpretation in the early Church makes evident . . . [it was] the entire Patristic tradition, East and West, that carried on such study of the foreshadowing of Mary in the Old Testament.[101]

Seeking to understand the Incarnation of God's eternal Word, early Christians scoured the Old Testament for clues and metaphors beyond the literal reading of Scripture. As Jon Sweeney—another Lutheran—concludes,

The dictum of the Protestant Reformation as to what makes for religious truth did not exist before the sixteenth century. In other words, the notion that, in order for a religious statement to be true it must be verifiable in the Bible, did not exist. Many of the first Protestants used this measure as a way of eradicating beliefs that had become dangerous. . . . Similarly, other early Protestants used this dictum to declare that all statuary of Mary, hymnbooks, and other religious articles should be stripped from the churches because the Bible does not make mention of them.[102]

For Sweeney, a strict, literal approach to the Bible misses the broader reading found in the early Church and its centuries of art, literature, and music. He and Pelikan found types and metaphors for Mary, including the Bride of the

Song of Solomon[103] and these words: "Surely you are a bridegroom of blood to me!" (Exod. 4:25), linking Mary to Christ's crucifixion.[104]

Scripture Types

Early Christians routinely explored how Old Testament "types" foreshadowed New Testament persons and events, revealing how Christ fulfilled Scripture.[105] Paul explains,

> Therefore as sin came into the world through one man and death through sin, and so death spread to all men because all men sinned—sin indeed was in the world before the law was given, but sin is not counted where there is no law. Yet death reigned from Adam to Moses, even over those whose sins were not like the transgression of Adam, who was a *type* of the one who was to come (Rom. 5:12–14).

In Acts 7:44, Stephen uses the word *pattern* to refer to types, as does Hebrews 8:5. Paul also uses the word *shadow* or *copies* to refer to, for example, the Old Testament Sabbath and festivals foreshadowing the Lord's Day and New Testament feasts. Similarly, Hebrews describes the Old Testament Law, high priesthood, sacrifices, the Temple, the Sanctuary, etc. as *copies* or *shadows* of Christ and of other New Testament realities.[106]

Types are real, historical persons, institutions, places, things, or events that prophetically prefigure and find fulfillment in Christ, or in real, historical New Testament counterparts. The fulfillment of a type is the *antitype*, which is always greater than the type. Parallel facts or similarities link the two, transferring the type's meaning to the antitype. It is God—Scripture's true author—who gives the type-antitype link its foundation in his intended meaning of the Scripture passage.

Some types are *positive*: Jonah's three days in the fish prefigures our Lord's three days in the tomb; the Great Flood, Noah's Ark, and circumcision prefigure Christian baptism.[107] In such types we see a positive link and parallel between the type and its fulfillment.

Yet the type-antitype link may also be negative and *antithetical*. Adam is an antithetical type of Christ (Rom. 5:12–21, 1 Cor. 15:20–50), since Christ fulfills the type by his exact opposite effect: Adam condemns all men by his disobedience; Christ saves all men by his obedience.

To read a type or prophecy properly, we must identify the true subject and event being prophesied or foreshadowed, which is often quite hidden. For example, Jeremiah 31:15 prophesies, "Thus says the Lord: 'A voice is heard in Ramah, lamentation and bitter weeping. Rachel is weeping for her children; she refuses to be comforted for her children, because they are not.'" Who is Rachel? What event is this foretelling? The prophecy's Old Testament context points us to the exile of Israel. But Matthew point us to Herod's attempt to destroy the Messiah by killing the innocent children in Bethlehem (Matt. 2:13–18). This means that prophecies and types—especially those involving the Messiah—can have multiple fulfillments, one that is immediate and others that come later. Thus, Rachel prefigures the people of Israel, the town of Bethlehem, *and* the Virgin Mary.

> **KEY 8:**
> *Prophecies and types may have multiple fulfillments.*

Mary as *Woman*, Eve

Marian types are identified in relation to those prefiguring Jesus. A well-developed type for Jesus is Adam. The name *Adam* is Hebrew for *man* (Gen. 1:26–27; 3:17), making him—prior to eating the forbidden fruit—the father and archetype for all men. Christ replaces Adam as man's archetype. As in this archetype, whenever Scripture compliments, praises, or blesses any human being, it implies that Jesus is even more blessed and worthy of praise.

As Eve was an important protagonist, although secondary to Adam (Gen. 2:18–25), early Christians saw Mary as Jesus' helper and partner. Thus, Mary was *the Lord's handmaid* (Luke 1:38,48) just as Eve was Adam's. Eve's name is also important. Originally, Adam named her *Woman* (Gen. 2:23), *Ishshah* in Hebrew, revealing that she was the archetype for woman prior to the Fall. She is renamed Eve (Gen. 3:20), losing her archetype role.

Jesus renames his mother *Woman* as woman's new archetype. This first occurs at the wedding feast of Cana (John 2:1–12), on the seventh day of the new creation.[108] Mary draws Jesus' attention to the lack of wine, and Jesus says to her, "Woman, what is this to me and to you, my hour has not yet come?" (John 2:4, literal translation). This phraseology seems a bit awkward and impersonal, both in English and in Greek; to Roberts it "seems curious, even disrespectful, though he does the miracle."[109] However, if we replace *Woman* with a proper name, it reads better: "O Eve, what is this to me and to you?" As *Woman*, *gyne* in Greek, Mary is "an instigator of Jesus' first miracle at Cana in Galilee,"[110] launching Jesus' public ministry.

Giving Mary a *new name* (Isa. 62:2; Rev. 2:17, 3:12) is especially significant because it is connected to our Lord's *hour* of suffering, as disciple and mother.[111] Timothy George considers Mary's response truly Christian:

Mary's second exemplary saying comes at the wedding at Cana. First Jesus has this little, almost, tussle with his mother, saying, "Woman, my hour has not yet come"—which sounds a little bit gruff, Jesus speaking to his mama like that. But then she says to the wine stewards, "Whatever he says unto you, do it." Well, again, this is the call to, as Evangelical Protestants sing, "trust and obey."[112]

Jesus again identifies his mother as *Woman* while on the cross as he looks upon the apostle John and his mother: "Woman, behold, your son!" (John 19:26). Again, we resolve the awkwardness of this phrase by substituting *Woman* with a proper name, making it read better: "Mary, behold, your son!" Mary is *Woman* because our Lord's *hour* is also her *hour* of travail. Jason Byassee marvels at Mary's strength and courage, as "she and other women are present at the cross, when the male disciples flee."[113] In this, Gaventa sees Mary as a model of Christian discipleship.[114] *Woman* stands at the cross without uttering a word. She stands. She watches. She fulfills Jesus' command: watch and pray (Matt. 24:42, 26:41, etc.). She listens to Jesus, and she receives his beloved disciple, given her as a son.

For Byassee, this makes Mary "an image of the Church, the mother of believers."[115] Migliore sees the symbolism of Jesus, dying for love of the Church (as represented in Mary), expanding the role of Mary, whom he then entrusts to the Church's pastors (represented by John).[116] Yet Jesus' love and sacrifice remain personal: on the cross, Jesus gives himself to Mary, telling her, "I'm here on the cross for you, Mother, for your salvation." As Kubiak notes,

> yes, God called a girl. But more important, he loved a girl. He loved Mary—and when Jesus was hanging on the cross he sure let her know it. . . . As he hung on the cross dying, Jesus had one final phrase to utter to Mary . . . *I will never leave you or forsake you.*[117]

Is this not love? Yet Kubiak captures the conflicting emotions Mary could have had when Jesus called her *Woman* and not *mother*: sorrow mixed with intimate joy.

Oh, how joy must have mingled with Mary's pain in that moment. Her heart must have warmed as the gaze of her beloved Jesus met hers one last time. His face was beaten and marred beyond recognition, but his lingering eye contact must have spoken volumes to the one who knew him well.

Her heart must have danced as the voice of the One she knew well addressed her one final time. Jesus was dying—but he was thinking of Mary and how he loved her so. Have you ever had a moment that powerful, that poetic, that piercing?[118]

Mary is a real, human example of a true Christian who accepts salvation in faithfully standing by Jesus in his last agony and in taking John as her son. "Mary exemplifies Christian faith and discipleship in her location at the foot of the cross and in her call to ministry with and for others."[119]

As woman is made for man—that is, for Christ (1 Cor. 11:8–9)—feminine roles, figures, and types, especially in supporting men, can give us salient insights into Mary. Tertullian[120] (d. 250) also identifies Mary as the archetype of *Woman*:

The apostle [Paul] also restricts the term [*woman*] to the same meaning it has in Genesis . . . when he calls the Virgin Mary "woman" (cf. Gal. 4:4), just as Genesis called Eve "woman." Writing to the Galatians, he says, "God sent his Son, born of a woman," which establishes that she is a virgin.[121]

KEY 9:

Old Testament types of women supporting men may apply to Mary in relation to Christ, such as Eve alongside Adam: Christ became the New Adam and archetype for all men as Mary becomes the New Eve and Woman, the archetype and courageous model for women.

Beverly Gaventa, Jaroslav Pelikan, David Jeffrey, and others describe how early Christians saw the virgin Eve as the *antithetical type* of the Virgin Mary: [122] Eve is disobedient, Mary obedient; a fallen angel tempts Eve to transgress God's will, whereas a faithful angel calls Mary to do God's will; Eve brings death, Mary brings life—Christ's incarnation and redemption. Irenaeus of Lyons (d. 202) also used this parallel: "Thus, the knot of Eve's disobedience was loosed by the obedience of Mary. What the virgin Eve had bound in unbelief, the Virgin Mary loosed through faith."[123] Justin Martyr (d. 165) also identified Eve as the antithetical type of Mary.[124]

Irenaeus of Lyons (d. 202)—a disciple of John's disciple, Polycarp—develops this parallel: Eve was betrothed to Adam, Mary to Joseph; Eve disbelieved, Mary believed; Eve leads humanity into bondage, Mary loosed those bonds through her faith.[125]

Identifying Mary as the New Eve came as naturally to early Christians as it did to identify Christ as the New Adam. As Farkasfalvy notes,

> the Mary/Eve parallelism is neither forced nor off-beat. It is nothing more than an extension of an apostolic exegesis of the Scriptures, reaching back to the first pages of Genesis. Its theological content vindicates the universality of Christ's redemptive work and thus, by the same logic, asserts the universality of Mary's motherhood.[126]

The *Woman* of Revelation 12

The typology linking Mary to Eve was no innovation. The
apostle John started it in the book of Revelation:

> Then God's temple in heaven was opened, and the ark of
> his covenant was seen within his temple. . . . And a great
> portent appeared in heaven, a *woman clothed with the sun*
> . . . on her head a crown of twelve stars; *she was with child*
> and she cried out in her *pangs of birth, in anguish for delivery.*
> And another portent appeared in heaven; behold, a great
> red dragon. . . . And the dragon stood before the *woman*
> who was about to bear a child, that he might devour her
> child when she brought it forth; *she brought forth a male
> child, one who is to rule all the nations with a rod of iron*, but
> her child was caught up to God and to his throne, and the
> woman fled into the wilderness. . . .
>
> Now war arose in heaven, Michael and his angels
> fighting against the dragon; and the dragon and his an-
> gels fought, but they were defeated and there was no
> longer any place for them in heaven. . . . And I heard
> a loud voice in heaven, saying, "Now the salvation and
> the power and the kingdom of our God and the au-
> thority of his Christ have come, for the accuser of our
> brethren has been thrown down. . . . And they have
> conquered him by the blood of the Lamb and by the
> word of their testimony, for they loved not their lives
> even unto death." . . .
>
> And when the dragon saw that he had been thrown
> down to the earth, he pursued the woman who had borne
> the male child. But the woman was given the two wings
> of the great eagle that she might fly from the serpent into
> the wilderness. . . . But the earth came to the help of the
> woman, and the earth opened its mouth and swallowed

the river which the dragon had poured from his mouth. Then the dragon was angry with the woman, and went off to make war on the rest of her offspring, on those who keep the commandments of God and bear testimony to Jesus (Rev. 11:19–12:17).

When God reveals the heavenly ark, it appears as a pregnant *woman clothed with the sun*. This is a *great sign in heaven*, in whom *the male child who will rule the nations* dwells. Parallels between this passage and Genesis 3 suggest that *Woman* is the New Eve: in this passage God clothes *Woman* with the sun, whereas God in Genesis 3:21 clothes Eve with skins. God curses Eve with birth pangs (Gen. 3:16); the Messiah's mother is with birth pangs as in Micah (5:2–3).[127]

In both Genesis and Revelation, the serpent battles the woman and her seed. In both, God curses the serpent. God promises to put enmity between the serpent and the woman in Genesis and fulfills that promise in Revelation by giving her "the two wings of a great eagle that she might fly from the serpent." Eve is "mother of the living" (Gen. 3:20) according to the flesh, yet *Woman* is mother of the true living, the mother of those who keep God's commandments (Rev. 12:17). We are *Woman's* children because we are brothers and sisters of Christ, "doing God's will" (Mark 3:33–35) by keeping his commandments.

Gen. 3	Parallels	Rev. 12
v. 1	Serpent (dragon) is subtle (slithery, cunning) . . . pours out a serpentine river	vv. 9, 15
v. 1	Serpent confronts Woman	v. 4
v. 8	Woman hides from God vs. being in the center of God's temple	vv. 11:19
v. 14	God curses serpent . . . banishes him from heaven	vv. 8-9

v. 14	To crawl on its belly, to eat dirt (below animals) . . . to the earth	vv. 9-10, 12-13
v. 15	God puts enmity between the serpent and Woman . . . on eagle's wings	v. 14
v. 15	Between Woman's and the serpent's seeds . . . he tries to devour her seed	v. 4
v. 15	Serpent snipes at . . . pursues Woman and wars against Woman's seed	vv. 13, 19
v. 15	Salvation: serpent's head is crushed . . . by the seed's blood and testimony	vv. 10-11
v. 16	God curses Woman with birth pangs . . . pangs in birthing Messiah	v. 2
vv. 17-19	Ground is cursed against Woman vs. protects Woman	v. 16
v. 20	Woman becomes mother of the living . . . of those alive in Christ	v. 19
v. 21	God clothes Woman with skins . . . with the sun	v. 1

Gaventa summarizes Protestants' quandary over Revelation 12 and their tentativeness to connect the Messiah's mother with Mary.[128] Although John Macquarrie is less tentative, he sees Revelation offering little insight.[129] But Perry sees it differently. He notes how, historically, Christians consistently applied Revelation 12 to Mary, as soon as the New Testament canon was finalized to include this text, drawing out theological consequences.[130]

Blessed Among God's *Handmaids*

Mary humbly and proudly recognizes herself as *God's handmaid*, *servant*, *and slave*, characterizing her response to God. John Macquarrie explains the significance:

The word translated "handmaid" is in Greek *doule*, and might be translated "slave." It is the feminine form of the noun *doulos*, "slave," the word used by Paul about

Jesus Christ, "who, though he was in the form of God, did not count equality with God a thing to be grasped, but emptied himself, taking the form of a slave (*doulos*)" (Phil. 2:6–7) The point cannot be made too strongly, for the Christian commendation of humility is not addressed primarily to women but to all human beings. Its principal exemplar is not Mary but Jesus Christ himself "who humbled himself and became obedient unto death, even death on a cross," but whose humble obedience wins for him in the transformed scale of values "the name which is above every name" (Phil. 2:8–9).[131]

Mary's response complements Christ's and anticipates our own, embracing God's will and his word, making it an honor to be *the Lord's slave*. For Dick McClain, she is "a model of submission,"[132] submitting to the Father as one who "came not to be served but to serve, and to give his life as a ransom for many" (Matt. 20:28).

For Pelikan, Mary's title *Handmaid of the Lord* links her to several Old Testament prophecies—Isaiah 45:9, 64:8—making Jesus the son of the handmaid.[133] Tim Perry adds other passages where *doulos* links Mary to Abraham, Moses, Joshua, David, Daniel, and the Messiah, along with Shiphrah and Puah, Deborah, Jael, and Esther. He also adds to Macquarrie's New Testament *doulos* texts, showing how early Christians would have understood Mary's *doule*.[134]

Mary was God's favored daughter, graced with his Spirit and prophecy. He clothed her with strength, dignity, and righteousness. Yet Mary saw herself as God's handmaid, as other women had, such as Abigail.[135] Christ loved Mary and the Church as a bride. Mary was faithful to Christ as to her love. She was a virgin bride fit for a priest, a good and obedient wife—a real treasure—worthy of his honor.[136]

As a good mother with a fruitful womb, Mary loved, nursed, and fed the infant Christ, and was ready to die for him. Christ, as the Son of God, honored and obeyed his mother, refusing her nothing, fulfilling the commandments to honor his parents, respecting her and her counsels.[137] God attested to Mary's faith by raising her son from death, as he had for other women who "received their dead by resurrection" (Heb. 11:35, 39).

Paul praises the women who helped him in his mission (Rom. 16:1–2), as does our Lord: "He who receives a prophet because he is a prophet shall receive a prophet's reward, and he who receives a righteous man because he is a righteous man shall receive a righteous man's reward" (Matt. 10:41). Mary assisted Jesus, receiving him not only as a righteous prophet, but also as her Savior, Messiah, Son of the Most High God, son of David, and as her everlasting King (Luke 1:31–38, 47). Imagine her reward! In effect, Mary is the archetype of Christian service: "Whoever receives one such child in my name receives me" (Matt. 18:5); Mary received Jesus as her child-Lord, child-God, and child-King!

Mary was generous in giving her gifts to God, to her son, and to her spiritual children, teaching her children what is good. We should praise her as we do other charitable and hospitable women, who care for the afflicted and the poor, putting the needs of the poor before their own. She accompanies Jesus' disciples from adversaries, as Rahab did for Joshua's spies.[138] As the Holy Spirit blesses great women for their good works, which shine before men and give glory to God, he does so to Mary: indeed, *all generations* shall bless her for how she glorifies God:[139]

The princess is decked in her chamber. . . . In many-colored robes she is led to the king, with her virgin companions, her escort, in her train. . . . I will cause your name to be celebrated in all generations; therefore the peoples will praise you forever and ever (Ps. 45:13–17).

For early Christians, Mary was particularly linked to the miracle of barren women conceiving through divine intervention, often communicated to them through angels. Whereas we don't usually associate the Virgin Mary with barrenness, Scripture does. Barrenness is a curse (2 Sam. 6:16, 23), associated with pride, disbelief, sin, and covenantal disobedience (Deut. 7:12–15; Prov. 30:16), an extension of Eve's original sinfulness. Yet, in the Bible, it is the holiest and most faith-filled women who suffered this curse: Sarah, Rebekah, Rachel, Samson's mother, Hannah, and Mary's cousin Elizabeth. All the barren women are old and had tried to conceive; Mary is young and did not know man. Yet both Mary and barren women could conceive only with God's miraculous intervention. As John Chrysostom (d. 407) concluded, "in this way, the barren woman [in Scripture] prepares the way for the Virgin . . . so that the virginal birth might be believed in."[140]

The Holy Spirit invites us to link Mary to these barren women through Mary's hymn of praise (Luke 1:46–55). The Magnificat parallels Hannah's song (1 Sam. 2:1–10), which reflects her joy and gratitude for having conceived in her barrenness. Although Mary is not strictly barren, the Holy Spirit does move her to rejoice in gratitude for miraculously conceiving. Mary praises God for lifting up "those of low degree" to place them on the thrones of the mighty (Luke 1:52), allowing a virgin to conceive and "rejoice in God" her Savior.

KEY 10:
*Women in Scripture are types of Mary,
especially other "handmaids" and "servants of the Lord"
who cooperated with God with their feminine
generosity. Women who miraculously conceive
prefigure Mary's virginal conception of Jesus.*

Abraham's wife, Sarah, is the paradigm of barren women (Gen. 11:29–23:2), remaining childless long past her child-bearing years. Even after God promises Abraham copious offspring, she continues to wait with faith. God twice preserves her pure relationship with Abraham from violation. Sarah's great faith makes her the mother of all believers. Similarly, the archangel Gabriel appears to both Mary's and Elizabeth's husbands to announce the miraculous birth of their sons, Jesus and John the Baptist.[141] As Sweeney notes,

> Sarah was the mother of Isaac, who then fathered Jacob, and who then became "Israel." Mary later became mother of the new Israel. But Mary's faith was an improvement over Sarah's, who according to the text, laughed at the notion of her giving birth at such an advanced age. Mary, on the other hand, rejoiced and had immediate faith in the words of the archangel.[142]

Isaac's wife, Rebekah, is a virgin *who had never known man,* anticipating Mary. She remains barren until miraculously conceiving Jacob and Esau. Jacob's beloved spouse, Rachel, remains barren until miraculously conceiving Joseph and Benjamin, becoming permanently associated with the Messiah's birthplace.[143]

Samson's mother is particularly striking: an angel appears both to her and to her husband, Manoah (Judg. 13:3–24), as Gabriel does to Mary and Joseph (Matt. 1:18–25; Luke 1:26–39). The angel tells Manoah's wife, "Behold . . . you shall conceive and bear a son," as Gabriel tells Mary, "Behold, you will conceive in your womb and bear a son."

A barren Shunammite woman also miraculously conceives, through Elisha's intercession (2 Kings 4:8–37). Later, when her son dies, God—through Elisha—raises him from the dead, as God would Mary's son (Acts 2:24, 10:40, etc.).

Pope John Paul II shows how miraculous motherhood links a mother to her son whom God chose for a special mission:

> In the accounts of miraculous motherhood which we have recalled, it is easy to discover the important place the Bible assigns to mothers in the mission of their sons. . . . That maternal intervention, described by the Bible, can be interpreted as the sign of being chosen as an instrument in God's sovereign plan. . . . Indeed, [miraculous motherhood] sheds light on the dimension of gratuitousness, which is especially apparent in the case of barren women, God's particular covenant with woman and the special bond between the destiny of the mother and that of the son.[144]

Scripture and early Christians also relate widows to Mary. Of course, widowhood occurs with the curse of death as the result of Adam's and Eve's sin (Rom. 5:12–21), yet the Bible presents widows of great faith (Luke 18:1–8) who are hospitable, who wash the feet of saints and relieve the afflicted, who are thus worthy of honor (1 Tim. 5:3–10).

Ruth was a barren widow (Ruth 1:1–4:17). Like Mary, she is a *handmaid* (2:13), who finds favor in Boaz's eyes as Mary had in God's. Ruth does not pursue young men but relies on God's goodness, graciously responding to God's messenger, Naomi, "All that you say I will do" (3:5). Mary similarly responds to Gabriel: "Let it be done unto me according to your word" (Luke 1:38). Ruth thus becomes the great-grandmother of David, another type for Christ.

At the gates of Zarephath, Elijah saves a widow's only son from starvation (1 Kings 17:10–24). At the gates of Naim, Jesus does the same (Luke 7:11–15). God would raise Mary's only son on Easter morning. The widowed prophetess Anna exemplifies a life of prayer (Luke 2:36–38), as the widow Tabitha, whom Peter brings back from the dead (Acts 9:36–41), exemplifies charity and good works.

As Paul relates Old Testament figures to Christ—Adam, Melchizedek, Isaac, Jacob[145]—early Christians do the same with Mary. Sweeney links Mary to Hannah in offering her first son to God.[146] Pelikan admires how Augustine (d. 430) links Mary to Moses' sister, Miriam, and to other women who praise the Lord.[147] Even Pharaoh's daughter, considering herself blessed in finding one of the Hebrew children in the river (Exod. 2:1–9), raising him as her own, naming him Moses, one of the greatest precursors of Mary, who raised Jesus.

The Evangelical Tim Perry justifies this Marian typology, though still needing development.[148] Mary's feminine qualities could have been so great only in relationship to Christ, who was their source. Lutheran Jaroslav Pelikan and Evangelical Tim Perry ponder this expanded focus of early Christians, giving Athanasius as an example:

The core of Athanasius's Mariology lies in his exhortations on the Christian ascetic life. *The Letter to the Virgins* commends Mary as an example of consecrated virginity . . . just as Mary had no other children after Jesus, so the nuns to whom [Athanasius] writes should follow in her footsteps, taking a vow of lifelong chastity. . . .

On its face[, Tim Perry continues,] Athanasius's strategy seems to suffer a serious drawback: the lack of biblical material concerning Mary's character and actions. And yet, chastity is merely the beginning of a long list of virginal qualities that the nuns are expected to embody. . . . Like Mary, [Athanasius thinks,] nuns are to be hard-working, generous, devout, modest, humble, progressing in sanctification and yearning for eternity with God. None of these virtues, as Athanasius well knew, are found in the New Testament. On what basis does he say such things? According to Pelikan, he does so by "what might be called development of doctrine by extrapolation," or a reapplication of the hermeneutic of "prophecy fulfillment," from the Old Testament to the New Testament to the Church.

This move requires a brief explanation. The prophecy-fulfillment hermeneutic allowed the Church Fathers to find in the Old Testament statements about Christ [and Mary] that were not explicitly reaffirmed in the New . . . [permitting them, as Pelikan explains,] "to amplify the teachings of the New Testament on the basis of what had become explicit in the history of salvation since the New Testament."[149]

So, using this hermeneutic of prophecy fulfillment, Athanasius justified applying to Mary the feminine qualities of working hard, generosity, yearning for eternity with God, etc. The Bible does not explicitly apply these virtues to Mary, but it does to other women. Yet, as *blessed among women*, Mary too has these qualities.

Personifications of the Feminine: Lady Wisdom

Poetry is a non-literal style that uses literary devices to express different levels of meaning simultaneously. People in love often use poetry to express their complex feelings for each other. In the Bible we find poetry in the Psalms as well as in the Song of Solomon. Through poetry, the Holy Spirit speaks something uniquely personal in his love toward each individual.

Christian Fathers such as Gregory of Nyssa (d. 394)[150] and Ambrose (d. 397)[151] applied the praises of the bride in the Song of Solomon to the Virgin Mary and to the Church. This helps develop the complete scriptural picture of Mary, as, for example, "my dove, my perfect one, is only one, the darling of her mother, flawless to her that bore her. The maidens saw her and called her happy [blessed]" (Song of Sol. 6:9). Since Mary is more blessed than any woman, poetic passages extolling feminine virtues may apply to her.

In isolation, such texts are not a definitive formulation of Marian teachings. Yet they can confirm and illuminate other texts. Although the sacred writers did not directly intend to describe Mary by these passages, the Holy Spirit was also at work, moving these authors to use this style and to apply them to Mary, giving them new and deep insights—insights that only the Spirit can discern (Rom. 8:26–27).

They did not fear misapplication of poetic verses to Mary because it was always consistent with other passages, coherently fitting the content within the context of all Scripture. If applying such texts to Mary contradicted Scripture, then the key would fail to unlock the true mystery of Mary.

One area where the Holy Spirit takes poetic license to express divine truths is in the personification of wisdom as a fine woman, such as in Proverbs. Early Christians often applied these praises of the extraordinary woman, *Lady Wisdom*, to Mary:

Because his Spirit had prepared her, the Father found the dwelling place where his Son and his Spirit could dwell among men. In this sense the Church's Tradition has often read the most beautiful texts on wisdom in relation to Mary (CCC 721; cf. Prov. 8:1–9:6, Sir. 24).

Wisdom is personified as a mother, wife, and queen, typifying traits of a created woman—not a divine, uncreated person who took male flesh. The Holy Spirit seems to say that he intended to prefigure Mary, which is confirmed by the coherence and consistency of such connections with the rest of Scripture. The key to applying Wisdom's attributes to Mary resides in how these texts fit with other biblical passages that typify Mary, as we have already identified.

Wisdom has similar physical and social virtues found in other types for Mary. *Lady Wisdom* is beautiful and graceful, which makes her precious and pleasant. God also blesses Lady Wisdom with the moral and intellectual virtues of righteousness and justice. She feeds her children with right knowledge, understanding, and prudence, with truth and righteousness, as a discreet sister and intimate friend.[152]

God loves Mary as a tree or fountain of life and associates her with his creative work. As a mother, Lady Wisdom protects her children from sin. Wisdom's children seek her out, listening to and loving her. When her children prize their mother, she honors them in return and rewards them with a crown of holiness.[153] Wisdom also maternally bears fruit, as Mary did Jesus: "But the wisdom from above is first pure, then peaceable, gentle, open to reason, full of mercy and good fruits, without uncertainty or insincerity" (James 3:17). Such parallels of Wisdom to types of Mary were so "tight"—consistent with other Scripture passages—that early Christians saw them as inspired by the Holy Spirit.

Even Protestant scholars, such as Jaroslav Pelikan, recognized how early Christians identified Mary with Lady

Wisdom.[154] John Macquarrie supports this early Christian insight:

> *[The Lord created Wisdom]* . . . *from eternity, and of old, before the earth was made. The depths were not as yet, and I was already conceived* (Prov. 8:22ff). . . . Originally, of course, these words were intended to refer to the divine Wisdom, metaphorically personified. . . .
>
> *The depths were not as yet, and I was already conceived.* The words, when applied to Mary, are not intended to suggest any pre-existence. But her ultimate metaphysical conception had taken place in the beginning of the salvific purposes of God. We are thinking here of the mystery of election. Already in the beginning God had elected Mary to her unique vocation in the scheme of salvation. Not only Mary originates in this divine conception. The whole human race is embraced within the divine election.[155]

God chose Mary, us, and Lady Wisdom in him "from the foundation of the world" (Eph. 1:4; Matt. 25:34). Applying these texts to Mary also makes sense to Macquarrie.[156]

> **KEY 11:**
> *As coherent and consistent with the rest of Scripture, poetic texts extolling feminine virtues, such as personifications of Wisdom, may portray Mary.*

QUESTIONS AND ANSWERS

Q: This use of allegory—Mary as prefigured by Eve, Miriam, etc.—is interesting and nice for piety, but we shouldn't overemphsize it. Isn't relying on allegory likely to lead to doctrinal errors?

A: How did Jesus use typology (allegory, as you put it)? Didn't he tell how his death and resurrection were foretold by Jonah being in the belly of a fish for three days (Matt. 12:38–40)? And Paul, who developed typology, called Adam a type of Christ because through Adam sin entered the world and infected us all, and through Christ salvation was offered to all (Rom. 5:12–21; 1 Cor. 15:20–50). He also applied typology to the Church (Gal. 4:19–31). If we want to know the truth about Mary, we must also apply typology to her, just as early Christians did.

Now we are simply using typology to identify prophetic statements that may refer to Mary. In the next section, we will consider dogmatic statements regarding her.

Q: These efforts to apply Old Testament Scripture to Mary seem quite arbitrary. How is this going to resolve the doctrinal disagreements between Catholics and Protestants?

A: This approach to reading Scripture is a fact of history, not of necessity. It may or may not resolve the doctrinal disagreements, but it can help us understand how such disagreements came from distinct ways of reading Scripture. With a bit of openness, we can discover how early Christians learned to apply these Scripture passages to Mary.

Q: You say Jesus renames his mother *Woman* in John 2:4 and John 19:26. Yet Jesus also calls Mary Magdalene *Woman*: "Jesus said to her, 'Woman, why are you weeping? Whom do you seek?'" (John 20:15). Is Mary Magdalene also a New Eve?

A: We could make a case that our Lord, after he rose from the dead, is indicating how all Christian women are called to be like Eve (before the Fall): pure and holy, his mother and sister by faith (Matt. 12:50). Nevertheless, we also have to acknowledge that Jesus may have used the term *woman* in a form of anonymous address of a woman, as we would use the term *madam* or *miss*. Certainly, when our Lord first addresses Mary Magdalene, he is hiding his identity and avoids calling her by name, until her tears and anguish move him to reveal himself (John 20:16).

Woman can have different applications in different contexts in Scripture, as with the name *Jesus* itself. Others too were named *Jesus* or *Joshua* or *Jesua*—which means *Yahweh-saves* (CCC 452)—such as the son of Nun, son of Bethshemesh, the governor of Jerusalem, the great high priest and the son of Sirach.[157] Nevertheless, the name especially applies to Christ, "for he will save his people from their sins" (Matt. 1:21).

So let's not be surprised that *Woman* is used differently when applied to different individuals. It can still have special significance for the Virgin Mary, the mother of Jesus.

Q: Only John mentions Mary at the foot of the cross. Doesn't this mean that the other Evangelists are downplaying this event?

A: Mary's presence at the foot of the cross fulfills God's prophecy in Luke:

> Simeon blessed them and said to Mary his mother, "Behold, this child is set for the fall and rising of many in Israel, and for a sign that is spoken against (and a sword will pierce through your own soul also), that thoughts out of many hearts may be revealed" (Luke 2:34–35).

Mary's suffering alongside the Messiah is significant enough to be prophesied.

Only Matthew mentions the trinitarian formula for baptism (Matt. 28:19). Does that mean that other Evangelists are down playing its importance? No. Likewise, only Luke gives us the parable of the Good Samaritan (Luke 10:29–37). All of God's words are significant, precisely in relationship to God's plan of salvation.

Q: You say the woman of Revelation 12 is Mary. But it is obvious that she refers to the Old Testament people of God. Are you not distorting the text with this interpretation?

A: In Revelation 5:5, the elder tells us that we can expect to see "the Lion of the tribe of Judah, the Root of David" opening the scroll sealed with seven seals. But instead of a lion, we see the "Lamb standing, as though it had been slain" (v. 6). Similarly, Revelation 11:19 has us peering into the holiest place of the heavenly temple. Expecting to see a golden ark, we see a woman clothed with the sun instead (12:1), the mother of the Messiah as well as of all Christians (v. 17). But is she Mary?

Some Catholic authors—including some Church Fathers—identify the woman as a collective personification of the people of Israel and of the Church. Though plausible, this does not seem to be the best interpretation. Note that all the other protagonists in this vision are real individuals: the child is the Messiah (Ps. 2:7–9), the dragon is Satan, and Michael is an individual archangel (Dan. 10, 12; Jude 8–10). We should expect the woman to be an individual, too, rather than a collective person.

Also, in Isaiah 7:11, God encourages King Ahaz to ask for a *sign* (Greek: *semeion*). Despite the king's refusal, God gives him one: "A young woman [virgin in Greek] shall conceive and bear a son, and shall call his name Immanuel." In Revelation 12:1, a great sign—*semeion mega*—appears in heaven as a woman with child, who is *Immanuel*. As John Paul II explains,

> current exegesis agrees in seeing in this woman the community of God's people, giving birth in pain to the risen Messiah. Along with the collective interpretation, however, the text suggests an individual one in the statement: "She brought forth a male child, one who is to rule all the nations with a rod of iron" (Rev. 12:5). With this reference to childbirth, it is acknowledged that the woman clothed with the sun is in a certain sense identified with Mary, the woman who gave birth to the Messiah. The woman-community is actually described with the features of the woman-mother of Jesus.
>
> Identified by her motherhood, the woman was with child and she cried out in her pangs of birth, "in anguish for her delivery" (Rev. 12:2). This note refers to the mother of Jesus at the cross (cf. John 19:25), where she shares in anguish for the delivery of the community of disciples with a soul pierced by the sword (cf. Luke 2:35). Despite her sufferings, she is "clothed with the sun"—that is, she reflects the divine splendor—and appears as a "great sign" of God's spousal relationship with his people.[158]

At least such evidence reaffirms that this interpretation does not distort the text in any way. In fact, it seems to be the principal interpretation intended by the Holy Spirit.

Q: John identifies Wisdom with Christ, the divine Word, not with Mary, saying, "In the beginning was the Word, and the

Word was with God, and the Word was God" (John 1:1). Proverbs does the same: "The Lord created me [Wisdom] at the beginning of his work, the first of his acts of old" (Prov. 8:22–23). Doesn't Wisdom refer to Christ, not Mary?

A: Church Fathers are mixed on this. Justin Martyr (d. 165) linked Wisdom to "the Word" of John's Gospel in order to defend Christ's divinity.[159] So does Augustine (d. 430)[160] to explain the incarnation of the Word and the Holy Trinity. Origen (d. 253),[161] not a Church Father but still an important ecclesiastical writer, does as well. In 537, the emperor Justinian I honored Christ with a church in Constantinople, calling it *Hagia Sophia—Holy Wisdom*. But since *Sophia* is feminine, it evoked the image of a female saint, so Christians began applying it to Mary under the title *Seat of Wisdom*.

Wisdom—as with other types—can have multiple fulfillments, one referring to Christ and another to Mary. As Athanasius (d. 373) explains in his exposition against the Arians:

> The true Wisdom which shaped the world claims for himself all that bears his image, and rightly says, "The Lord created me in his works." . . . Wisdom himself is not created, because he is the Creator, but by reason of the created image of himself found in his works, he speaks thus as though he were speaking of himself. . . . The likeness of Wisdom has been stamped upon creatures in order that the world may recognize in it the Word who was its maker.[162]

Some of Wisdom's attributes are more applicable to the eternal and uncreated Word of God, whereas those referring to Wisdom as created are more appropriate for Mary, a creature. Athanasius would apply these to all creation as an image of the Word.[163] When heretics, such as the Ebionites, Adoptionists, and Arianists, used those passages to assert that the Word was a creature—the first and greatest, but still a creature—Christians countered with the interpretation that applies Wisdom to Mary.

5

Keys to Other Marian Types and Figures

Christ wants to abide in us and us in him (John 15:4). To abide in Christ, we must obey his commandment (v. 10) to love one another (v. 12), which will yield much joyful fruit. Thus, St. Paul encourages us to become of one mind and one heart in love:

> So if there is any encouragement in Christ, any incentive of love, any participation in the Spirit, any affection and sympathy, complete my joy by being of the same mind, having the same love, being in full accord and of one mind. Do nothing from selfishness or conceit, but in humility count others better than yourselves. Let each of you look not only to his own interests, but also to the interests of others (Phil. 2:1–4).

Let's explore, with love and humility, other Scripture passages that prefigure Mary, starting with those related to her pregnancy, when Immanuel, *God with us*, dwelt in her womb.

God's Miraculous Dwelling

For early Christians, Marian typology wove together a wonderful, tight-fitting tapestry, opening additional insights into Mary and her role in salvation.

God etches in a woman's nature the facility to develop intense and intimate emotional bonds and spiritual relationships with the children she conceives and nurtures in her womb. Mary formed a particularly intense bond and relationship with the Word incarnate—Immanuel, *God with us* (Isa. 7:14, 8:8; CCC 744)—who dwelt in her womb and then in her home. This was key to Mary's personal identity as well as Christ's identity as a child and as a man. Jon Sweeney summarizes their reasoning:

> God had an unusual home for those nine months, feeding on blood and partaking of flesh, while still very much of heaven . . . important clues to how Christians would perceive [Mary's] role in the history of salvation.[164]

As the incarnate Word's dwelling place, Mary was prefigured in Old Testament images of God dwelling among us, as on his holy mount, on his temple house, and in his chosen city.[165] Accordingly . . .

KEY 12:
Persons, objects, or places where God dwells may be types for God dwelling in Mary. Those that God abandons may be types antithetical to Mary.

This key helped early Christians identify more Marian Bible passages. Sweeney notes how they used it to identify Mary with the Ark of the Covenant,[166] the privileged dwelling of God. The letter to the Hebrews describes how this gold vessel contained "the manna, and Aaron's rod that budded, and the tablets of the covenant" (Heb. 9:1–5).* Yet Mary's womb was the vessel for the true manna and bread from heaven, Christ's body (John 6:48–51); for the true high priest; and for God's one, incarnate Word—versus, in the *Decalogue*, God's *ten words*.

Ark Contained:	Mary's Womb Contained:
Manna: bread from heaven	Christ's flesh: true bread from heaven
Rod of Aaron's high priesthood that budded	Christ, the true, eternal high priest
The Decalogue: God's ten words	The Word of God

God overshadowed Mary, as he had the Ark of the Covenant and, like the ark, Mary's womb was God's resting place. John himself—moved by love—identified the Ark of the New Covenant with a woman, the mother of the Redeemer.[167] Early Christians, such as Hippolytus (d. 235),[168] made this connection quite naturally, as does Athanasius (d. 373).[169] Maximus of Turin (d. 465) parallels the ark's trip to Jerusalem to Mary's trip to her relative Elizabeth.[170]

Gregory Nazianzen (d. 390) also describes Mary as the temple,[171] the place of God's special presence. The sanctuary is God's holy and beautiful bride, the place of his glorious throne, and seat of his power. This earthly sanctuary is a place to contemplate, praise God, and pray, since it is where God hears our prayers, speaks to us, and makes known his promises. The temple sanctuary is a sign of the eternal covenant and blessing, a source of help and support, from which the waters of the Spirit emanate. God calls us to revere this creature.[172]

---

* Compare Numbers 17:1–11 for the budding of Aaron's rod.

The Blessed Fruit of Mary's Womb

Evangelical Scot McKnight notes the importance of Christ's dwelling in Mary:

> For Jesus to be really human he had to be born, as the apostle Paul wrote in the fourth chapter of his letter to the Galatians, *of* a woman and not just *through* a woman. God didn't just use Mary as a "rent-a-womb," and the underlying principle is this: what God becomes, God redeems. . . . That's why Jesus' real body is important for our faith.[173]

Although the key to understanding Mary is her spiritual relationship to Christ through faith, the Holy Spirit also blesses her physical relationship to him: "Elizabeth was filled with the Holy Spirit and she exclaimed . . . 'blessed is the fruit of your womb!'" (Luke 1:41–42). The fruit and its shoot are found in ancient messianic prophecies (Isa. 27:6–9; Ezek. 36:8–11, etc.), starting with the fruit of the tree of life (Gen. 3:13–18; Rev. 22:2, 14, 19).

KEY 13:
The fruit of a tree (vine, stalk, etc.) may prefigure Christ in relationship to Mary.

With this key, the Holy Spirit guides us to many rich passages of Scripture, as Jesus tells us: "Either make the tree good, and its fruit good; or make the tree bad, and its fruit bad; for the tree is known by its fruit" (Matt. 12:33–34). Of Mary's womb is "the first fruits of those who have fallen asleep" (1 Cor. 15:20), which suggests that Mary's relationship with Christ extends to all believers through his death and resurrection: the fruitfulness of her faith foreshadows ours.

Thus God prepared a precious tree with holy roots (Rom. 11:16)—Mary—for the precious fruit of Jesus Christ, the incarnate Word. As Tertullian (d. 250) wrote,

[Christ] is the blossom of the shoot sprung from the root of Jesse. But just as the root of Jesse is the family of David, and the shoot sprung from the root is Mary, a descendant of David, and the blossom of the shoot is the son of Mary, called Jesus Christ, is he not the fruit?[174]

Hippolytus offers us similar words:

In calling him who descended from Judah and David "the lion's cub," the prophet [Jacob] indicated the Son of God become man; and by saying, "From a sprout, my son, you went up" (Gen. 49:9, Septuagint), he foretold the fruit that flowered from the holy Virgin, not generated from David's seed, but conceived by the working of the Holy Spirit. . . . For Isaiah says, "A shoot shall sprout from the stump of Jesse, and a branch shall flower forth from his roots" (11:1).[175]

Early Christians used this interpretive key freely to express the mysteries of Christ's relationship to his mother. Along this same line, they saw Mary as the mountain from which the little stone (Jesus) was cut "by no human hand," who would become an eternal kingdom (the Church) and smite the lower kingdoms (Dan. 2:31–45).

A Great Sign

Simeon prophesied that Christ was the *sign* to be contradicted. Christ confirmed that he is a *sign* for an unbelieving generation, the *sign* of Jonah, which is fulfilled on the cross.[176]

Mary is intimately linked to Christ also as a sign, a virgin conceiving and bearing a son (Isa. 7:11–14). This prophecy occurs when the northern kingdom, allied with Damascus, besieges Jerusalem, threatening to depose King Ahaz. God offers to give him a sign of reassurance, but Ahaz dares not ask for one. Then, through Isaiah, God promises him a great sign: a young woman—a virgin—shall conceive and bear a son. Historically and literally, the prophecy is partially fulfilled when Ahaz's young wife conceives their son, Hezekiah. Yet, in our Lord's time, both Jews and Christians also considered this prophecy messianic:

> All this took place to fulfill what the Lord had spoken by the prophet: "Behold, a virgin shall conceive and bear a son, and his name shall be called Immanuel" (which means *God with us*) (Matt. 1:22–23).

A virgin who conceives is a great sign, first to Joseph, then to the nations (Isa. 11:10). Angels tell the shepherds that the *sign* of the Savior would be a babe in the manger (Luke 2:12), which they find with Mary and Joseph (v. 16). Simeon's prophecy also links Christ, the sign that will be contradicted, to Mary, whose soul will be pierced with a sword (vv. 34-35), fulfilled at Calvary. The sign of Christ and of his mother is found at his conception, birth, and crucifixion. This is how early Christians saw Isaiah's prophecy fulfilled:

> A virgin conceived, bore a son, and yet remained a virgin. This is no common occurrence, but a sign; no reason here, but God's power, for he is the cause, and not nature. It is a special event, not shared by others; it is divine, not human. Christ's birth was not necessity, but an expression of omnipotence, a sacrament of piety for the redemption of men.[177]

KEY 14:
*Signs and miraculous works that elicit
faith may prefigure Mary.*

John sees Mary with Christ as a sign in heaven. When God reveals the heavenly ark, John sees as a great sign—a woman clothed with the sun, the mother of the Redeemer (Rev. 11:19–12:6)—the virgin with child of Isaiah 7:14.

God performs signs to reinforce people's faith. Early Christians associated such signs with Mary. For example, the rainbow was God's sign of assurance to Noah (Gen. 9:8–17); early Christians saw Mary as the true rainbow, the sign of hope that Christ's covenant has saved humanity from the Flood, the condemnation of sin. Severus of Antioch (d. 538) linked Mary to Jacob's ladder, a sign of assurance to him (Gen. 28:10–22).[178] Gregory of Nyssa (d. 394) saw Mary in the burning bush, God's sign to Moses (Exod. 3:1–12).[179]

Some find these Scripture links odd, yet we can learn from the early Christians who made them naturally.

Collective Persons and Places

Scripture often personifies both nations and cities as women. For example, Judah and Jerusalem are often called *daughter, daughter Zion,* or *daughter Jerusalem,* and Israel is depicted as a mother. Scripture also links collective attributes to a single person. For example, Jeremiah links the northern kingdom of Ephraim to the image of Rachel wailing in childbirth (Gen. 35:16–20). His prophecy foretells the people of Israel going into exile and returning:

> Thus says the Lord: "A voice is heard in Ramah, lamentation and bitter weeping. Rachel is weeping for her

children; she refuses to be comforted for her children, because they are not."

Thus says the Lord: "Keep your voice from weeping . . . and they shall come back from the land of the enemy . . . and your children shall come back to their own country" (Jer. 31:15–17).

Earlier, when Jerusalem is under siege, a woman of the city asks Joab to preserve Jerusalem, the *mother in Israel*, linking the city to Deborah, who similarly saved God's people. Jeremiah was also called *a fortified city* due to his great strength.[180] So Scripture often describes individuals as cities and cities as individuals.

God dwelt in a special way in Israel and in Jerusalem, making them types of Mary. This holy city was foreshadowed before Israel entered the promised land. Jerusalem is linked to holy barren women when Scripture describes the city forsaken, barren, and a widow, but promising to redeem her by conceiving many children in her. Yet it is not this earthly city that is great, but the heavenly city that she prefigures.[181]

> ### KEY 15:
> *Collective persons portrayed as feminine may be types for Mary.*

Jerusalem has certain feminine qualities that fit the Virgin Mary: her exalted maternity, her physical radiance, and her beauty, giving joy as God's delight. God loves her faithfulness and holiness. She is God's virgin daughter and Christ's virgin bride, as she becomes part of the Church (CCC 773). Finally, she is a mother who teaches all nations, glorious and blessed for all generations.[182]

Some Protestants also connect Jerusalem, Israel, and Zion to Mary. Jon Sweeney notes that God's people were also "a virgin waiting, full of hope for the birth of a child. She was like Mary."[183] Timothy George concurs: "As the daughter of Zion, Mary also represents the eschatological and redeemed people of God."[184]

St. Peter speaks of the lady *Elect* church in Babylon, which scholars tend to identify with the church in Rome (1 Pet. 5:13). John greets one church as *Elect* and shares blessings from her sister church, also named *Elect* (2 John 1, 13). Clement of Alexandria (d. 215) saw Mary as the fulfillment of the Old Testament people of God and archetype for the Church. Just as Mary, a virgin mother, nursed the Word incarnate, the Church is a virgin mother who nurses her children with the body of Christ.[185] Ephraim the Syrian (d. 373)[186] and Ambrose (d. 397)[187] also saw Mary as a figure of the Church.

Objects that Typify Mary

Objects can typify Mary, just as they do Christ. Our forebears in the Faith compared Mary's womb to such images as "a tabernacle, an unopened gate, a sealed fountain, a tower, a holy field, a palace." Sweeney notes how Ambrose exemplifies this form of reasoning in applying the title *unopened gate* to Mary:

Ambrose of Milan, the great teacher of Augustine, interprets one of the prophecies of Ezekiel as telling of Mary, God, and her virginity forever. Ezekiel 44:2–4 reads, "And he said to me, 'This gate shall remain shut; it shall not be opened, and no one shall enter by it; for the Lord, the God of Israel, has entered by it; therefore it shall remain shut. Only the prince may sit in it to eat bread before the Lord; he shall enter by way of the vestibule of the gate, and shall go out by the same way'" (RSV). To Ambrose, Mary's womb and chastity are that gate.[188]

KEY 16:

Objects may be types for Mary by reflecting her perfections.

Pelikan sees how Christians applied other figures to Mary, such as the morning star (of the sea),[189] "Poor of the Lord,"[190] Noah's ark (an ark to save humanity), and Jacob's ladder.

As the sun is a type for Jesus, for example, so the moon may typify Mary, having a lesser glory and clothed with the sun's light, which she reflects but doesn't generate. Similar texts portray John the Baptist and all Christians as lights and lamps for the world.[191]

Also, "in the beginning," the earth was barren—"without form and void" and in darkness—yet the Spirit of God moved over the waters of the earth, and the earth was filled with life and light (Gen. 1:1–13). Whereas in the new beginning (John 1:1), Mary was a virgin—without child—when the Holy Spirit overshadowed her (Luke 1:27,35), and she conceived the Light and the Life (John 1:4–15)

Early Christians also associated Mary with Gideon's dew-soaked fleece (Judg. 6:36–40) insofar as Mary was "soaked" with God's Spirit. Others saw Mary as the little cloud that came to cover the whole earth, bringing refreshing rain to end the drought (1 Kings 18:44). She is also a rose amidst thorns, myrtle instead of brier (Isa. 55:12–13). When the Jews receive a savior, an altar and pillar to the Lord in Egypt will be a sign to the nations (19:19–22); Mary and Jesus were in Egypt as a sign of hope for the Jews while Herod terrorized Bethlehem.

Antithetical Women

Scripture contrasts Mary with wicked and cursed women, antithetical to the kind of person women should be, representing Mary's opposite. Antithetical types of Mary include figures such as Miriam, who became leprous due to challenging legitimate authority (Num. 12:1–15). Yet prior to her sin of presumption, being a prophetess (Exod. 15:20–21) and leader (Mic. 6:4), Miriam was a positive figure or type of Mary.

> **KEY 17:**
> *Evil and cursed women may be antithetical types for Mary.*

Harlots, unclean and impure women, who discharge blood, or who are deceitful and idolatrous, or who are slaves to drink, have bad doctrine, are immoral, or tempt others to curse God, may also be antithetical to Mary.[192] The woman most antithetical to Mary is the idolatrous Jezebel, the great manipulator of power, who persecutes and kills God's prophets. Though God attempts to win her back, she refuses. Jezebel is an anti-Mary as her husband Ahab is an Antichrist. In contrast to *Wisdom*, Scripture personifies *Folly* and *Wickedness* to refer to women who are antithetical to Mary.[193]

Although Jerusalem (daughter Zion) originally typifies Mary, other texts curse Jerusalem as a faithless daughter, who is repulsed by her husband, God, choosing to become a whore. This once sacred city is now rebellious, blaspheming God with her idolatry, defiling his sanctuary, killing his prophets. She is now contemptuous, full of abominations and impurities, a false sister, and a widow.[194]

So Jerusalem is a type, both positive and antithetical, of Mary. She continues to be called Jerusalem a virgin daughter (Lam. 2:13) to express her call to be holy, although she later becomes the whore of Babylon instead (Rev. 17:1–19:3). Thus, she is named *Oholibah* (Ezek. 23:2–48), meaning *my tent* (or *sanctuary*) *is in her*. Many Old Testament cities or nations are personified with antithetical qualities.[195]

Antithetical women help us to form a contrasting picture. If an antithetical type of Mary, such as sinful Jerusalem, plays the harlot, then Mary should be pure. As unbelievers are cursed, Mary is blessed for her faith.

Marian Teachings and Biblical Reflections

Jesus and his apostles used the Old Testament extensively, calling it the Word of God (Mark 7:13), God's oracles (Rom. 3:2), and divinely inspired (2 Tim. 3:16), yet they left us no list of inspired books. Determining the canon of Scripture is a complicated matter, since the Jews were divided into dissenting groups, each with a different set of scriptures. Sadducees only considered the Mosaic Law as authoritative. Palestinian Pharisees included the prophets, the Psalms, and some other books. Finally, Greek-speaking Jews relied on the *Septuagint*, named for the *seventy* translators of the Hebrew Scriptures into Greek.[196]

Although Jesus and his apostles gave us no list, they did use the *Septuagint* for most of their quotations. The New Testament cites the Old some 300 times, about 250 of which are from the *Septuagint* translation.[197] Early Christians regarded the *Septuagint* so highly and authoritative that some (including Jews) even considered the translation as being divinely inspired.[198]

As most early Christians spoke and wrote Greek, they generally accepted the *Septuagint* as canonical:

KEY 18:

*Texts in the Septuagint canon follow the same keys
and principles as the rest of Scripture.*

So, early Christians would read Isaiah 7:14—"a virgin shall conceive and bear a son"—and concluded that Mary had to be ever virgin.[199] They found confirmation of this in other passages, such as "sealed fountain" and "locked garden" of Song of Songs 4:12. According to Pelikan, early Christians found scriptural rationale for Mary's sinlessness[200] and for her Assumption[201] as the true fulfillment of Christ's victory over Satan (Gen. 3:15) and death: "He will swallow up death forever, and the Lord God will wipe away tears from all faces, and the reproach of his people he will take away from all the earth" (Isa. 25:8).

In this way, early Christians expanded their application of Scripture to Mary, inspired in their understanding of her special condition as mother of the Word incarnate. Sweeney considers Luther's preaching and writing about Mary very Catholic:

> Luther continued to see [Mary] as a primary means by which sinners may come to God. She points the way to God. . . . [Luther] also could not help praising Mary's huge heart and ready acceptance of that grace, which was not at all ordinary: "Oh, how simple and pure a heart was hers, how strange a soul was this! What great things are hidden here under this lowly exterior!"
>
> Perhaps this is the point on which Luther's reforms most benefited the Church, both then and now.[202]

The Reformation's approach to Scripture found Luther's Marian piety and teaching too Catholic. Yet a mysterious attraction to Marian teachings has begun to move some Protestants to overcome their fears to return to them, as Sweeney notes:

> Many Protestants are increasingly willing to accept Catholic teaching about Mary that had previously been considered too troublesome. Lutheran, Anglican, and Evangelical theologians, in particular, have been meeting in ecumenical dialogue with their Catholic counterparts. . . . Dogma can make sense to people simply because it is beautiful . . . [such as] the spirit and the beauty of the mother of God.[203]

For Catholics, Marian teachings involve both captivating mystery and powerful truth, impacting Christian life in a positive way. It is not an "either/or," but a "both/and"—a rich scriptural basis for appreciating the beauty of the mystery *and* the truth as God has revealed it to us.

By reflecting on early Christians' scriptural musings, we can learn to read Scripture anew, finding its deeper meaning, as did the ancient Beroeans. As Pelikan concludes,

> the explicit references in the New Testament to Mary the mother of Jesus were few in number, and most were quite brief. Even when, by typology or allegory, various statements were applied to her that were taken from earlier biblical books, relatively little amplification was supplied. From this sparse evidence, however, Christian thought almost from the beginning was moved to reflect on its hidden and deeper meanings and on its potential implications. The methods of such reflection were many and various, but at their core they constituted an effort to find and to formulate her place within the themes of the biblical message.[204]

KEY 19:
*Early Marian teaching always resulted
from scriptural reflections.*

Exciting insights are being discovered from exploring Old and New Testament teachings on Mary, which is also refreshing our understanding of early Christian tradition. This effort to uncover their "methods of reflection" will help us discover the *Bible Mary.*

QUESTIONS AND ANSWERS

Q: Why don't we just focus on Scripture's literal description of Mary? Do all these types and figures really help us understand the issues?

A: There is no question that we need to start with the Bible's literal descriptions of Mary because they are the basis for all the others. However, we can't limit ourselves to those literal descriptions. We don't limit ourselves to the literal descriptions of Christ, of the blessed Trinity, or of the Church. If we did, we would end up discarding some 90 percent or more of the Old Testament. But Christ tells us that we can't do that:

> Think not that I have come to abolish the law and the prophets; I have come not to abolish them but to fulfill them. For truly, I say to you, till heaven and earth pass away, not an iota, not a dot, will pass from the law until all is accomplished (Matt. 5:17–18).

In addition, we would also not be able to understand many New Testament texts without types and figures. For example, without the history of the term "covenant of blood" found in Exodus 24:1–11 and Zechariah 9:9–11, we would not understand the full significance of our Lord's expression over the cup at the Last Supper: "This cup is the New Covenant in my blood."[205]

Scripture's literal descriptions of Mary are extremely important and are the starting point for understanding Mary. We can't ignore them, but it would be wrong to limit ourselves to them. Nor can we contradict them. A literalist approach to Scripture puts much more emphasis and weight on our process of logical reasoning. It also forces us to rely heavily on a handful of statements, often taking those statements out of their original context. Finally, we may be more easily influenced by particular philosophies, translations, or theological definitions that are human traditions, clouding our thinking from what the Spirit is trying to say.

Effectively, the literalist approach produces a logical logjam, with opposing sides disagreeing on what Scripture actually says. The way to break this logjam is to discern how the Holy Spirit portrays Mary in the whole of Scripture, not just in part of it.

Q: Most people seem to think that our modern way is better, even more systematic and scientific. Why don't you?

A: There is nothing essentially wrong with the "modern" or literal interpretation. But our interpretation changes as the interpreter changes—that is, as an individual's needs change, as he matures and develops sensitivities in new areas, etc. We can read the same passage and get very different messages over time; Scripture has not changed, but the interpreter has. This is especially true as we grow in faith and love. Imagine how much Peter got out of Scripture before he met our Lord; then, after he first met him; then after the Resurrection; and finally, after years of evangelization (1 Pet. 2:2; Heb. 5:12–14).

You can imagine a middle-aged man, perhaps going through a midlife crisis, stumbling across a stack of love letters he wrote to and received from his wife in their courtship. As he rereads those letters years after they were written, they still strike his heart, and they may shed light that he never saw before as he interprets them in light of the sacrifice and support his wife has had for him, the children they brought into the world and raised together, etc. Now the words mean so much more.

The Holy Spirit was indeed working thousands of years ago. Returning to ancient ways of reading Scripture can help us discover how coherent the Holy Spirit is in the diverse ways he works. It may help us cultivate an openness to *all* that the Spirit has said, with *all* its ramifications. Pride makes us think our "modern" way is the *only* way, or the *best* way. Paul wrote to the Corinthians that they were not ready for solid food, but only for milk because they were still spiritual infants (1 Cor. 3:1–4). They were infants because they were doctrinally divided. Perhaps this is why modern Christians are not ready for typology.

Q: If ancient Jews considered certain books apocryphal, why shouldn't we?

A: Why should we adopt a later, Palestinian Bible that removed books from the early Christian Bible? Should we also go contrary to the New Testament? Whom should we take as authoritative: Jewish rabbis or the early Church established by Christ?

The oldest Jewish manuscripts (codices—parchment copies of the Bible made centuries ago) are the *Allepo* and *Leningrad Codices*, dating back to the tenth and eleventh centuries. These are the sources for the Jewish *Masoretic* text, which is used for translations.

The oldest Christian manuscripts of the Old Testament, however, are much older: complete Greek texts date back to the fourth century. All of these old Bibles contain the Septuagint books. The *Codex Vaticanus* contains the complete version of the Septuagint, except for 1 and 2 Maccabees and the Prayer of Manasseh. Though half of the *Codex Sinaiticus*—also from the fourth century—has been lost, the part that remains includes the books of Maccabees and other books of the Septuagint canon.

In citing Isaiah 7:14, Matthew uses the Septuagint Bible: "Behold, a *virgin* shall conceive and bear a son, and his name shall be called Immanuel" (Matt. 1:23); the Masoretic Hebrew text has *almah*, "young woman," instead of "virgin." So if early (and subsequent) Christians didn't restrict themselves to the Palestinian Bible (until the Reformation), why should we?

Q: Well, if you must use apocryphal books, look at what Baruch says about *Wisdom*:

> You [Israel] have forsaken the fountain of wisdom. If you had walked in the way of God, you would be dwelling in peace forever. Learn where there is wisdom, where there is strength. . . . She is the book of the commandments of God, and the law that endures forever. All who hold her fast will live, and those who forsake her will die (3:12–14, 4:1).

Clearly Baruch identifies Wisdom with Scripture, not Mary. Shouldn't we do likewise?

A: No doubt Wisdom can be identified with Scripture, as with Christ. Yet Mary is more blessed than the woman portrayed as Wisdom. This shows that prophecies, types, and figures can have multiple fulfillments.

Consider this parallel: Christ says John the Baptist fulfills the type of Elijah (Matt. 11:12–14), whereas John denies it (John 1:19–23, Matt. 17:10–13). Both must be right if Scripture doesn't contradict itself. How?

John denies being Elijah, the great prophet, as he was keen to emphasize: "I am not the Christ, but I have been sent before him" (John 3:28). That's his message by saying he is not Elijah.

Jesus teaches us to see John the Baptist as his precursor, anticipating the Messiah as Elijah anticipates Elisha, a prophet with double his spirit and who raises a woman's only son, feeds the multitude with few loaves, and heals leprosy.[206]

So, in a similar way, Wisdom can apply to Scripture *and* to Christ *and* to Mary.

Part II

MARY'S SCRIPTURAL PORTRAIT

Having identified a significant body of scriptural texts referring to Mary, we now turn to Marian teachings, which rose not in isolation, but in direct connection with revealed truths and traditional interpretations about Christ and God's plan for salvation.

Christian doctrinal formulations were developed as the most thoughtful response to heresies or dogmatic misunderstandings. Here is a list of some of these early heresies and some modern counterparts:

Regarding the nature of Christ and the Trinity:

- *Ebionite Jews* (first century)—Christ is not divine; the *Arians* (fourth century)—Christ is only a creature; later *Jehovah's Witnesses* (1852)

- *Gnostics* (first century)—apply to Jesus a materialist dualism (matter and body are evil), leading to *Marcionites* (second century)—two gods, one good and the other evil, declaring Jesus' incarnation impossible; later *Albiguenses* (thirteenth century); *Wicca* (1949); *Satanism* (1966)

- *Docetism* (first century)—Jesus' body is an illusion; *Apollinarianism* (fourth century)—Jesus is only part man (his divine intellect and will replace his human ones); *Monophysitism* (fifth century)—Jesus has only one nature (divine); *Nestorianism* (fifth century)—Jesus is two separate persons: human and divine; Mary is only mother of the human person, not of God; *Adoptionism* (eighth century)—Christ was born man and became divine when God the Father adopted him at his baptism

- *Monarchians* (second century)—God the Father and the Son are the same person; *Modalism* (third century)—the one person of God manifests himself in three modes: Father, Son, and Holy Spirit

- *Mormonism* (1830)—the Trinity is three separate gods

Regarding the nature of salvation:
- *Montanism* with Tertullian (third century)—adultery and flight from persecution are unforgiveable; *Novatians* (third century)—idolatry and mortal sins committed after baptism are unforgiveable

- *Pelagianism* (fifth century)—children need good example, not redemption

- *Semipelagians* (fifth century)—grace is God's response to man's seeking (not God's invitation eliciting man's response)

- *Unitarians* (1774)—Jesus is not God, and his atonement is useless

We will begin considering each Marian doctrine as it arose, often in response to heresy. This will show us, I believe, how early Christians discerned Marian doctrines while clarifying teachings on Christ and God's plan for redemption from Scripture.

Understanding Scripture Anew Through Mary

In discussing Marian teaching and devotion, the Catholic Church sees a wonderful opportunity to deepen her own approach to Scripture:

> The Sacred Scriptures, of both the Old and the New Testaments, as well as ancient Tradition, show the role of the Mother of the Savior in the economy of salvation in an ever clearer light and draw attention to it. The books of the Old Testament describe the history of salvation, by which the coming of Christ into the world was slowly prepared. These earliest documents, as they are read in the Church and are understood in the light of a further and full revelation, bring the figure of the woman, mother of the Redeemer, into a gradually clearer light (*Lumen Gentium* 55).

As we strive to apply Scripture to the mother of the Redeemer, we can improve how we understand other issues scripturally, as the same Holy Spirit moved men to author and interpret Scripture (2 Pet. 1:20–21). Scripture is "the speech of God as it is put down in writing under the breath of the Holy Spirit" (CCC 81, quoting *Dei Verbum* 9). "God communicates himself to man gradually . . . [culminating] in the person and mission of the incarnate Word, Jesus Christ" (CCC 53). Thus "God speaks only one single Word" (CCC 102): Christ whom Mary bore. Any reflection on Scripture relating to Mary opens us to the Spirit of truth (John 14:17, 15:26) who continues to guide his people into all truth (16:13). Thus, the Second Vatican Council encourages a Scripture-based study of Mary:

> Following the study of Sacred Scripture, the Holy Fathers, the doctors and liturgy of the Church, and under the guidance of the Church's Magisterium, let them rightly illustrate the duties and privileges of the Blessed Virgin which always look to Christ, the source of all truth, sanctity and piety (*Lumen Gentium* 67).

For Catholics and Protestants, this advice is both a challenge and an opportunity. As we have seen, there is much more to Mary than is usually told. Many Protestant scholars—in their sensitivity to the Bible—can help make us aware of this new depth.

Mary's Virginity

Early Christians are a wonderful example of the unity for which Christ prayed at the Last Supper:

> And they devoted themselves to the apostles' teaching and fellowship, to the breaking of bread and the prayers. . . . And all who believed were together and had all things in common (Acts 2:42–44).

Their unity grew from reading the Old Testament and receiving the teachings of those in authority. It was expressed in their fellowship—"those who believed were of one heart and soul" (v. 32)—and in the breaking of the bread, fulfilling Christ's Last Supper command: "Do this in remembrance of me" (Luke 22:19).

Mary was a component of this unity: "All these with one accord devoted themselves to prayer, together with the women and Mary the mother of Jesus" (Acts 1:14).

The earliest teaching about Mary is that she was a virgin *before*, *during*, and *after* Christ's birth (CCC 499), which—for early Christians—confirmed Christ's divinity (CCC 496). Vehemently opposing these teachings, unconverted Jews saw Christ as an ordinary man—not God—conceived through a physical sexual union and uterine birth.

Though questioning the teaching, Evangelical Scot McKnight notes that

> with very few exceptions, all Christians from the second or third century onward believed that Mary was perpetually virginal. That is . . . "ever-virgin." . . . This surprises many of us. What may surprise us even more is that three of the most significant Protestant leaders—Martin Luther, John Calvin, and John Wesley—who in their own way were also very critical of what Catholics believed about Mary, each believed in Mary's perpetual virginity.[207]

Early Christians attest to Mary's virginity, describing how Mary conceived Jesus virginally[208]—that is, without male seed or marital intercourse.[209] Non-canonical Christian "scriptures" also refer to Mary miraculously giving birth without pain or shedding blood:

> Some said, "The Virgin Mary has given birth before she was married two months." And many said, "She has not given birth; the midwife has not gone up to her, and we heard no cries of pain."[210]
> So the Virgin became a mother with great mercies. And she labored and bore the Son, but without pain, because it did not occur without purpose. And she did not seek a midwife.[211]

Mary's virginity and Christ's virginal birth mean that Christ is truly divine because God is truly his father. That is why Ignatius of Antioch (d. 110) defended Mary's virginity: "In regard to our Lord . . . he is truly of the family of David according to the flesh, and God's Son by the will and power of God, truly born of a virgin."[212]

Mary's virginity is categorical, since Jesus is both true God and true man—i.e., "truly born of a virgin." Clement of Alexandria (d. 215) also witnesses to Mary's ongoing virginity:

> But, as appears, many even down to our own time regard Mary, on account of the birth of her child, as having been in the childlike state, although she was not. For some say that, after she brought forth, she was found, when examined, to be a virgin.
>
> Now such to us are the Scriptures of the Lord, [that she] gave birth to the truth and *continued virgin*, in the concealment of the mysteries of the truth. "And she brought forth, and yet brought not forth," says Scripture; as having conceived of herself, and not from intercourse. Wherefore the Scriptures have conceived to Gnostics; but the heresies, not having learned them, dismissed them as not having conceived.[213]

Gnostics denied Mary's virginity because it witnessed to Christ's divinity. Tertullian (d. 250) was one of the few Christians who doubted Mary's virginity. A lawyer with a keen mind, this convert produced one of the earliest systematic approaches to theology, yet he could not fathom how Mary could give birth without shedding blood or how to deal with Jesus' brothers.[214] Tertullian's doubts seem linked to his Montanist heresy and did little to influence Christians on the intimate link between Mary's virginity and the mystery of the Incarnation.

Athanasius (d. 373) called her the "Ever-Virgin Mary,"[215] countering those who denied the union of the Word's divine and human natures. Peter Chrysologus (d. 450) more explicitly delineated the theological distinction of Mary's virginity (before, during, and after Christ's birth), saying,

"She conceives as a virgin, she gives birth as a virgin, and she remains a virgin."[216] Augustine concurs (see CCC 510). The ecumenical council of Constantinople (553) bestowed the title "Ever-Virgin" upon Mary.[217]

Ambrose (d. 397)—the bishop of Milan who had to counter his Arian predecessor, Auxentius—considered the belief in Mary's virginity before, during, and after Christ's birth as universal. He used "this *common* belief" to support another belief, that our Lord transformed bread and wine into his flesh and blood at the Last Supper:

> Did the birth of the Lord Jesus from Mary come about in the course of nature? . . . It is clear then that the conception by the Virgin was above and beyond the course of nature. And this body that we make present [in the Eucharist] is the body born of the Virgin. Why do you expect to find in this case that nature takes its ordinary course in regard to the body of Christ when the Lord Jesus himself was born of the Virgin in a manner above and beyond the order of nature?[218]

He could make this bold analogy because the belief in Mary's virginity was so universal. Now it is our task here to investigate the scriptural evidence for these early intuitions.

Scripture's Explicit References

Matthew describes Joseph's quandary: his betrothed was "found to be with child" (Matt. 1:18). What should he do with his beloved wife and her mysterious pregnancy? The angel Gabriel appeared to resolve his agony: "That which is conceived in her is of the Holy Spirit" (Matt. 1:20). Gabriel declared this as the fulfillment of Isaiah's prophecy: "'Behold, a virgin shall conceive and bear a son, and his name shall be called Immanuel' (which means *God with us*)" (Matt. 1:23, Isa. 7:14).[219]

At face value, the prophecy says Mary *is* a virgin, both in *conceiving* and in *bearing* Immanuel. To the modern mind or Scripture scholar, it may seem a preposterous myth for Mary to remain a virgin while giving birth. But Scripture plainly says that a great sign of God's salvation is that "a virgin . . . shall *bear* a son."[220]

Scripture anticipates the possibility of virginal birthing when describing the amazing event of giving birth without labor or pain: "Before she was in labor she gave birth; before her pain came upon her she was delivered of a son. Who has heard such a thing? Who has seen such things?" (Isa. 66:7–8). Certainly, this would be a great sign, a miraculous birth without shedding blood.

Similarly, it was a marvel for the elderly Sarah to conceive a child in her old age: "Is anything too hard for the Lord? At the appointed time I will return to you, in the spring, and Sarah shall have a son" (Gen. 18:14). It was likewise incredible for Elizabeth to conceive. That is why Gabriel told Mary: "Behold, your kinswoman Elizabeth in her old age has also conceived a son; and this is the sixth month with her who was called barren. For with God nothing will be impossible" (Luke 1:36–37). All this was a confirmation to Mary of what God was doing in her, allowing her to conceive and give birth without "knowing man" (v. 34).

Early Christians concluded that "a virgin-for-life shall conceive and bear a son" gave Matthew 1:23 and Isaiah 7:14 their fullest meaning.

John's Account

Although John does not give us a full account of Christ's conception and birth, he does describe the Word's divinity

(John 1:1–5), who "became flesh and dwelt among us" (v. 14). Just before this, he says,

> But to all who received him, who believed in his name, he gave the power to become children of God; him who was born, not of human bloods [plural], nor of the will of the flesh, nor of the will of man, but of God (vv. 12-13, older Greek version).

This passage—*who is born not of human bloods*—is awkward. If the relative pronoun *who* is singular, as many old versions have it, it refers to *the Word.** Several Church Fathers—Justin Martyr (d. 165), Irenaeus (d. 202), Hippolytus (d. 235), etc.—witness to this passage with *who* in the singular, referring to the Word incarnate as being *born not of human bloods, etc., but of God*. These Fathers predate the oldest presently known manuscripts that contain this text. Tertullian accuses the Valentinians of inserting the plural form of *who* to support their Gnostic doctrines.[221] Ambrose also supported this reading:

> Even though [the Word] assumed the natural substance of this very flesh, he was not conceived in iniquity nor born in sin—he who was not born of blood nor of the will of the flesh nor of the will of a man, but of the Holy Spirit from a virgin.[222]

The plural use of *bloods* is awkward in English, Latin (*sanguinibus*), and Greek (*haimátôn*). Some suggest that the plural

---

* Most translations and ancient manuscripts—the oldest of which date from the fourth century—have the relative pronoun *who* rendered in the plural, referring to all Christians *who believe in his name*.

form may refer to the contribution of fluids from both parents in natural conception. Yet a more likely interpretation is that John is referencing the Hebrew Scriptures, which uses the plural *bloods* to describe the woman's menstrual and birthing issues of blood:

> The Lord said to Moses, "Say to the people of Israel, If a woman conceives, and bears a male child, then she shall be unclean seven days; as at the time of her menstruation. . . . Then she shall continue for thirty-three days in the bloods [Hebrew: *damîm*] of her purifying. . . .
>
> "And when the days of her purifying are completed . . . then she shall be clean from the flow of her bloods [*damîm*]" (Lev. 12:1–4, 6–7).

Purification for menstrual and birthing bloods was a consequence of Adam's and Eve's sin, as God said to Woman: "I will greatly multiply your pain in childbearing; in pain you shall bring forth children, yet your desire shall be for your husband, and he shall rule over you" (Gen. 3:16). But since Mary's child was to be God's Son, God restored his original design for women, allowing Mary to give birth without pain or bloods.

Eve's Children (Gen. 3:16)	Mary's Child (John 1:1213)
Born in pain and bloods.	Not born of human bloods.
Born of woman's desire for her husband.	Born not of the will of the flesh.
Born of man's will ruling over woman.	Not born of the will of man.
	Born of God.

Born not of human bloods means the Word incarnate was born without Mary having menstrual or childbearing bloods or pain, remaining a virgin before and during his birth. *Born not of the will of the flesh* means Mary conceived without desire for Joseph. *Born not of the will of man* means Joseph didn't force his will on Mary. In other words, God freed Mary of the curse of Eve: Mary virginally conceived and gave birth to the Word incarnate per God's original plan.

Luke 1:34

Luke gives us greater detail of Christ's conception and birth. Although he does not dwell on the length of Mary's virginity, he does relate Mary's reaction to God's plan, his call for her to give birth to the Messiah. Although written long after Mary's childbearing years, Luke calls Mary a virgin throughout his Gospel:

> In the sixth month the angel Gabriel was sent from God to a city of Galilee named Nazareth, to a virgin betrothed to a man whose name was Joseph, of the house of David; and the virgin's name was Mary. And he came to her and said, "Hail, O favored one [O full of grace or favor], the Lord is with you!" But she was greatly troubled at the saying, and considered in her mind what sort of greeting this might be.
>
> And the angel said to her, "Do not be afraid, Mary, for you have found favor with God. And behold, you will conceive in your womb and bear a son, and you shall call his name Jesus.
>
> "He will be great, and will be called the Son of the Most High; and the Lord God will give to him the throne of his father David, and he will reign over the house of Jacob forever; and of his kingdom there will be no end."
>
> And Mary said to the angel, "How shall this be, since I have no husband [literally, *since I do not know man*]?"
>
> And the angel said to her, "The Holy Spirit will come upon you, and the power of the Most High will

overshadow you; therefore the child to be born will be called holy, the Son of God.

"And behold, your kinswoman Elizabeth in her old age has also conceived a son; and this is the sixth month with her who was called barren. For with God nothing will be impossible."

And Mary said, "Behold, I am the handmaid of the Lord; let it be to me according to your word." And the angel departed from her (1:26–38).

This passage shows Joseph and Mary betrothed—having a covenant marriage, but not yet living together as man and wife. Normally, they wouldn't have marital relations until the marriage feast, which occurred after the husband had acquired a small house and sufficient livelihood to support a wife and children. So Mary is legally married to Joseph, but not living with him, when the angel Gabriel says to Mary, "You will conceive in your womb and bear a son." Mary replies, "How shall this be, since I do not know man?" In other words, she told Gabriel, "Hey, something doesn't add up. How can this happen?"[223]

The interpretation that Mary lost her virginity after Christ's birth holds that neither had any commitment to celibacy. Effectively, this scenario has Mary telling Gabriel, "What you say doesn't add up. How can I possibly conceive and bear a son if we're waiting until the marriage feast to have relations? Until Joseph and I do, which has not happened yet, I can't possibly conceive a child. Come back after the wedding, and I'll consider it." Gabriel would have replied, "You and Joseph will come to live together. You'll have plenty of children together, but first you must become God's spouse and conceive and bear his son. I'll convince him that it is okay. After that, you can become Joseph's wife and have as many children as you like together."

But Gabriel didn't say that. Can you imagine a normal girl engaged to be married saying, *How will I ever conceive a child, since I have never had sex?* In this scenario, neither Mary's nor Gabriel's response reasonably fits Luke 1:34.

This non-virginal scenario is physically possible but seems strange, and it was proposed, adopted, and defended only after the Reformation.

Luke 1:34—Virginal Commitment Scenario

The more traditional scenario views Mary and Joseph as betrothed, but with commitments or expectations to remain virgins. Had Mary and Joseph planned on children, then Mary would not have asked *how* she would conceive, because she would know *how*. She knew the facts of life. When the angel Gabriel tells Mary, "You will conceive in your womb and bear a son," Mary does *not* say, "Okay! Sure! After the wedding feast, we will come together as husband and wife and conceive the Messiah. That makes sense to me."

But that is not her reply. In fact, her reply—"How can this be since I do not know man?"—strongly suggests that marital relations were not even a possibility in her mind— not then, not later, not ever. Mary is saying, "This is impossible. How can this be?"

As Fr. Denis Farkasfalvy writes,

> when Mary objects to the angel that she does not "know man," her words must be logically taken as an objection to the angel's words about her offspring; for she rightly concludes that this child would be a son of David and thus, in view of her engagement to Joseph, Joseph's son.[224]

Let's suppose—as the early Christians did—that Mary and Joseph had discerned God's call to remain perfectly continent, committing themselves to virginity. If that were so, then how would Mary respond to Gabriel's message for her to conceive the Messiah? But "how can that be since I do not and will not know man, having this commitment to God to remain a virgin? How is it possible for a virgin to conceive and bear a child?" Gabriel's responds, "The Incarnation."

Augustine (d. 430) reasoned this way,[225] along with most early Christians, in reflecting on Luke. They deduced that Mary had vowed to remain a virgin, as Pope John Paul II notes:

> St. Augustine does not see in [Mary's] resolution the fulfill-ment of a divine precept, but a vow freely taken. . . . Mary "dedicated her virginity to God when she did not yet know whom she would conceive, so that the imitation of heavenly life in the earthly, mortal body would come about through a vow, not a precept, through a choice of love and not through the need to serve" (*De Sancta Virg.*, IV, PL 40:398). The an-gel does not ask Mary to remain a virgin; it is Mary who freely reveals her intention of virginity. The choice of love that leads her to consecrate herself totally to the Lord by a life of virginity is found in this commitment.[226]

Such vows were not unheard of; in fact, Scripture shows that a man is bound to such a vow (Num. 30:3), whereas father or husband can release a woman from her vow (vv. 4-16). If Joseph chose to go ahead with his betrothal to Mary after learning of her vow, then the vow would stand. Reasoning like this supports the truth that Mary remained a virgin after giving birth to Christ until her death.

Mary's Magnificat and Hannah's Song

Beyond the explicit references, there is plenty of supporting evidence in other Scripture passages for Mary's persistent virginity. For example, the Holy Spirit helps clarify this issue in Mary's song of praise. This canticle, recited after learning of God's plan, makes no direct reference to Mary's virginity, but any Jew who heard it would immediately recognize the parallel of Mary's song with Hannah's.

Of Elkanah's two wives, Hannah was barren, "because the Lord had closed her womb" (1 Sam. 1:6). His other wife, Peninnah, taunted Hannah for her barrenness. Hannah went yearly to the temple to beg God for a son, vowing to entrust her child entirely to him should he grant her prayer. Finally, God announces through the priest, Eli, that she will miraculously conceive; and she does, bearing the prophet-priest Samuel. Presenting her son to Eli, she praises God:

Hannah's Song (1 Sam. 2:1–11)	Mary's Song (Luke 1:46–55)
My heart exults in the Lord; my strength is exalted in the Lord. My mouth derides my enemies, because I rejoice in thy salvation.	My soul magnifies the Lord, and my spirit rejoices in God my Savior, for he has regarded the low estate of his handmaiden.
There is none holy like the Lord, there is none besides thee; there is no rock like our God.	For . . . he who is mighty has done great things for me, and holy is his name.
The bows of the mighty are broken, but the feeble gird on strength. Those who were full have hired themselves out for bread, but those who were hungry have ceased to hunger. . . . The Lord . . . brings low, he also exalts. He raises up the poor from the dust; he lifts the needy from the ash heap, to make them sit with princes and inherit a seat of honor.	And his mercy is on those who fear him from generation to generation. He has shown strength with his arm, he has scattered the proud in the imagination of their hearts, he has put down the mighty from their thrones, and exalted those of low degree; he has filled the hungry with good things, and the rich he has sent empty away.

He will guard the feet of his faithful ones ... for not by might shall a man prevail. . . . The Lord will judge the ends of the earth; he will give strength to his king, and exalt the power of his anointed.	He has helped his servant Israel, in remembrance of his mercy, as he spoke to our fathers, to Abraham and to his posterity forever.

One of the messianic Psalms echoes these two songs of praise:

He raises the poor from the dust, and lifts the needy from the ash heap, to make them sit with princes, with the princes of his people. He gives the barren woman a home, making her the joyous mother of children. Praise the Lord! (113:7-9).

Why would Mary, the young virgin, identify herself with an older barren woman, a *handmaid* like Hannah (1 Sam. 1:11, 16–18; Luke 1:38, 48)? It is simple! Mary applies this hymn to herself because she felt spiritually "barren," unable to have children due to her commitment to virginal "barrenness." Yet God "favored" or "graced" her (1 Sam. 1:18; Luke 1:28–30); it was his plan for her to miraculously conceive a prophet-priest in an impossible way.

Other holy barren women foreshadow the Messiah's mother. God blesses them with miraculous conceptions. Sarah is a barren, faith-filled woman who conceives her first and only son miraculously at the appointed *fullness of time* (Gen. 18:14, 21:2; Gal. 4:4). God preserves from violation Rebekah, "a virgin, *whom no man had known*," and opens her womb to conceive Jacob miraculously (Gen. 26:7–11). Rachel miraculously conceives Joseph; Manoah's wife miraculously conceives Samson, a type of Christ, after an angel announces to her, "You shall conceive and bear a son," prefiguring Gabriel's words to Mary.

Ruth is a widow without child. Though a non-Jew, she faithfully follows her Jewish mother-in-law Naomi back to Bethlehem. In Bethlehem, God guides her to marry Boaz. God guides her through Naomi, responding, "All that you say I will do," as Mary does to Gabriel: "Let it be done unto me according to your word." Also, Elisha's prayer allows a barren Shunammite *handmaid* to conceive. Elisha raises her son from the dead, just as God does Mary's. Likewise, Tobias's wife is "barren" (in a spiritual sense, due to a demon) until the angel Raphael brings Tobias to her. God listens to her persevering prayer, and she conceives and gives birth (Tob. 3:7–17, 6:9–11:19). Even Jerusalem is desolate without children but becomes a mother of all (Isa. 54:1, Gal. 4:26–27).

Thus, by prefiguring her miraculous conception to those of Old Testament women, who knew they could not conceive because they tried and tried and couldn't (or, for Tobias's wife, attempting marriage seven times without becoming a mother), the Holy Spirit clarifies Mary's intention in Luke 1:34: Mary knew she couldn't conceive naturally because she had become—and would remain—a spiritual eunuch for the sake of the kingdom.

Prophecies and Types for (or Antithetical to) Virginity

Other Old Testament prophecies and types prefigure Mary's virginity. Esther, for example, is crowned queen of King Ahasuerus after Vashti (Eve)'s disobedience. Esther is a beautiful young virgin who finds "grace" and "favor" in the king's eyes (Esther 2:1–18).

Jephthah sacrifices his daughter, the price required for victory over evil. She is a young woman "who never knew man" (Judg. 11:30–40), surrounded by unmarried virgin companions,* similar to the Messiah's spouse and queen (Ps. 45:1–17).

The early Church also applied the Old Testament ark to Mary. Objects used in worship—including the Ark of the Covenant—were holy and consecrated to God. The ark was so holy that any person, besides a consecrated priest, would die were he to touch it (Num. 4:15), as in fact happen to Uzzah when he reached out to steady it (2 Sam. 6:1–8). Mary, the vessel that carried the most sacred divine Word, was even more holy. Even the high priest could enter into the ark's presence but once a year, after offering purification for his sins (Heb. 9:7; Exod. 30:10; Lev. 16:2–10). Christ entered Mary's virginal womb once.

Mary was also more blessed than Solomon (Christ)'s bride, his "enclosed garden" (Song of Sol. 4:12), who belonged only to him (2:16; 7:10). In similar fashion, the Temple enclosed a special presence of the Almighty; the Temple's eastern gate was to remain shut because the Lord had entered by it (Ezek. 44:1–3). The early Christians saw Mary as that temple when God became incarnate by entering her womb. The gate of this temple—the gate of her womb—would forever remain shut because she would remain a virgin.[227] God's people prefigured Mary, too, especially as "Virgin Israel," who would become the "new thing on the earth" in order to "protect" (Hebrew: cabab, encompass) man—the New Adam, the Messiah (Jer. 31:21–22)—in her womb. This links us to the many passages of Scripture that call Israel or Jerusalem a virgin daughter (2 Kings 19:15–21). Mary is like Lady Wisdom, chaste and pure, who is clear, spotless as a virgin (Wis. 3:13).[228]

---

* Had she been married, Jephthah's daughter would most likely associate herself with other married women, not with virgins, since young virgins would be in competition to lure away her precious husband. Unmarried girls usually hang out with other similarly situated unmarried girls.

Priests were required to marry a virgin in order to remain undefiled (Lev. 21:7, 13–15; Ezek. 44:21–22; etc.). Our high priest, Christ, required a virginal spouse, who is the Church as prefigured in Mary: "For as a young man marries a virgin, so shall your sons marry you, and as the bridegroom rejoices over the bride, so shall your God rejoice over you" (Isa. 62:5). Early Christians saw how God, who called Israel to be his holy people and virgin bride, would choose Mary to be that creature to give birth to her creator, her God, and her bridegroom, thus fulfilling that call, which would also be extended to the whole Church, the bride of Christ.

Prior to the Fall, Adam called his wife *Woman*, as she was still a virgin (Gen. 2:23). The New Adam—the virginal Christ—calls his mother *Woman* as he begins and ends his public ministry (John 2:4, 19:26), suggesting that she—who is more blessed than the virgin Eve—is still a virgin.

Gideon's fleece is also a sign of Mary's virginity. Just as God caused the fleece to become dew-soaked while the ground around it remained dry, God causes Mary to conceive without man's seed (Judg. 6:36–38). Then, as God caused the fleece to remain dry while the ground became dew-soaked, she gave birth to a child without any bloodletting (vv. 39-40).

For early Christians, all these texts implied Mary's perpetual virginity.

The Meaning of Marital Relations and Virginity

In addition to prophecies and types that prefigure the virgin mother of the Messiah, we may also find feminine types and prophecies that are antithetical to the proper image of Mary.[229]

We are not suggesting that early Christians considered marital relations as something evil. It is true that some sects (such as the third-century Montanists) did hold such negative views, mixing Christianity with Gnosticism or Stoicism. However, the main body of Christians admired the holiness of the marital union alongside Mary's perpetual virginity, seeing marriage as a reflection of the love among the persons of the blessed Trinity. The physical, marital union of bodies is meant to reflect a true spiritual union (1 Cor. 6:15–17), especially as this physical union reflects Christ's pure love for the Church and the Church's pure love for Christ:

> Even so husbands should love their wives as their own bodies . . . as Christ does the Church. . . . "For this reason a man shall leave his father and mother and be joined to his wife, and the two shall become one flesh." This mystery is a profound one, and I am saying that it refers to Christ and the church (Eph. 5:28–32).

Christ was celibate, as were John the Baptist, Paul, and John the Apostle. Although some find it hard to imagine Mary's abiding commitment to virginity, our Lord anticipated how some men like himself would become eunuchs for the sake of the kingdom (Matt. 19:10–12), men "who have not defiled themselves with women, for they are chaste; it is these who follow the Lamb wherever he goes" (Rev. 14:4). Certainly this gave new meaning to chastity as a path of total self-giving to Christ, as a way of putting a man's life at the service of his kingdom. As John Paul II describes it,

> this confirms that these words were impressed in the conscience of the first generation of Christ's disciples and they repeatedly bore fruit in a manifold way in the generations of his confessors in the Church (and perhaps also outside it). So, from the viewpoint of theology—that is, of the revelation of the significance of the body, completely new

in respect to the Old Testament tradition—these words mark a turning point.[230]

We can safely assume that some women would also make themselves "barren" for the sake of the kingdom. Paul considers it a great blessing for a woman to remain like himself, a virgin, to focus and to be "anxious about the affairs of the Lord, how to be holy in body and spirit," whereas a woman with children is "anxious about worldly affairs, how to please her husband" (1 Cor. 7:32–35). If a woman could be blessed a hundredfold for forgoing house, spouse, or children for the sake of the kingdom of God (Luke 18:29–30), for remaining a virgin for the sake of God's kingdom, then Mary—most blessed among women (1:42)—would be pre-eminent among them.

Scripture honors modesty and purity, especially a virginity that frees a woman from worldly pursuits to follow the Lamb wherever he goes and to serve God's kingdom. God calls his people to be a virgin daughter and a pure bride.[231]

In addition, every child should be conceived in grace, of an act of pure love. It does an innocent child a grave injustice to be conceived merely through passion of lust, rape, or incest. Jesus had to be conceived in an act of pure, virginal love. In being conceived by the Holy Spirit, Jesus was the fruit of Mary's virginal love for God. To have it otherwise would be antithetical to Mary:

If a man divorces his wife and she goes from him and becomes another man's wife, will he return to her? . . . You have played the harlot with many lovers; and would you return to me? says the Lord (Jer. 3:1).

Ungrounded and false accusations against a woman for not being a virgin were a shameful crime offensive to God

(Deut. 22:13–21)—as would those against Jesus' mother be to Jesus—just as the king of Assyria offended God by mocking Jerusalem, God's virgin daughter (Isa. 37:21–24).

As early Christians considered Mary's womb a tabernacle of the Holy of Holies, then how could God allow something that is not holy (another human life that is not the sacred body of Christ) to enter this tabernacle? So let's take Scripture at its word: Scripture says Mary is a virgin, before conceiving our Lord (Luke 1:26–27) and while bearing him: "'Behold, a *virgin* shall *bear* a son'" (Matt. 1:23). Scripture never says that Mary ever had relations with a man, so neither should we, as the great Scripture scholar Jerome (d. 419) insists:

> Whereas on the one hand we do not deny what is written [in the Bible], on the other hand we do reject what is not written. We believe that God was born of a virgin, because we read it. We do not believe that Mary consummated her marriage after giving birth, because we do not read it.[232]

The *Catechism* speaks of several other important implications of Mary's virginity. It shows that salvation is God's absolute initiative (503); Jesus is truly the New Adam in a new creation (504); Christians are truly born again as God's children, through faith (505); her perpetual virginity is *the sign of a faith* "unadulterated by any doubt" (506), prefiguring the Church (507).

QUESTIONS AND ANSWERS

Q: Isaiah 7:14 uses the Hebrew word *almah*. So it is a *young woman* who conceives a son. Why then must you argue that Mary had to be a physical virgin to fulfill this prophecy?

A: Those who deny Jesus' divinity make this argument. Evangelical Tim Perry acknowledges that the great biblical scholar Jerome effectively resolved this question through comparative textual analysis:

> [Jerome] avoids allegory, choosing instead more textually based strategies. He presents an argument for understanding *'almah* to mean "virgin" in Isaiah 7:14, for example, not by arguing for what counts as a miracle or a sign but by examining how the word is used elsewhere in the Bible.[233]

Q: Micah 5:1–4 prophesies that in Bethlehem *she who was in travail* gives birth to the Messiah. Doesn't this mean that Mary delivered Jesus with normal birthing pains?

A: Woman's travail comes as the curse for Eve's sin. It also prefigures Jerusalem's destruction, the end of the world, and its redemption. Matthew links this travail to Bethlehem's at the slaughter of the infants; Jesus links it to his disciples'—including Mary's—suffering at his crucifixion; Paul links it to our suffering, the world's longing for the Messiah, and his redemption over sin.[234] So Mary's "travail" is not her labor pains, but her suffering and groaning for the fulfillment of her son's mission.

Q: Gabriel tells Mary, "Your kinswoman Elizabeth in her old age has also conceived a son; and this is the sixth month with her who was called barren. For with God nothing will be impossible" (Luke 1:36–37). Clearly, this is meant to be a sign to Mary. If Mary was a woman of faith and was committed to virginity, then why did she need a sign like Zechariah?

A: Mary is a woman of faith: "Blessed is she who believed" (Luke 1:45). God has granted her a sign—that her barren cousin will bear a son—not to help her believe, but to confirm his plan for her to conceive and bear a son miraculously while remaining a virgin.

Zechariah did ask for a sign to believe: "How shall I know this? For I am an old man, and my wife is advanced in years" (Luke 1:18), saying by this, "How can I be sure you are telling the truth?" The Jews will also ask, "What sign do you do, that we may see, and believe you? What work do you perform?" (John 6:30). But Mary asks no such question, needing no sign to bolster her faith; she doesn't ask for one; she doesn't doubt the possibility of a miraculous conception. In fact, Ahaz's refusal to ask for a sign seems somehow to prefigure Mary:

Ahaz said, "I will not ask, and I will not put the Lord to the test." And [Isaiah] said, "Hear then, O house of David! Is it too little for you to weary men, that you weary my God also? Therefore the Lord himself will give you a sign. Behold, a virgin shall conceive" (Isa. 7:12–14).

Mary too doesn't ask for a sign, but her strong faith simply seeks understanding to better correspond: "How shall this be since I do not know man?" How can this be, as God clearly wants me to remain a virgin? So Gabriel explains: you, a virgin, shall conceive in a miraculous and holy manner, as did barren women of old who bore great leaders, prophets, and messiahs. As a sign, Elizabeth is currently with child, the great precursor, similar to Hosea's marriage to Gomer (Hos. 1:1–10:15) and Ezekiel's many symbolic acts (Ezek. 4:1–8, 5:1–12, etc.): a living sign for God's people to understand his plan. Mary did understand and said "yes" to it: "Be it done unto me according to your word."

Q: If Mary did make a lifelong vow of virginity, then why would she marry Joseph?

A: Some suggest that Mary needed this to survive the harsh judgment of the people toward women with out-of-wedlock pregnancies; in fact, she would have been stoned (Deut. 22:20–29). Others suggest that God sought what was best for his Son: being part of a normal family with earthly parents who would mirror the Father's love for his Son and safeguard the mystery of who Jesus was, until the proper time to reveal himself to the world. Others suggest that this helps show Christians the goodness of virginity.

We could give other reasons, but, ultimately, it occurred the way it did so as to fulfill God's plan established from the beginning. We need to humbly respect this plan.

Q: Did Joseph know about Mary's lifelong commitment to virginity?

A: Scripture gives us few details, but Augustine insists that Joseph had to have known it. Perhaps he had even committed himself to virginity like Mary, as Pope John Paul II suggests: "The Holy Spirit, who had inspired Mary to choose virginity in view of the mystery of the Incarnation . . . was quite able to instill in Joseph the ideal of virginity as well."[235] That would also fit with the virginal commitment scenario we discussed above.

Yet we must admit and humbly respect the *mystery* of what remains hidden in Scripture.

Q: If Joseph and Mary didn't consummate their marriage, was it a true marriage, despite refusing each other the marital right?

A: Adam and Eve were truly man and wife (Gen. 2:24) before knowing each other (Gen. 4:1–2). Scripture says that

Joseph was betrothed to Mary—truly married—and was encouraged to take her into his home as his wife without "knowing" her (Matt. 1:20–25). It was indeed part of God's plan that the two would be husband and wife, Jesus' legitimate earthly father and mother.

This teaches us that true marriage entails pure and sacrificial love. It would be wrong to marry another for selfish sexual gratification (Eph. 5:21–33). Sexuality is good and beautiful, because God created it, yet it is not essential for a happy and wholesome marriage. Our Lord teaches us that virginity is a God-given gift to some (Matt. 19:10–12). True, Paul does say that couples should not refuse each other their marital right, "except by mutual agreement," in part to avoid temptations to be unfaithful (1 Cor. 7:5). These temptations hardly refer to Mary and Joseph, who had received a special grace from God to fulfill their calling.

Joseph and Mary could have made the mutual agreement, as proposed by Paul, before celebrating the wedding feast and living together. Such a mutual agreement would cause Mary to question Gabriel (Luke 1:34) and produce Joseph's anxiety before taking Mary into his home (Matt. 1:20–25).

Q: If truly married, why would Joseph divorce Mary quietly (Matt. 1:18–19)?

A: If Joseph were indeed "in on" Mary's commitment to virginity, then he would have realized that God was doing something very special in her. Perhaps he didn't feel worthy to be part of the mysterious intimacy between God and Mary. By leaving her quietly, he would accept the blame so she would be safe from public criticism, as people would think that he had abandoned his wife after—at least in their minds—having conceived a child with her.

Again, Scripture leaves the details of Joseph's plan hidden from us. Let's respect that.

Q: The New Testament explicitly states that Jesus had brothers and sisters (Mark 3:31–32; Gal. 1:19).[236] Doesn't this mean that Mary had other physical children?

A: Nowhere does the Bible say that Mary had other children or that Jesus' brothers and sisters were hers. Scholars agree that Jesus spoke Aramaic, which—like Hebrew—has no word for *cousin*. In these languages, cousins and other close relatives are called *brothers* and *sisters*. For example, Abraham calls his nephew Lot *'ach* (Hebrew for *brother*, Gen. 13:8).

Evangelical Tim Perry says there is no way to conclude from the context whether such brothers and sisters were children of Mary or not. In analyzing Galatians 1:19, he writes,

The obvious significance of *adelphos* is "uterine brother." . . . But is it possible that this conclusion is premature? It is, after all, widely agreed that the semantic range of *adelphos* encompasses meanings ranging from common ideological and religious adherences to various family relations. While Paul is not using "brother" to refer to James's and Jesus' common religion, it is not clear that he means uterine brother; legitimate alternatives are "cousin" or "stepbrother." Context (Gal. 1:11–24) does not permit a final determination. That James and Jesus are from the same family is indubitable; that they are both children of Mary is possible but not established. Thus this verse alone does not refute ancient beliefs regarding Mary's perpetual virginity.[237]

The Virgin Mary also had a "sister" named Mary (wife of Clopas, John 19:25, CCC 500). In the Bible we never see two blood sisters with the exact same name, but two cousins might share a name. Mary, the wife of Clopas, also happens to be the mother of James and Joseph (Matt. 27:56), *Jesus' brothers* (13:55). That Jesus had brothers and sisters born of the Virgin Mary's *sister* or cousin doesn't imply that she had other children.

Referring to the *brothers of Jesus*, John Chrysostom (d. 407) writes,

If [after Jesus' birth] Joseph had known Mary and lived with her as his wife, why would our Lord, on the cross, have entrusted her to his disciple, commanding him to take her into his own home, as if she had no one else to take care of her?

Why then, you ask, are James and others called the "brothers" of Jesus Christ? They are called brothers of Jesus in the same way that Joseph is called Mary's husband. God wanted to cover this great mystery with many veils, so that the divine birth might remain hidden for a time.[238]

James is "Jesus' brother" as much as Joseph is Jesus' father (Luke 2:33,48), without implying any blood relationship to Jesus.

Q: But the inspired New Testament was written not in Aramaic, but in Greek, which has a word for cousin (*anepsios*) as distinct from brother (*adelphos*). For example, Mark was Barnabas's cousin (*anepsios*, Col. 4:10). It specifically calls Jesus' brothers *adelphoi*.

A: The Bible is not a legal document; it does not use *adelphos* categorically. Christians call one another *adelphos* throughout the Bible: "Beloved, it is a loyal thing you do when you render any service to the brethren (*adelphoi*), especially to strangers" (3 John 5). *Adelphos* is used more than 300 times in the New Testament where it clearly does *not* mean sons of the same biological mother. For example, John the Baptist chastises Herod for marrying Herodias, "his brother (*adelphos*) Philip's wife" (Mark 6:17). Philip and Herod are "brothers," though, through different mothers: Herod's was Malthace; Philip's Mariamne.*

Obviously, Scripture uses the terms *brother* and *sister* differently from how we do. We must be sensitive to that. Tim Perry notes that only later theological debate

> has caused exegetes to try to determine just what the relationship was between Jesus and his siblings. We can conclude that . . . Jesus' "brothers and sisters" may or may not have been other children of Mary.[239]

Q: Matthew states that Joseph took Mary as his wife, "but knew her not until [Greek *eos*] she had borne a son" (Matt. 1:25), clearly implying subsequent union.

A: John Chrysostom (d. 407) addresses this logical inference and rejects it:

> The expression "until" need not lead you to believe that Joseph knew her subsequently; rather, it is used to inform you that the Virgin was untouched by man until the birth of Jesus. Scripture is accustomed to using the expression "until" without intending thereby to establish a limited period of time.[240]

---

*   The early second-century document the *Protoevangelium of James* (8-9, 17) suggests a different solution, although few hold it today: that Joseph was a widower, and Christ's *siblings* were his children by an earlier marriage (not to the Virgin Mary). Origen uses this to argue for Mary's perpetual virginity (*Commentary on Matthew 17*, quoted in Perry [2006] 141).

For example, in Matthew 28:20, Christ promises to remain with us "*until* [Greek *eos*] the completion of the age" (Darby Translation). Nobody thinks this implies that Christ will abandon us afterward, just as Matthew 1:25 doesn't infer that Mary lost her virginity. Likewise David's curse of Michal—"And Michal the daughter of Saul had no child to [*until*] the day of her death" (2 Sam. 6:23)—doesn't say that Michal had children after she died. So Perry concludes,

> Readers may infer that Matthew 1:25 assumes that Joseph and Mary engaged in sexual intercourse after Jesus' birth, as a normal part of their marriage. However legitimate the inference, it is just that—an inference. Grammar and context both suggest that Matthew's point is not to allude to Mary and Joseph's assumption of a normal sexual relationship after Jesus' birth, but to explicitly affirm one of chastity prior to it. It thus re-emphasizes that Jesus can in no way be biologically connected to Joseph.[241]

Q: Scripture doesn't usually put women in genealogies, yet Matthew puts four women of ill repute—Tamar, Rahab, Ruth, and Bathsheba—in Jesus' lineage (Matt. 1:3–5). Doesn't this indicate that Mary was, like these women, not a virgin?

A: Matthew focuses on Joseph's perspective of Jesus' nativity, Luke on Mary's. This is important for drawing the correct implications from this passage.

When Judah's twice-widowed daughter-in-law Tamar becomes pregnant, he must "put her away" for conceiving by harlotry. When Judah learns that the twins she is carrying are actually his, he acknowledges her righteousness, legitimatizing her boys (Gen. 38:6–30).

Salmon—son of Nahshon, head of the tribe of Judah (Num. 1:7, 2:3)—is sent to spy on Jericho. Apparently, when Salmon meets Rahab, a harlot, the two fall in love, since she takes him into her home. Salmon's future child Boaz is doomed to die with Rahab and all of Jericho, but the two spies save them during the attack of the city (Josh. 2:1–21, 6:17–25).

Ruth—a childless widow—follows her mother-in-law's instruction and compromises herself with Boaz. Boaz loves her, yet another man has rights over her. To avoid Ruth being condemned to death, Boaz redeems her and marries her so she can bear his son (Ruth 3:1–4:17).

Finally, king David has an affair with Bathsheba that puts him in a serious dilemma: let Bathsheba be stoned for conceiving a child through adultery or try to put her away by tricking Bathsheba's husband Urriah into thinking the child is his own. David attempts the latter, but his plans fail, so David has Urriah killed in battle. David then takes Bathsheba into his home, and she bears his son, Solomon (2 Sam. 11:1–12:25).

When Joseph learns that Mary is with child, he is in a similar situation to Judah, Salmon, Boaz, and David. Perhaps God used these Scripture passages to confirm what the angel told him, showing Joseph that he, too, should acknowledge Mary's righteousness, take her to be his wife, and thus make Jesus legitimate. Certainly, this is what Joseph did. Joseph gives us a wonderful model of using Scripture to "test the spirits" (1 John 4:1).

Q: Jesus is Mary's firstborn (Luke 2:7), implying that she had other children.

A: Not necessarily. Jesus could be Mary's first and last.[242] In fact, Christ is God the Father's firstborn (Heb. 1:6),[243] without implying that God had other divine sons by other women.

Jesus is God's only son (John 1:14)[244]—"*the* son of Mary" (Mark 6:3), i.e., *the only* son of Mary but still her firstborn (CCC 501)—fulfilling Zechariah's messianic prophecy:

> And I will pour out on the house of David and the inhabitants of Jerusalem a spirit of compassion and supplication, so that, when they look on him whom they have pierced, they shall mourn for him, as one mourns for an *only* child, and weep bitterly over him, as one weeps over a *firstborn* (Zech. 12:10).

As Christ's mother, Mary mourns her son pierced on the cross; she mourns for her *only* child; she weeps over her *first-born*. As Perry explains,

> the Greek term translated "firstborn," *prototokos*, does not necessarily imply the births of subsequent children but means only that no children preceded Jesus. It "establishes for this child the status and privileges in Mosaic Law of the firstborn child (Exod. 13:2; Num. 3:12–13; 18:15–16; Deut. 21:15–17)."[245]

Q: You say that Mary remained a virgin during childbirth. How is that possible? Couldn't Jesus come into the world like any other baby?

A: Virgin childbirth can occur only by a miracle. For Christians, miracles are never out of the question. Christ's incarnation is quite a miracle, too.

Remember that birthing pain and bloods are associated with sin. Jesus had no sin and could not be tainted by sin. Gregory of Nyssa (d. 394) likened Mary's virginity in giving birth to God's appearance to Moses in the burning bush of Exodus 3:1–3.

God passed through the womb of Mary without corrupting her body, just as he appeared to Moses without consuming the bush (CCC 724).[246] Jerome (d. 419) explains it this way:

> Do you want to know how he was born of a virgin and how, after his birth, his mother remained a virgin? The doors were locked, yet Jesus entered. There is no doubt that the doors were locked. He who entered through the locked doors was not a phantasm or a ghost but a true body. For what did he say? "Look at me and see that a ghost does not have flesh and bone as I do" (Luke 24:39).[247]

Q: Your view of sex and marriage seems very negative and puritanical. God created sex as good, even for Mary and Joseph. Isn't the dogma of Mary's perpetual virginity rooted in Augustine's theory that sex is inherently bad, that it taints the body and is the cause of all sin? So Augustine needed Mary to break this cycle, as Jon Sweeney discovered.[248]

A: The teaching of Mary's perpetual virginity doesn't consider sexual desire and union to be bad. It simply affirms Mary's unique relationship with God and her son being the Son of God. This teaching preceded Augustine by hundreds of years. Tertullian was the first to doubt it, falling into a form of Puritanism called Montanism. Sweeney notes that the *Protoevangelium of James*—written around 150—defended Mary's perpetual virginity as a teaching accepted by all Christians.[249] So Augustine did not invent it in the fifth century as a way of defending his supposed anti-sex theories.

Q: Yet didn't Origen and Jerome defend Mary's virginity to support their celibacy and to exalt the dignity of their way of life?

A: Jesus Christ and Paul are better examples to justify this way of life. So early Christians didn't need to invent any rationale to justify their decision to remain celibate. In addition, long before Origen, Christians—as opposed to unconverted Jews—almost unanimously affirmed that Mary remained a lifelong virgin. With the Protestant Reformation, some began to say that Mary had sex with Joseph. Did this happen to justify their abandoning of celibacy?

Q: Yet Scripture never says that Mary was a lifelong virgin. The Reformers taught us to base our teaching on Scripture, not on human authority.

A: We haven't brought in human authority to establish this teaching, but we have focused on discovering the full biblical picture of Mary, which means bringing out what Scripture says that includes types and prophecies. We only introduced the early Christian writers, who are commonly esteemed by virtue of their being closer in time to the actual events and informed more directly by the living tradition of the Faith, to confirm that this was indeed how they read Scripture. What this means for us is that we need to develop the humility to read Scripture as those who wrote it, although this may be different from the approach to which we have become accustomed in the past 500 years.

Even the Protestant Reformers were comfortable with reading Scripture this way. For example, Martin Luther wrote, "Christ, we believe, came forth from a womb left perfectly intact. . . . It is an article of faith that Mary is Mother of the Lord and still a virgin."[250] Calvin knew that the use of "brothers" in Scripture could also mean cousins or relatives. He agreed with Jerome: "Helvidius has shown himself too ignorant, in saying that Mary had several sons, because mention is made in some passages of the brothers of Christ."[251] Zwingli also had clear ideas regarding Mary's virginity:

> I firmly believe that Mary, according to the words of the gospel, as a pure virgin brought forth for us the Son of God and in childbirth and after childbirth forever remained a pure, intact virgin.[252]

Mary's Divine and Spiritual Motherhood

No mother likes to see children argue and fight. Instead, she fosters sympathy and mutual love. Having a mother makes it easier for us to avoid differences and live together in the harmony to which Paul exhorts us:

> Above all these put on love, which binds everything together in perfect harmony. And let the peace of Christ rule in your hearts, to which indeed you were called in the one body (Col. 3:14–5; see Rom. 15:5–6).

Mary's spiritual maternity ought to motivate us to live out this ideal with humility, charity, and unity by living compassion, kindness, etc. toward one another (Col. 3:12–13).

Just as the early Church vigorously defended Christ's divinity by affirming Mary's virginity, the Church also defended his humanity by calling Mary *the Mother of God—Theotokos*. These first Christians did so not to elevate Mary to the divine, but to confess their belief that God truly became man. As Ignatius of Antioch (d. 110) said, "for our God, Jesus Christ, was conceived by Mary in accord with

God's plan: of the seed of David, it is true, but also of the Holy Spirit."[253] Irenaeus of Lyon (d. 202) also made this link: "The Virgin Mary . . . would bear God."[254] Tertullian also embraced her title *Mother of God*.

According to the early Christian historian Socrates, Origen (d. 253) used the title *Theotokos* to defend the true Christian belief that there are not two beings in Jesus Christ (one human and one divine), but one single human person, who is also divine. As mother to this single divine person, Mary is the mother of God.[255] Mary's divine maternity is thus key to a true understanding of the Incarnation.

Heresies increased in the fourth century, attacking the dual natures of Christ as both God and man. For example, Theodotus taught *Adoptionism*, that God the Father adopted the man Jesus at his baptism; Mary was only the mother of the man. Later, Arius taught that Christ is not one substance with the Father, but half Creator and half creature. The Christian teaching that Mary is Mother of God, *Theotokos*, maintains Christ's divinity while affirming his humanity of the Virgin Mary, as the early creeds reflect (CCC 456).

To counter Arianism—which proposes that Christ, the Son of God, was distinct from and subordinate to the Father—Athanasius (d. 373) vigorously defended the fullness of Christ's deity (Col. 2:9), finding the title *Theotokos—Mother of God*—a clear standard for truth.[256] The Syrian deacon Ephraim of Nisibis (d. 373) wrote a hymn praising God that included some words about the interconnection between Mary and Christ's humanity:

In the womb of Mary the Infant was formed, / who from eternity is equal to the Father . . . / And the handmaid and work of his wisdom / became the mother of God.[257]

Gregory Nazianzen (d. 390) found *Theotokos* to be a sure guide to the truth of Christ's two natures in the one person.[258] Ambrose (d. 397) used the title *Mother of God* to counter the Manichean teaching that Christ was human in appearance only, that his human nature didn't just *appear* from heaven, but was truly from the Virgin.[259] Cyril (d. 444) defended Christ the God-Man and Mary the *Theotokos*, the mother of the God-Man, against Nestorius (d. 451). He taught that Christ was two distinct persons: the divine Word and the human person of Jesus, making Christ a God-bearing man. The Council of Ephesus (431) condemned Nestorius, declaring,

> Canon 1: If anyone does not confess that God is truly Immanuel, and that on this account the Holy Virgin is the Mother of God [*Theotokos*] (for according to the flesh she gave birth to the Word of God become flesh by birth), let him be anathema.[260]

The Council of Chalcedon, in 451, condemned Monophysitism—the heresy that Christ has only one nature, the divine. The council reaffirmed the title *Mother of God* (CCC 466).

There are other examples, but now let's focus on what Scripture says about Mary's divine maternity.

The Mother-Son Relationship

The Bible calls Mary the *mother of Jesus Christ* or the *mother of Jesus* or simply *his mother*, but never the *mother of God*. Yet Jesus is *Son of God* and *Son of the Most High*, while remaining *son of Mary*.[261] She conceives of the Holy Spirit and bears *Immanuel*,[262] making her *mother of Immanuel*, mother of *God with us*. Shortening that description, we arrive at *mother of God*.

Paul describes Christ's birth, saying that God sent forth his son, born of woman (Gal. 4:4–5), at the *fullness of time* (Eph. 1:10), linking Mary to Jesus' divinity. He did this to emphasize that God's Son is man, not that Mary is divine. John describes his birth: "And the Word became flesh . . . the only Son from the Father" (John 1:14). Mary is thus *the mother of the Word incarnate*, of God, who becomes fully human through her (CCC 509). Christ was born not of bloods, nor of the will of the flesh, nor of the will of man, but of God, through faith.*

How did Mary treat Jesus and Jesus, Mary? The Bible hints that Mary treated Jesus as any good mother would. She naturally loved her only son, nursing and feeding him. She sacrificed everything for him, interceding for him to obtain his promised inheritance and kingship, even if it meant dying for the salvation of others—she believed that God would raise him from the dead.[263] If other women were saved through bearing children (1 Tim. 2:15), how much more was Mary! She pondered Jesus' childhood words and actions to discern God's will (Luke 2:19, 33, 51); she would have pondered his preaching, teaching, and miraculous deeds as well.

As an example for us, Jesus fulfilled all of God's law and commandments: he showed us how to inherit eternal life, being a good son of Mary and Joseph. Jesus must have honored, revered, glorified, and supported her as his mother in faith, since the Father confirmed her rights over him.[264] Jesus gladdened Mary by his wise conduct, attentively listening to this blessed woman, her wise counsels and good doctrine, obeying his mother's voice:[265] "He who obeys her

---

* Comparing John 1:13 to Wisdom 7:1–2, we see Solomon was born of bloods; the "children of God" are born through faith (Gal. 4:23).

will judge the nations, and whoever gives heed to her will dwell secure" (Sir. 4:15). Jesus never behaved badly toward his mother.[266] Alongside her, he "grew and became strong, filled with wisdom," and he "increased in wisdom and in stature, and in favor with God and man" (Luke 2:40, 52), just as Samson, Samuel, and John the Baptist had done beside their mothers (Judg. 13:24, 1 Sam. 2:26, Luke 1:80).

Mary's identity is found in relationship to her son, who is the Christ, the anointed one, God's consecrated prophet and savior (John 10:36). Scripture prefigures the Savior not in isolation, but in relation to God's people and to his mother. As the Psalmist writes,

> upon thee I have leaned from my birth; thou art he who took me from my mother's womb. My praise is continually of thee. I have been as a portent to many; but thou art my strong refuge (Ps. 71:6–7).

The Father destined Christ for his mission from all eternity, forming and knitting him in the womb (Ps. 139:13). His mission began in that womb, linking his mother to the plan of salvation. Jeremiah prefigures Christ by his consecration in the womb: "Before I formed you in the womb I knew you, and before you were born I consecrated you; I appointed you a prophet to the nations" (1:5). Isaiah (49:1–18) and John the Baptist (Luke 1:13, 31) were also called and named while in their mothers' wombs, prefiguring Christ.

Although all Jewish priests and kings were consecrated to God, the Christ—the crucified one, the sign of contradiction (Luke 2:34)—would be consecrated in Mary's womb: "For they had afflicted him; yet he had been consecrated in the womb as prophet, to pluck up and afflict and destroy, and likewise to build and to plant" (Sir. 49:7). The mother of God's consecrated one also shares in his affliction, with a heart pierced by the sword (Luke 2:35).

All this shows that we should not neglect Christ's relationship with his mother that began at the moment of the Incarnation.

Mother of All Christians

Mary's relationship with Jesus reaches its high point at his crucifixion, when he says his parting words to her and his disciple John: "Woman, behold, your son!" "Behold your mother!" (John 19:26, 27).

John is the "disciple whom Jesus loved," yet early Christians saw an ongoing fulfillment of this passage, as every Christian is called to be a "beloved disciple." Origen (d. 253) saw this as key to understanding John's Gospel:

> Thus we should be bold and say that . . . the firstfruits of the Gospels is the Gospel of John, whose profound meaning cannot be perceived except by him who rested his head on Jesus' breast (see John 13:23) and who received Mary to be his mother also.[267]

Christ is the only-begotten Son of the Father. To image our firstborn brother as God's children, we must embrace God as our spiritual father. But to fully image Christ, we must also have the same spiritual mother—otherwise, Christ would be only our half-brother. So, following Origen's interpretation, we must honor Mary as Jesus would, so as to be fully Christlike.

In this interpretation, the Holy Spirit seems to call every Christian to be a beloved disciple (John 19:25–27, CCC 964), with Jesus applying the words "behold your mother" to each one of us. To be a beloved disciple is to accept Mary as his mother; to reject Mary would be to disobey and reject Christ.

Pope John Paul II links this interpretation to the prophecy that one man "should die for the nation . . . to gather into one the children of God" (John 11:51–52):

On Calvary, Mary united herself to the sacrifice of her son and made her own maternal contribution to the work of salvation, which took the form of labor pains, the birth of the new humanity. In addressing the words "woman, behold your son" to Mary, the crucified one proclaims her motherhood not only in relation to the apostle John but also to every disciple. The Evangelist himself, by saying that Jesus had to die "to gather into one the children of God who are scattered abroad" (John 11:52), indicates the Church's birth as the fruit of the redemptive sacrifice with which Mary is maternally associated.[268]

Typology confirms this maternity over all Christians. Mary is more blessed than Eve, who became the mother of all the living according to the flesh; therefore, as a mother blessed with many children, she is the mother in Israel for all Christians.[269] God promised that Sarah would become mother of all nations and of his people, not according to the flesh, but according to the promise. This is fulfilled in the mother of the true Isaac, Jesus—truly sacrificed on Mount Moriah, Calvary,[270] where our Lord becomes "the firstborn among many brethren" (Rom. 8:29) and where Mary becomes the mother of all his descendants (Isa. 44:1–3, 24–28).

Paul alludes to the common parentage of all the baptized: "For as many of you as were baptized into Christ have put on Christ"; thus, there is no longer distinction of Jew or Greek, male or female, slave or free, because we "are all one in Christ Jesus" as Abraham's children (Gal. 3:27–29). Like Mary, Abraham was blessed for his faith as the father of all believers:

Thus Abraham "believed God, and it was reckoned to him as righteousness." So you see that it is men of faith who are the sons of Abraham. And the Scripture, foreseeing that God would justify the Gentiles by faith, preached the gospel beforehand to Abraham, saying, "In you shall all the nations be blessed" (Gal. 3:6–8).

The Word became a son of Abraham by taking on our human form. By faith and baptism we put on Christ, becoming children of Abraham and of *Woman*—that is, of Mary. With Christ, the first fruit of those who have fallen asleep, we belong to Christ and become fruit of Mary's womb, born again not by entering that womb, but by spiritual rebirth of water and the spirit at baptism.[271]

Scripture also prefigures Mary as Lady Wisdom, mother of all good things, mother of all. She satisfies our spiritual needs with good fruits and produce, filling our storehouses with an abundance that we can share with others. As a good mother, she protects us, shelters us, and gives rest to those who seek and obey her in serving God.[272]

Mother of the Church

Abraham and Sarah "believed against hope," becoming the father and mother "of many nations" (Rom. 4:18). As Jacob's mother, Rebekah is forever associated with God's Old Covenant people. After a wrestling bout, God changes Jacob's name to *Israel* to represent his people and the company of nations and kings.[273] Consequently, the mother of Jesus (the New Testament Jacob, who wrestled with death and came back to life) is associated with his descendants, the Church. The New Jerusalem is also the mother of many children and nations, and of us, too. In a single moment, she becomes the mother of a nation, when

Jesus dies on the cross.[274] This gives new meaning to Isaiah's prophecy:

> It shall come to pass in the latter days that the mountain of the house of the Lord shall be established as the highest of the mountains, and shall be raised above the hills; and all the nations shall flow to it, and many peoples shall come, and say: "Come, let us go up to the mountain of the Lord, to the house of the God of Jacob; that he may teach us his ways and that we may walk in his paths."
>
> For out of Zion shall go forth the law, and the word of the Lord from Jerusalem. He shall judge between the nations, and shall decide for many peoples; and they shall beat their swords into plowshares. . . . Nation shall not lift up sword against nation, neither shall they learn war any more (Isa. 2:2–5).

Like Paul, Mary loved the Church—Christ's body (Rom. 12:45)—as a parent loves his children (1 Cor. 4:14–15). They had similar sentiments for the people Israel: "I have great sorrow and unceasing anguish in my heart. For I could wish that I myself were accursed and cut off from Christ for the sake of my brethren, my kinsmen by race" (Rom. 9:2–3).

Ambrose (d. 397) saw Mary and the Church as our mother:

> [Mary] is the type of the Church, which is also married but remains immaculate. The Virgin [Church] conceived us by the Holy Spirit and, as a virgin, gave birth to us without pain.[275]

Augustine (d. 430) developed this idea, describing Mary as a type of the Church because both are holy, a virgin, a mother (CCC 829, 867), and Christ's bride.[276] The Church can even be called the mother of Christ in a certain sense,[277] because Mary is a member and part of the Church.[278] This links Mary to us as our spiritual mother:

> She [Mary] is clearly the mother of his members; that is, of ourselves, because she cooperated by her charity, so that faithful Christians, members of the Head, might be born in the Church. As for the body, she is the mother of its head.[279]

A model of faith and adherence to God, Mary is a type of the Church (CCC 967). The Second Vatican Council called her mother of the Church, an instrument of Christian unity.

QUESTIONS AND ANSWERS

Q: Isn't calling a creature the *mother of God* idolizing her, putting her on the level of God and turning Mary into a goddess?

A: Jews found the expression *the Lord* a reverent substitute for *YHWH*, God's sacred name. There are many instances wherein a creature is connected to God, as when Scripture describes the Temple or tabernacle as the *House of the Lord*, which is found upon the *Mountain of the Lord*, in Jerusalem, the *City of the Lord*. Nevertheless, the terms *House of God*, *Mountain of God*, and *City of God* do indeed refer to the same reality (yet these terms are used less frequently).[280] So a creature (whether house, city, or mountain) can be linked to God without being idolized. Calling Jerusalem *the City of God* doesn't put it on the same level as God. Neither does the expression *Mother of God*.

Likewise, the expression *Mother of God* is no more unacceptable than the term *son of God* for Christians (Rom. 8:14–25, Gal. 3:24–4:7). No one thinks this makes Christians into gods, yet we do "become partakers of the divine nature" (2 Pet. 1:3–4). If the Holy Spirit himself bears witness that we are children of God, moving us to call God our Father, bestowing on us the great dignity of being *children of God* (1 John 3:1–3), then we should not be surprised that he moves us to call Mary *the mother of God*. Mary can be called *daughter of God* or *mother of God* without breaking the First Commandment.

Q: Calling Mary the *mother of God* can cause confusion, especially to those who don't know the Bible well. It seems to make her superior to Christ, as a mother is over her son. Shouldn't we restrict ourselves to what Scripture explicitly says?

A: We may become confused when first hearing the title *Mother of God*, yet that is true about most Christian teachings. For example, Scripture affirms that there is but one God, but also that the Father is God, the Son is God, and the Holy Spirit is God. Yet there are not three gods, but three persons in one God. So we must qualify what we say so as to teach the full gospel, avoiding mixed-up versions of Christianity. As Pope John Paul II says,

> now, the difficulties and objections raised by Nestorius offer us the opportunity to make several useful reflections for correctly understanding and interpreting this title. . . . The Church's faith is clear: Mary's divine motherhood refers only to the human begetting of the Son of God but not, however, to his divine birth. The Son of God was eternally begotten of God the Father, and is consubstantial with him. Mary, of course, has no part in this eternal birth.

However, the Son of God assumed our human nature 2,000 years ago and was conceived by and born of Mary.

In proclaiming Mary "Mother of God," the Church thus intends to affirm that she is the "mother of the incarnate Word, who is God." Her motherhood does not, therefore, extend to all the Trinity, but only to the Second Person, the Son, who, in becoming incarnate, took his human nature from her.[281]

Scripture never says that Mary is *not* the mother of God. An expression doesn't contradict Scripture simply because it is not found explicitly there. In fact, the Holy Spirit moved Elizabeth to proclaim Mary the *mother of my Lord* (Luke 1:41–43), which indeed is another way of saying *mother of God*. In Luke 1, the word *Lord* is used seventeen times, all referring to God: the word *God* could replace each instance of *Lord*. Thus, Elizabeth effectively addresses Mary as *mother of my Lord who is my God*. Due to the young age of Jesus and his young mother, the only way that Jesus would be Elizabeth's "lord" would be if he were her God (CCC 495). Thus, Elizabeth is effectively saying, "And whence is this to me, that the *mother of YHWH* should come to me?"

As we saw, historically, Christians used the title of *Mother of God* or *God-bearer* (Greek: *Theotokos*) not to emphasize Mary's separateness from humanity, but to reaffirm Christ's true humanity against the heresies of Arias and Nestorius. Nestorius argued that calling Mary *Theotokos* made her into some kind of goddess or semi-goddess. Such an interpretation is heretical and foreign to historical Christianity.

Q: But the Reformers insist on not going beyond Scripture. Wouldn't it just be safer to stick to the titles for Mary that are explicit in Scripture?

A: Many Reformers accepted Mary as the mother of God.
Luther wrote,

> God is born . . . the child who drinks his mother's milk
> is eternal; he existed before the world's beginning and he
> created heaven and earth. . . . These two natures are so
> united that there is only one God and Lord, that Mary
> suckles God with her breasts, bathes God, rocks him, and
> carries him.[282]

> She is rightly called not only the mother of the man, but
> also the mother of God. . . . It is certain that Mary is the
> mother of the real and true God.[283]

Calvin worked out the scriptural implications of several
Bible passages, observing,

> Elizabeth called Mary mother of the Lord because the uni-
> ty of the person in the two natures of Christ was such that
> she could have said that the mortal man engendered in the
> womb of Mary was at the same time the eternal God.[284]

Likewise, Zwingli wrote, "It was given to her what belongs to no creature, that in the flesh she should bring forth
the Son of God."[285]

Q: Mary mothered Jesus' humanity, whereas his divinity comes
from the Father. Doesn't this make it inappropriate to call Mary
Mother of God?

A: This question implies that we can separate the divine and
human natures united in the person of Jesus. But we cannot.
Jesus is simultaneously true God and true man. Mary is the

mother of the person of Jesus, not the mother of his human nature. When we say that Mary is the *mother of God*, we do not mean that Mary is the mother of Christ's divine nature, which is impossible. Ambrose (d. 397) aptly put it this way: "Mary was the temple of God, not the God of the temple. And therefore he alone is to be worshiped who was working in his temple."[286]

The person of Jesus is divine; Mary is the mother of that divine person by mothering him in his humanity. In saying that Mary, a human being, is God's mother, we are affirming with Christians of the earliest times that she is the mother of Christ, in whom the "whole fullness of deity dwells bodily" (Col. 2:9; CCC 484, 722).

What would Mary say? Would she not call Jesus (the incarnate Word) *her son*, or would she call *Jesus' humanity* her son? Would Mary call herself *mother of the Word* or *mother of the Word's humanity*? Would Mary say, *My son Jesus is God*, or would she say, *My son Jesus is only man; I am not related to his divinity*? Obviously, Mary would use the first expression in each pairing. In Luke 2:48, Mary calls Jesus "Son." After Jesus rises from the dead and Thomas acknowledges his divinity by saying, "My Lord and my God" (John 20:28), Mary is still called his mother (Acts 1:14). Had Mary witnessed Thomas's act of faith, she could have followed it with her own: "My son, my Lord, and my God."

A comparison may be helpful: Bathsheba was Solomon's mother long before he became the king of Israel. She did not mother Solomon's kingship, yet she is still called the king's mother (1 Kings 2:19). Likewise, Jehoiachin's mother is called the king's mother (2 King 24:15). Following Scripture's lead, we call Mary the mother of the King of Kings— that is, the *mother of God*.

Q: Jesus' relationship with Mary as her son was unique. Why should we try to imitate him in honoring and obeying his mother as our own?

A: Jesus' relationship with each person is unique. His relationship with Paul was unique, yet Paul suggests that we imitate him in imitating Christ. Christ's relationship of sonship to the Father is unique, as is his relationship to his mother. Yet he is the firstborn of many brothers and sisters (Heb. 2:11–15). For us to be his true brothers and sisters, we need to have the same father and mother as he did: God our heavenly Father and Mary our spiritual mother.

8

Mary's Immaculate Origen

What impedes Christian unity is sin, especially pride that produces division:

> I do not commend you, because when you come together it is not for the better but for the worse. For . . . I hear that there are divisions [Greek: *schismata*] among you; and . . . there must be factions [Greek: *haireseis*] among you in order that those who are genuine among you may be recognized (1 Cor. 11:17–18).

To avoid such *heresies* and *schisms*, Paul ceaselessly urges, "by the name of our Lord Jesus Christ, that all of you agree and that there be no dissensions among you, but that you be united in the same mind and the same judgment" (vv. 9-10). We need humility to overcome doctrinal factions (i.e., heresies) that divide Catholics and Protestants. Scriptural reflections, such as what we are attempting, should help us reach a united mind and judgment.

We have seen how doctrinal errors and heresies lead to defining Christian dogmas. Centuries of misunderstandings over Christ's divinity and humanity, and over the Holy Spirit, forged the doctrine of the Trinity. Likewise, the Pelagian error helped develop the doctrine of original sin, which is essential to a right understanding of the immaculate conception of Mary and her role as the New Eve (CCC 411).

The *Immaculate Conception* means that God preserved Mary from original sin at conception in her mother's womb and that she remained free from sin throughout her life. This special grace prepared her for her mission as mother of the Redeemer (CCC 493).

Around 400, influenced by Stoicism, Pelagius taught that man's nature and relationship with God were harmed by Adam and Eve's bad example, not their sin. Christ redeemed us through his good example. We can avoid sin with a good family and cultural environment. In 416, Pope Innocent I ratified the synods of Carthage and of Milevum, where Augustine (d. 430) and his fellow bishops championed orthodoxy, condemning these errors:

- Adam's sin harmed not the human race, but himself only.

- Newly born children are in the same state as Adam before his fall.

- Man does not die through Adam's sin or death, nor is he raised again through Christ's resurrection.

- The Mosaic Law is as good a guide to heaven as the gospel.[287]

Augustine explains how all are born with original sin, lacking a relationship with God and with a proclivity to further sin. This affects everyone—it is universal—"with the exception of the holy Virgin Mary,"[288] recognizing the Tradition that Mary was always free from sin.

This doctrine was taught in different parts of the world. Origen (d. 253) records the title for Mary used in Alexandria, which had spread throughout the East: *All-Holy* (Greek: *panaghía*).[289] Eastern liturgical prayers still use it today. Didymus the Blind (d. 398) wrote,

> For neither did Mary, who is to be honored and praised above all others, marry anyone, nor did she ever become the mother of anyone else, but even after childbirth she remained always and forever an immaculate virgin.[290]

In Syria, Ephraim (d. 373) wrote poems and ancient Christian hymns, including this one: "For on you, O Lord, there is no mark; neither is there any stain in your mother."[291] In Northern Italy, Ambrose (d. 397) wrote that Mary "alone is called 'full of grace,' since only she obtained that grace which no one else had merited: to be filled with the author of grace,"[292] and that Mary is "a virgin not only undefiled but a virgin whom grace has made inviolate, free of every stain of sin."[293] In Asia Minor, Gregory Nazianzen (d. 390) said the Holy Spirit purified Mary so that Christ's spirit could deify the flesh.[294] Gregory of Nyssa (d. 394) linked the virgin birth of Christ (virginity *in partu*) to Mary's freedom from sin, as non-virginal birthing arose from the curse of Eve's sin.[295] Mary is not an exception to "all have sinned and fall short of the glory of God" (Rom. 3:23), but God had to prepare her for an exceptional mission with the "gift of purifying grace at or before the incarnation."[296]

In the East, Bishop Theoteknos of Livias (d. 650) wrote, "She is born like the cherubim, she who is a pure, immaculate clay," linking God's formation of Adam from the clay of the earth to the Incarnation.[297] Andrew of Crete (d. 740) continues the thought: "The Virgin's body is ground which

God has tilled, the first fruits of Adam's soil divinized by Christ, the image truly like the former beauty, the clay kneaded by the divine artist."[298]

Though the Immaculate Conception was officially defined as Catholic doctrine in 1854, the idea that Rome "invented" it in the nineteenth century ignores history. The dogma of original sin had to be defined before the Immaculate Conception could be fully expounded. Once that dogma became clear, more explicit statements appeared in the Fathers: Theodotus of Ancyra (d. 446), Romanos the Melodist (d. 560), Germain I of Constantinople (d. 733), and John Damascene (d. 749).[299]

Pelagianism reappeared with Enlightenment thinkers in the eighteenth and nineteenth centuries, proposing new myths, such as that of the innocent savage—natives raised without the violence and sin of Western civilization. Thinkers such as Rousseau blamed evil on society and religion—not original sin—such that man needs no redemption. The Immaculate Conception counters this error, reaffirming the Christian dogmas of original sin and redemption.

So the early Christians saw how this doctrine reaffirms the proper understanding of essential elements of the Faith. Let's explore what Scripture passages may have inspired these early Christians, using their principles and the keys we have uncovered.

Full of Grace

The passage most associated with the Immaculate Conception is Luke 1:28–30, where Gabriel addresses Mary with the title (or proper name) of *Full of Grace* or *Highly Favored One*—[Greek: *Kécharitôméne*]. *Kécharitôméne* is the passive perfect participle form of the verb *charitoo*, expressing a completed action or definitive perfection. The verb's root is *charis*, Greek for *grace* or *favor*. The full literal translation of *Kécharitôméne* would be *oh, one who is completely graced* or *favored*. It is followed by "you have found favor [Greek: *charis*, grace] with God."

In the fourth century, Jerome translated *Kécharitôméne* as *gratia plena*—*full of grace*—since God had blessed Mary "in Christ with every spiritual blessing," having chosen her and us in Christ "before the foundation of the world . . . [to] be holy and blameless [Latin: *immaculati*]" (Eph. 1:3–4).

If God fully favored or graced Mary, she needed to be free of sin, of any alienation from God. Mary is fully graced, as she is fully a virgin. Had she been "unvirginal" in any moment of her existence, then she would not be fully a virgin. Likewise, had Mary been disfavored (i.e., in sin) at any moment, then she would not have been fully graced by God or "filled with all the fullness of God" (Eph. 3:19).

Light is an image for grace. Being clothed with the sun indicates that Christ shared with Mary his glory, favor, and grace in God, just as he will with all Christians: "the righteous will shine like the sun in the kingdom of their Father" (Matt. 13:43), when we shall be full of grace. God did this with Mary in anticipation of the redemption, of her becoming the mother of God. This fulfilled his promise: to pour out his Spirit upon his maidservants and handmaids—upon the *handmaid of the Lord*.[300] The Spirit both purified and filled Mary at her conception so she could be called *full of grace* and *most blessed of women*. Gregory Nazianzen (d. 390) explains,

> He was conceived by the Virgin, who had first been purified by the Spirit in soul and body; for, as it was fitting that childbearing should receive its share of honor, so it was necessary that virginity should receive even greater honor.[301]

Mary was more blessed, spiritually holy, clear, pure, and spotless than Lady Wisdom (Wis. 7:23–24). God sought Mary—as he does every Christian—to be Christ's pure bride (2 Cor. 11:2–3), just as Abraham sought a pure bride for his son Isaac (Gen. 24:3, 37; 28:1–2): she must not be a daughter of Canaanites—of sinners descended from Cain. No, Christ's bride must be immaculate: spiritually holy, spotless, without blemish or wrinkle (Eph. 5:25–27), just as every Christian must be washed clean of any stain so as to form the spotless bride. So it is impossible that Mary had any sin affecting her relationship with God.

God goes to great lengths to preserve women from defilement, prefiguring how God would preserve Mary from the spiritual defilement of sin.[302] Sinful and defiled women are antithetical to Mary (as we saw on page 109). Sin is linked to shame. We contract sin at conception and experience shame as we grow. Scripture praises Susanna "because nothing shameful was found in her" (Dan. 13:63). In fact, she freely faced death rather "than to sin in the sight of the Lord." v.23. God vanquished the tempting adversaries of Mary, more blessed than Susanna. So describing Mary as immaculate, free from all sin, best fits Scripture.

Eve: From Shamelessness to Shameful Sin

Key to understanding the Immaculate Conception is how Scripture prefigures Mary in Eve. Exploring early Christian writings, John Henry Newman (d. 1890) noticed how God created both Adam and Eve fully graced and favored, with no stain of sin or shame. This meant their human nature could reflect God's image and likeness perfectly. The New Adam typology suggests that the New Eve would also be fully graced and immaculate. In fact, God calls all of us, "before the foundation of the world, that we should be holy and blameless [Latin: *immaculati*] before him" (Eph. 1:3–4). Human nature doesn't necessitate sin: God calls all to be immaculate, free from sin and its effects. So Mary could be.

As the Word of God and source of all grace (John 1:14–17), Christ was conceived in Mary without sin. Since he is eternally God, he is also eternally holy and without sin. This radically differs from Adam, Eve, and Mary, all of whom had the capacity to sin, whereas Christ did not. Although her immaculate conception differs from her son's, Mary is more blessed than Eve, even before the Fall! "Blessed is the man [or the woman] to whom the Lord imputes no iniquity, and in whose spirit there is no deceit" (Ps. 32:2).

Justin Martyr (d. 165) compares Mary to the immaculate, undefiled virgin Eve.[303] In Scripture, virginity affirms something beyond the physical: it represents freedom from sin.* As more blessed than Eve, Mary is more fully a virgin and free from sin; she is fully graced with a favorable relationship with her heavenly Father (Luke 1:28–30).

Ill favor is sin. For John, sin and virginity are mutually exclusive:

Then I looked, and lo, on Mount Zion stood the Lamb, and with him a hundred and forty-four thousand who . . . have not defiled themselves with women, for they are chaste . . . and in their mouth no lie was found, for they are spotless (Rev. 14:1-5).

---

* Scripture does not say that every person who is sexually a virgin is free from sin or immaculately conceived. The Bible makes only a negative assertion: the loss of virginity is connected with sin and impurity. Where there is sin, there is a loss of virginal love of God and a loss of the wholesome relationship with God the Father.

Comparing the Conceptions of
Eve, Mary, John the Baptist, and Christ

	Adam and Eve	Mary	John the Baptist	Christ
Originally Without Sin?	Conceived without	Conceived without	Born without*	Inconceivable in him
Conceived Holy?	Due to God's grace	God filled her with grace	Filled with Holy Spirit in the womb	Holy in himself
Is the Source of that Grace?	No	No	No	Yes
Is Full of Grace?	Not stated in Scripture	Yes	Filled with the Holy Spirit	Yes
Created Sinless?	Yes	Yes	Yes	Not created, but eternally sinless
In God's Image and Likeness?	Yes	Yes	Yes	Yes, image of the Father
Had Free Will?	Yes	Yes	Yes	Yes
Tempted?	Yes, by Satan	Yes	Yes	Yes, by Satan, as man
Could Sin?	Yes, and did	Yes, but didn't; could "become sin" in association with Christ	Yes, but didn't**	As God, no, but "became sin" by taking on our form

* Theologians conclude that John the Baptist was sanctified in the womb of his mother, since he was "filled with the Holy Spirit, even from his mother's womb" (Luke 1:15). See Aquinas, *S. Th.* III.27.1.

** If truly "filled with the Holy Spirit . . . from his mother's womb" onward, then he would not have sinned.

Adam and Eve lose this immaculate grace and shameless-ness when they freely disobey God.[304] God curses Eve's sin: "I will greatly multiply your pain in childbearing; in pain you shall bring forth children, yet your desire shall be for your husband, and he shall rule over you" (Gen. 3:16). Eve, and all women stained with original sin, are cursed with birthing pain and menstrual and birthing bloods, associating these with sin and a need for purification.

As God puts enmity between the devil and the Messiah's mother (Gen. 3:15), so Satan does not break through God's protection of Mary. John Paul II explains:

> The absolute hostility put between the woman and the devil thus demands in Mary the Immaculate Conception, that is, a total absence of sin, from the very beginning of her life. The son of Mary won the definitive victory over Satan and enabled his mother to receive its benefits in advance by preserving her from sin. As a result, the son granted her the power to resist the devil, thus achieving in the mystery of the Immaculate Conception the most notable effect of his redeeming work . . . the beginning of a new order which is the result of friendship with God and which, as a consequence, entails a profound enmity between the serpent and men.[305]

Mary is blessed because of her faith (Luke 1:41–45), and "whatever does not proceed from faith is sin" (Rom. 14:23). So fullness of faith means fullness of sinlessness and grace. Christ's mother is "a lily among brambles, so is my love among maidens" (Song of Sol. 2:2), oh, blessed among women!

Other Types for Mary's Sinlessness

Christ, the Word of God, is "such a high priest, holy, blame-less, unstained, separated from sinners" (Heb. 7:26)—greater than the Temple (Matt. 12:6)—requiring a vessel holier than the Ark of the Covenant in the Holy of Holies, which prefigures Mary. God overshadowed Mary as he had the ark; both were special places of God's presence, of Immanuel, *God with us*. The ark carried the tablets of the Law (God's ten words or commandments), manna (bread from heaven), and Aaron's rod that had budded (a sign of the high priest); Mary was the holy vessel of God's one Word, the true heavenly bread, and the eternal high priest.[306]

The Old Testament ark was covered with gold (Exod. 25:10–22, Heb. 9:4), a sign of divinity, royalty, purity, and holiness. Mary, the Ark of the New Covenant, was not covered with gold, but overshadowed by the Holy Spirit, and thus full of grace, of God's pure, sinless favor.

Since God alone is holy, the city or vessel in which God dwells must be holy: nothing unclean can enter it. Mary is such a vessel. God re-established in Mary his original plan for humanity, making her immaculate and more blessed than Solomon's bride: "You are all fair, my love; *there is no flaw in you*" (Song of Sol. 4:7). She is perfect: "My dove, *my perfect one*, is only one, the darling of her mother, *flawless* to her that bore her" (6:9).[307] The Immaculate Conception is a great grace that God gave Mary (CCC 508). She received this grace to fulfill her mission to be the sacred vessel of God's presence among us.

As God is holy (Rev. 15:4), anything touching him must also be holy. As Moses approaches the burning bush, God says: "Do not come near . . . for the place on which you are standing is holy ground" (Exod. 3:5). As his people approach Mount Sinai, God warns them not to touch the mountain "lest they die," since his presence makes it holy (19:12–13). God promises to sanctify them if they stay in the camp, refrain from sin, and keep themselves holy (Deut. 23:10–15).

The camp is an image of the Church. God continues to challenge us: "This is the will of God, your sanctification" (1 Thess. 4:3); "therefore, be holy, for I am holy" (Lev. 11:44–45, Matt. 5:48). To reach heaven we all need "the holiness without which no one will see the Lord" (Heb. 12:14).

God's dwelling place is holy (Bar. 2:16–18): "Who shall ascend the hill of the Lord? And who shall stand in his holy place?" (Ps. 24:3). Similarly, early Christians asked: who can touch God? Who has the holiness to conceive and bear the incarnate Word? Who is worthy to be the Lord's mountain, where he will dwell for nine months? Who is prepared to receive the all-holy God, who descends from heaven (John 3:13) and become "the fruit of her womb" (Luke 1:42)? Even Isaiah lacks the holiness to be in God's presence and to carry out his mission:

> I saw the Lord sitting upon a throne, high and lifted up; and his train filled the temple. . . . And I said: "Woe is me! For I am lost; for I am a man of unclean lips, and I dwell in the midst of a people of unclean lips; for my eyes have seen the King, the Lord of hosts!"
>
> Then flew one of the seraphim to me, having in his hand a burning coal which he had taken with tongs from the altar. And he touched my mouth, and said: "Behold, this has touched your lips; your guilt is taken away, and your sin forgiven."
>
> And I heard the voice of the Lord saying, "Whom shall I send, and who will go for us?" Then I said, "Here am I! Send me" (Isa. 6:1–8).

Purified of his sin, Isaiah could then serve the Lord and fulfill his prophetic mission. Certainly Mary must be purified before conceiving and bearing Jesus, and touching the incarnate

Word; she too had to be freed from any guilt. As John says,

> no one who abides in him sins; no one who sins has either seen him or known him. . . . No one born of God commits sin; for God's nature abides in him, and he cannot sin because he is born of God (1 John 3:6, 9).

So, in light of her mission, God made Mary holy: "If the root is holy, so are the branches" (Rom. 11:16); "every sound tree bears good fruit, but the bad tree bears evil fruit" (Matt. 7:17); "make the tree good, and its fruit good" (12:33). In this God reveals his plan when conceiving Mary: before he founded the world (Eph. 1:4), he knew he would become the blessed incarnate fruit of Mary's womb (Luke 1:42). As the Psalmist says,

> he who has clean hands and a pure heart, who does not lift up his soul to what is false, and does not swear deceitfully. He will receive blessing from the Lord, and vindication from the God of his salvation (Ps. 24:4–5).

By giving her "clean hands and a pure heart," freeing her from any sin, God prepared Mary to receive a great "blessing from the Lord": the indwelling of her Lord, God, and savior. Couldn't this have happened at the moment she was conceived?

Romans 3:23—the Non-Categorical Context: *All Jews* AND *Gentiles*

Romans 3:19–26 reads, "*All have sinned* and fall short of the glory of God." John adds, "If we say we have no sin, we deceive ourselves, and the truth is not in us" (1 John 1:8). This seems to contradict the teaching on Mary's immaculate conception. Let's explore how the Holy Spirit, through

Paul, intended to apply this to Mary, beginning by putting it in its full context.

The passage reads,

> Now we know that whatever the Law says it speaks to those who are under the law, so that every mouth may be stopped, and the whole world may be held accountable to God. For no human being will be justified in his sight by works of the law, since through the law comes knowledge of sin.
>
> But now the righteousness of God has been manifested apart from law, although the law and the prophets bear witness to it, the righteousness of God through faith in Jesus Christ for all who believe. For there is no distinction; *since all have sinned* and fall short of the glory of God, they are justified by his grace as a gift, through the redemption which is in Christ Jesus, whom God put forward as an expiation by his blood, to be received by faith.
>
> This was to show God's righteousness, because in his divine forbearance he had passed over former sins; it was to prove at the present time that he himself is righteous and that he justifies him who has faith in Jesus.

Key to understanding this passage is the proper meaning of *all have sinned*. Does the Holy Spirit intend for us to read it categorically—*all* human beings *without exception*—or to read it non-categorically—people *in general*, at the same time admitting of exceptions, such as the incarnate Word, Adam and Eve before the Fall, and perhaps others?

Here's the context: Paul wrote to the Christians before his extradition to Rome in A.D. 59. The Christian community contained mostly (if not exclusively) Jewish converts (see RSV note to Rom. 1:13). To avoid scandalizing his Christian brethren with his preaching (vv. 14-17), Paul sought to prepare these Christians for his eventual arrival (v. 10) and his work with Gentiles (v. 13). As Jews would be more receptive to Scripture than to human arguments, he cites the Old Testament extensively.

Familiar with Rome's moral decadence, Paul doesn't excuse Gentile immorality since Gentiles can know God in creation (vv. 18-28). Thus, *all*—both Jew and Gentile—are responsible for their immorality, since God judges each person according to his works, rewarding those who do good—whether Jew or Gentile—and punishing those who do evil (2:1–11). God will judge each, but differently:

- the Jews, on fulfilling the *written Law* (vv. 12-13, 17-24), not on their physical circumcision (vv. 25-29), and

- the Gentiles, on fulfilling the *law written on their hearts*, which is circumcised (vv. 14-16, 26-27, 29) through faith in Jesus Christ (3:27–31).

So God shows no partiality (2:11). Both Jew and Gentile must follow the law: the Jew, the Old Testament; the Gentile, the law written in his heart. Some Jews fail to follow Scripture, and some Gentiles fail to follow their conscience. God entrusted to the Jews his promises, which are not nullified despite the unfaithfulness of some (3:1–4), bringing condemnation (vv. 5-8). A Jewish Christian has no advantage (vv. 1, 9, 27-31), since "all have sinned and fall short of the glory of God" (v. 23). In other words, *all* means *Jews and Gentiles alike,* since "both Jews and Greeks are under the power of sin" (v. 9).

In this context, *all* does not refer to *all men* categorically, not even *all human beings with the exception of Christ*, which would include Adam and Eve before the Fall. Nor does he consider the question of original sin of newborn children, such as Jacob and Esau, who "had done nothing either good or bad" (9:11). He is simply summarizing that *both Jew* and *Gentile* alike need to be redeemed from sin through faith in Jesus Christ, because *both* "have sinned and fall short of the glory of God."

The whole world—*all*—is accountable to God (3:19–20): his righteousness is seen in the Law for the *Jew* and apart from the law for the *Gentile* (vv. 21-22), eliminating distinctions between *Jew* and *Gentile*, for *both* are under the power of sin, and *both* need redeeming grace and the forgiveness of sin through faith in Christ (vv. 24-26). Jews thus have no advantage.

Continuing this argument, Paul shows how Abraham was justified by faith before being circumcised (4:1–25), such that *both* circumcised *Jew* and uncircumcised *Gentile* will receive David's blessing: the forgiveness of sin (vv. 6-9). Thus, there is no difference between Jew and Gentile with regard to redemption.

The *all* of Romans 3:23 is the same *all* of Romans 2:12: "*All* who have sinned without the Law [i.e., Gentiles] will also perish without the Law, and all who have sinned under the Law [Jews] will be judged by the Law." Romans 3:9 specifies that the *all* refers to "*all* men, *both Jews* and *Greeks*, [who] are under the power of sin." *All*, *every man*, and *human being* refer to "the *Jew* first and also the *Greek* . . . for God shows no partiality" (2:6, 9, 10-11) or "distinction" (3:22) between *Jew* and *Gentile*. Romans 3:10–12 paraphrases Psalm 14:1–7 or Psalm 53:1–4, connecting the *all* of Romans 3:23 to *the fool*, who says, "There is no God." This passage also refers to the *corrupt* who *do the abominable* and who do not *act wisely* or *seek God*, but have *gone astray*. They are *corrupt evildoers*, the *ungodly* and *depraved*, who *have all fallen away* because they *do not call upon the Lord*. So *all* does not include *the generation of the righteous*, the *poor, his people, Jacob*, or *Israel* mentioned in the same passages.

Romans 3:13 paraphrases two more psalms: "For there is no truth in their mouth; their heart is destruction, their throat is an open sepulcher, they flatter with their tongue" (Ps. 5:9), and "they make their tongue sharp as a serpent's, and under their lips is the poison of vipers" (Ps. 140:3). Paul thus connects his *all* to the *boastful evildoers* who *speak lies* and *flatter, bloodthirsty and deceitful men, my enemies*, who have *many transgressions* in *rebelling* against God. They are *wicked, arrogant, evil*, and *violent* men who *plan evil* and *stir up wars*, to *trip up my feet*—but not the *righteous, afflicted, needy*, or the *upright* who *worship* in God's holy temple and take *refuge in him* by *loving his name*.[308]

So the Old Testament context shows *all* referring to all sorts of evildoers and explicitly excluding the innocent.

A few lines down from Romans 3:23, we read,

> Is God the God of Jews only? Is he not the God of Gentiles also? Yes, of Gentiles also, since God is one; and he will justify the circumcised on the ground of their faith and the uncircumcised through their faith (vv. 29-30).

God is the God of *all*, of both *Jew* and *Gentile*, of the circumcised and uncircumcised.

This non-categorical interpretation is often found in early Christian writings. Augustine (d. 430), bishop of Hippo, dealt precisely with this topic in his work against Pelagius, who thought all infants were conceived and born without sin:

> This grace of Christ, however, without which neither infants nor those of more mature age are able to be saved, is not given in view of merits; rather it is given gratuitously,

which, indeed, is why it is called grace. "They are," he says, "justified freely by his blood" (see Rom. 3:24–25). Those, therefore, who are not liberated through that blood . . . are justly condemned, because they are not without sin, either that which they originally bore, or which they have added by their own wicked practices. "For all have sinned," whether in Adam or whether in themselves, "and need the glory of God" (Rom. 3:23).[309]

Augustine appears to apply Romans 3:23 to every human being without exception, but he goes on to exclude Mary:

Having excepted the holy Virgin Mary, concerning whom, on account of the honor of the Lord, I wish to have absolutely no question when treating of sin—for how do we know what abundance of grace for the total overcoming of sin was conferred upon her, who merited to conceive and bear Him in whom there was no sin?— so, I say, with the exception of the Virgin, if we could have gathered together all those holy men and women, when they were living here, and had asked them whether they were without sin, what do we suppose would have been their answer? Would it be what Pelagius says, or would it be what the apostle John says?

I ask you, however, excellent might their holiness have been when in the body, if they had been so questioned, would they not have declared in a single voice, "If we say we have no sin, we deceive ourselves, and the truth is not in us" (1 John 1:8)?[310]

Augustine exempts Mary from both Romans 3:23 and 1 John 1:8, sure evidence that the non-categorical understanding of Romans 3:23 is quite ancient.

Romans 3:23—the Categorical Reading: "All" Really Means All

Although the context and hermeneutics of Romans 3:23 seem to indicate that Paul's "all have sinned" is not a categorical affirmation, it can still be read that way.

Most people consider the categorical reading of Romans 3:23 as Protestant. In reality, it is a very Catholic reading. An anti-Catholic bias typically skirts the ramifications implied in the categorical reading. A truly categorical reading of Romans 3:23 would say that all human beings—every man, woman, and child, including Adam, Eve, Mary, and Jesus Christ—have sinned.

Applying Romans 3:23 to Adam and Eve is not hard since, although conceived without sin and living some time without sin, they eventually do sin (Gen. 3). Indeed, sin comes into this world through one man, Adam (Rom. 5:12–14), and with sin, death (1 Cor. 15:21–22), and thus all bear the image of Adam (1 Cor. 15:45–49), which now includes sin.

We can also apply this passage to Jesus Christ, the Word incarnate, for although he "is light and in him is no darkness" (1 John 1:5) and cannot sin (1 Pet. 2:22),[311] nevertheless,

> though he was in the form of God, [he] did not count equality with God a thing to be grasped, but emptied himself, taking the form of a servant, being born in the likeness of men. And being found in human form he humbled himself and became obedient unto death, even death on a cross. Therefore God has highly exalted him and bestowed on him the name which is above every name (Phil. 2:6–9).

The Word redeems us in an unexpected manner, abandoning his equality with the Father to become a slave ("servant" in the RSV). Slavery is associated with sin and sin with slavery (Rom. 6:16–20). So the eternal Word associates himself with sin by becoming man, "obedient unto death, even death on a cross."

Paul makes this point even more emphatically: "For our sake he *made him to be sin who knew no sin*, so that in him we might become the righteousness of God" (2 Cor. 5:21). The Word, as God, who "knew no sin" made himself "to be sin" by becoming a slave—a human—by embracing the cross, "so that in him we might become the righteousness of God." "Christ redeemed us from the curse of the law, having become a curse for us—for it is written, 'Cursed be every one who hangs on a tree'" (Gal. 3:13, quoting Deuteronomy 21:23). When he is baptized by John, Jesus links himself to the sins of all the baptized (Matt. 3:6, 13–17). Christ, our high priest, takes on the curse of our sin, sympathizes with our weaknesses, "one who in every respect has been tempted as we are, yet without sin" (Heb. 4:15), but he took our sinfulness upon himself:

> He has borne our griefs and carried our sorrows; yet we esteemed him stricken, smitten by God, and afflicted. But he was wounded for our transgressions, he was bruised for our iniquities; upon him was the chastisement that made us whole, and with his stripes we are healed. All we like sheep have gone astray . . . and *the Lord has laid on him the iniquity of us all* (Isa. 53:4–6).

Thus, there is more than one way to "have sinned." One way is by offending God; another is by emptying oneself, becoming stricken, smitten by God, embracing death on a cross—becoming sin. So *all have sinned* can include Christ, but certainly not in the same way that it includes almost all other men.

Mary is closely linked with Christ's cross and thus with Christ's "sin": "Behold, this child is set for the fall and rising of many in Israel, and for a sign that is spoken against" (Luke 2:34). Christ will "become sin" for "the fall and rise of many in Israel" that "we might become the righteousness of God." And of Mary: "A sword will pierce through your own soul also, that thoughts out of many hearts may be revealed" (Luke 2:35). Mary's heart is pierced by sin at the foot of the cross, united to Christ, who became sin.

Romans 3:23 is really a wonderful description of Mary's relationship with Christ's redemptive sacrifice on the cross. So we should respect what God told Peter: "What God has cleansed, you must not call common" (Acts 10:15, 11:9). In other words, with regard to sin, we must not automatically treat Mary as we do everyone else.

QUESTIONS AND ANSWERS

Q: Can Mary be conceived without sin if no one else ever received such an exceptional grace?

A: Looking at Mary as an exception to all humanity misses an important truth: Mary is an exemplar for each of us. As Evangelical Tim Perry explains,

> what makes her *all-holy*—for this title does convey deep theological truth—is not the way in which God graciously removes her from the rest of the race, but the way in which his electing and equipping grace grants her the ability to persevere to the end, to fulfill her vocation completely.[312]

John Henry Newman noted how God's original plan was for all to be conceived immaculate, as Adam and Eve had been.[313] Adam's sin foiled that plan. Yet God still chose Mary from "before the foundation of the world" (Eph. 1:4) to be his mother to restore his original plan in her. She is not the exception; we are!

Even Martin Luther considered Mary's origin something to be expected:

> The infusion of [Mary's] soul, it is piously and suitably believed, was without any sin, so that while the soul was being infused, she would at the same time be cleansed from original sin and adorned with the gifts of God to receive the holy soul thus infused. And thus, in the very moment in which she began to live, she was without all sin.[314]

Q: Mary describes herself in "the low estate of his handmaiden" (Luke 1:48), like every sinner, and then goes to the temple to be purified after Christ's birth (2:22–24). Doesn't this mean Mary had sins needing purification?

A: Sin is not the only motive for lowliness. Any creature, Mary included—no matter how great, powerful, or perfect—is lowly compared to God. Even Jesus calls himself lowly in his human nature: "Learn from me; for I am gentle and lowly in heart" (Matt. 11:29). He who was without sin lowered himself, taking on the form of a slave (Phil. 2:6–8); so did Mary. It is precisely her freedom from sin that leads Mary to adopt such a humble attitude.

Jesus was circumcised on the eighth day (Luke 2:21), the purification for boys initiated into a Covenant relationship with their heavenly Father. Jesus was also baptized by John in the river Jordan (Mark 1:9). John's baptism was "a baptism of repentance for the forgiveness of sins" (v. 4). No one claims that either event indicates that Jesus had sin.

Q: If Mary says, "My spirit rejoices in God my savior" (Luke 1:47), doesn't this mean that Mary needed salvation from her sin?

A: We saw how Mary's song of praise parallels Hannah's, who says, "My heart exults in the Lord . . . because I rejoice in thy salvation" (2 Sam. 2:1). Hannah uses the Hebrew word *yeshuw`ah*, meaning *God's salvation* or *deliverance*. Her "salvation" is in God's miraculous deliverance from barrenness and from Peninnah's derision by allowing her to conceive and give birth. *Salvation* may mean military deliverance, such as God's delivering Israel from captivity in Egypt, or personal deliverance from evildoers or enemies.[315] Later the word *salvation* is connected with eternity: "Israel is saved by the Lord with everlasting salvation" (Isa. 45:17).

God is Mary's savior because he "saves" her from barrenness by miraculously conceiving in her a child named *Jesus—Yeshuw`ah*, or *God saves* (Matt. 1:21, Luke 1:31). The Holy Spirit moves her to say, "My soul magnifies the Lord, and my spirit rejoices in God my savior" (Luke 1:46–47), which could read: "My spirit rejoices in God, my Jesus— *God saves.*" Mary magnifies and rejoices because God her savior has taken flesh in her womb, having filled her with his grace (Luke 1:28) and favor (v. 30).

Q: But Mary needs *eternal* salvation. If Christ tells us, "He who believes and is baptized will be saved" (Mark 16:16), then didn't Mary need Christ to establish baptism first?

A: We all need an eternal savior (CCC 411, 491–2), but salvation is more than wiping away sins: God is her savior even before Christ's death and resurrection, *before redemption from sin*. Christ redeemed her in anticipation of his passion on the cross. She believed (Luke 1:45) and was saved, even before Christ was conceived. The Immaculate Conception truly fulfills Luke 1:47 in advance, as Isaiah foretells:

> I will greatly rejoice in the Lord, my soul shall exult in my God; for he has clothed me with the garments of salvation, he has covered me with the robe of righteousness, as a bridegroom decks himself with a garland, and as a bride adorns herself with her jewels (Isa. 61:10).

God saved Mary by *clothing* her with grace, salvation, and righteousness, allowing her soul to rejoice, magnify, and exult in God her savior. Salvation is a right relationship with Christ. As he told his apostles, "no longer do I call you servants, for the servant does not know what his master is doing; but I have called you friends, for all that I have heard from my Father I have made known to you" (John 15:15). Mary was his friend—salvation is eternal friendship with God. She could become a friend without having sinned, because friendship is a gift freely given. Mary needed God's offer of friendship for him to be her savior.

Salvation is even more. It means relating to Christ as his bride (Eph. 5:28–32). Christ must invite a person—even those without sin—to be his bride. *This invitation is salvation!* Adam and Eve needed a savior—even had they not sinned*—

★ Thomas Aquinas acknowledges that there are differing opinions on this point. He thought that the Word would not have become incarnate had Adam and Eve not sinned, though recognizing that "even had sin not existed, God could have become incarnate" (Aquinas, *S. Th.* III.1.3). Aquinas also thought that the Virgin Mary was sanctified in her mother's womb, but not at conception, because she needed to be sanctified *from sin* for Christ to be her savior (cf. *Ibid.* 27.2). Duns Scotus showed how Christ could be the Virgin's savior by saving since they too were invited (ransomed by Christ) "before the foundation of the world"—before sin! (1 Pet. 1:18–21). Although God "favored" her at her conception, Mary still needed to be invited to be Christ's bride, to be part of his Church. Her whole life was a "yes" to that invitation.

Q: This seems to require two forms of salvation: one *from sin* and another *of friendship.* Wouldn't it be easier to say that Mary was saved from sin like everyone else?

A: It would be even easier had Adam and Eve not sinned. Then salvation would be only God's friendship freely given. But Scripture tells us things happened differently.

Here is an often-used example to explain how Christ saved Mary. Suppose a man falls into a pit or well—"he who misleads the upright into an evil way will fall into his own pit" (Prov. 28:10). When some would-be rescuer hears the man's pleas, he lowers a rope to the man, pulls him up to safety, and washes him clean. In this way, God saves the sinner by drawing him up from the pit (Ps. 40:1–2), forgiving his sins (103:2–5), applying the fruits of Christ's cross to the sinner.

Now suppose we have another person—a woman, let's say—who is walking along toward the same pit. However, before she reaches the pit, her rescuer catches her and prevents her from falling in. She has been "saved," in fact, in a much better way, since God prevented her from getting muddied and from ever seeing or falling into the pit (Ps.

her from ever being tainted by sin and by being the person through whom she achieves complete union with God. Nevertheless, even Aquinas acknowledged that the angels were created happy and in grace while still needing to be granted the beatific vision. They received this gift not by salvation from having sinned, but by salvation to avoid sin by saying yes to God's invitation (see Aquinas, *Ibid.* I.62.1–8).

49:7–9). This gives Mary more reason to call God her savior, who saved her from any stain of sin.

Q: Why does Mary have to be holy at the moment of her conception instead of being purified shortly before God chooses her to be his mother?

A: God chooses and elects those who are to cooperate in his plan of redemption from before the foundation of the world (Eph. 1:4), anticipating his plan. The Old Testament constantly shows how God chose his prophets and leaders at birth or while in their mothers' wombs. This applies to individual prophets, to the people of Jacob, and to the city of Jerusalem, all types of Mary. But God goes beyond just calling them; he consecrates and sanctifies them in the womb.[316] The same is true with the New Testament Holy of Holies, the womb that would carry the Redeemer, Immanuel, *God with us.*

Q: If Mary was free from sin, did she have temptations or have to suffer?

A: The devil tempted sinless Jesus (Matt. 4:1–11): "Because he himself has suffered and been tempted, he is able to help those who are tempted" (Heb. 2:18), and "we have not a high priest who is unable to sympathize with our weaknesses, but one who in every respect has been tempted as we are, yet without sin" (4:15). The same may apply to Mary since, as his mother, she was fully human in every respect.

Another of Jesus' temptations is his agony in the garden, which likely has a parallel in Mary's heart as the cross draws near (Luke 2:35). In addition, when Mary and Joseph lose track of Jesus in Jerusalem (vv. 41-52), she suffers dearly: "Son, why have you treated us so? Behold, your father and

I have been looking for you anxiously." Mary doesn't understand Jesus and perhaps is tempted to lose faith, but she ponders his words and remains faithful.

Q: There's kind of a domino effect here: if Jesus needed an immaculate mother, then Mary too would need an immaculate mother, who also needed an immaculate mother, and so on. How do we avoid someone, such as Adam and Eve, not tainting Mary's line?

A: Jesus could have become man without being born at all, but raised directly from the earth: "God is able from these stones to raise up children to Abraham" (Matt. 3:9). But the most appropriate way for God to show himself to be fully man without tainting his divinity with sin is by being born of a sinless virgin.

Mary didn't need a sinless mother, because she was not God; she did not possess the divinity that would necessitate a sinless mother. It is Jesus Christ, the Word incarnate, whose divinity requires sinlessness. It is God who sanctifies Mary, not the other way around: "For which is greater, the gold or the temple that has made the gold sacred . . . the gift or the altar that makes the gift sacred?" (Matt. 23:17, 19). It is not Mary herself, nor her parents, grandparents, etc., who make her sinless, but God.

Q: In 2 Corinthians 5:21, Paul excludes sin from Jesus but not Mary, so how do you?

A: Paul says nothing directly of Mary, that she knew or did not know sin. Sin is darkness, a negative reality, an absence of grace, a lack of a relationship with God. Yes, Jesus "knew no sin," and "no darkness was in him," because he is the light, "full of grace and truth." God fully graced Mary with his favor and clothed her with the sun, that she too may shine before all: "Her lamp does not go out at night"— that is, her holiness is not extinguished by a sinful world.[317] Neither 2 Corinthians 5:21 nor Romans 3:23 says anything about Mary and her relationship with Jesus.

The Anglican scholar John Macquarrie acknowledges that the meaning of the doctrine of Mary's immaculate conception is that she always had a right relationship with God.[318] As Luther also acknowledges, "she is full of grace, proclaimed to be entirely without sin . . . devoid of all evil."[319]

It was God's plan from "before the foundation of the world, that we should be holy and blameless" (Eph. 1:4). Jesus and Mary became the Adam and Eve of God's new creation; they were made "holy and blameless" in anticipation of the Redemption. *All others*—both Jew and Gentile—"fall short" of God's glory . . . of God's favor . . . of God's grace . . . of being *Kécharitôméne* (Luke 1:28–30). Scripture describes only Jesus and Mary as full of grace (CCC 491).

As all generations of Christians are to call Mary blessed (Luke 1:48) among all women (v. 42), we must be able to say of Mary what the Psalmist says:

Blessed are those whose way is *blameless*, who walk in the law of the Lord! Blessed are those who keep his testimonies, who seek him with their whole heart, *who also do no wrong*, but walk in his ways! (Ps. 119:1–3).

9

Mediating Cooperation

Christians should seek unity and peace in one faith, hope, and love, patiently building up Christ's unified body in a mature knowledge of Christ (Eph. 4:1–6, 11–16). Everyone is called to use his gifts generously to serve others in building up the Church. As we explore Mary's mission in Christ's body, perhaps we can better understand our own.

For early Christians, Mary's role in Christ's redemption was a direct consequence of her relationship with our Lord and his work. Ignatius of Antioch (d. 110), for example, connects Mary's motherhood to God's economy of salvation, as do Athanasius (d. 373), Ambrose (d. 397), and Leo the Great (d. 461).[320] Augustine (d. 430) called Mary "cooperator" in Christ's redemption.[321] Gregory Nazianzen (d. 390) describes how St. Justina implored "the Virgin Mary to bring her assistance," and Gregory of Tours (d. 594) recalls countless miracles attributed to Mary's intercession.[322] Germanus of Constantinople (d. 733) describes Mary:

May the Ever-Virgin—radiant with divine light and full of grace, mediatrix first through her supernatural birth and now because of the intercession of her maternal as-sistance—be crowned with never-ending blessings.[323]

Should Christians go to God through Jesus through Mary? Does God send graces to us through Jesus through Mary? Would this detract from Christ's unique mediating role? This is how the Second Vatican Council explains it:

This maternity of Mary in the order of grace began with the consent which she gave in faith at the Annunciation and which she sustained without wavering beneath the cross, and lasts until the eternal fulfillment of all the elect. . . . By her maternal charity, she cares for the brethren of her son, who still journey on earth surrounded by dan-gers and difficulties, until they are led into the happiness of their true home. Therefore the Blessed Virgin is in-voked by the Church under the titles of *Advocate*, *Aux-iliatrix*, *Adjutrix*, and *Mediatrix*. This, however, is to be so understood that it neither takes away from nor adds anything to the dignity and efficaciousness of Christ the one mediator (*Lumen Gentium* 62).

Critics ask: How can it not take away from "the dignity and efficaciousness of Christ the one mediator"? Is this not trusting Mary rather than Jesus? To resolve this apparent "scandal," we must explore the meaning of mediation and intercession in Scripture.

Let's now consider Mary's role in Christ's redemption that she shares with all Christians in spreading the gospel to others. Next we will explore the uniqueness of Mary's role alongside Christ, as the New Eve alongside the New Adam. Then chapter twelve will consider her heavenly cooperation alongside Christ.

Prayer and Christ's Unique Mediation

Jesus is our "advocate with the Father" (1 John 2:1), mediating righteousness:

> As sin came into the world through one man and death through sin . . . much more have the grace of God and the free gift in the grace of that one man Jesus Christ abounded for many. . . . If, because of one man's trespass, death reigned through that one man, much more will . . . righteousness reign in life through the one man Jesus Christ . . . [for] acquittal and life for all men. For . . . by one man's obedience many will be made righteous (Rom. 5:12–19).

Christ's obedience to the Father unto death brings about the acquittal of sin, which alone communicates God's free gift of grace, making him the sole mediator between God and man: "For there is one God, and there is one mediator between God and men, the man Christ Jesus, who gave himself as a ransom for all" (1 Tim. 2:5–6). This seems quite categorical, excluding any other form of mediation, yet in almost the same breath Paul had just urged Timothy to exhort Christians to pray and intercede for others:

> I urge that supplications, prayers, *intercessions*, and thanksgivings be made for all men. . . . This is good, and it is acceptable in the sight of God our Savior, who desires all men to be saved and to come to the knowledge of the truth (vv. 1-4).

Intercessory prayer pleases God and is connected with saving others. This would require two distinct kinds of mediation: one that is unique to Christ and another that applies to everyone else in union with him. Christ's mediation is the "ransom for all," thus *primary* or *uncreated*. No one could ever substitute or supplant him in this. John Paul II explains:

> Are not prayers a form of mediation? Indeed, according to St. Paul, the unique mediation of Christ is meant to encourage other dependent, ministerial forms of mediation. By proclaiming the uniqueness of Christ's mediation, the Apostle intends only to exclude any autonomous or rival mediation, and not other forms compatible with the infinite value of the Savior's work.[324]

The Holy Spirit also exercises *primary* mediation, moving us to pray and intercede for one another (Rom. 8:26–27). Our efforts to pray are *secondary* intercession, as we can do nothing without Christ and his Spirit (John 15:5) and as God doesn't need our prayer and sacrifices (Ps. 50:8–15), yet he encourages us in these, glorifying him in thanksgiving.

Paul: A Coworker with Christ

Christ uniquely reveals the Father, since "no one knows the Father except the Son and any one to whom the Son chooses to reveal him" (Matt. 11:25–27). As God, Jesus has unique access to the Father, but then he reveals the Father to his disciples: "No longer do I call you servants, for the servant does not know what his master is doing; but I have called you friends, for all that I have heard from my Father I have made known to you" (John 15:15). Christ's mediation is *primary* or *uncreated*, revealing the Father to us—thus, we can call God *Father* (Rom. 8:14–25, Gal. 4:6–7).[325]

Having receiving knowledge of the Father—in union with Christ and through the Holy Spirit—we too can witness, evangelize, pray for, and teach others, making them disciples (Matt. 28:18–20), "that all might believe" (John

1:7). Thus we reveal the Father to others: "He who hears you hears me, and he who rejects you rejects me, and he who rejects me rejects him who sent me" (Luke 10:16). All this is *secondary* or *created* mediation.

Paul understood well his own role as a secondary mediator. He realized that he, and all believers, are called to be Christ's coworkers, even to work miracles (Matt. 17:14–20). Reflecting on Paul's cooperation with Christ can help us understand how God plans for all his creatures to cooperate in redeeming others.

Paul describes himself and all Christians as "God's fellow workers. . . . According to the grace of God given to me, like a skilled master builder I laid a foundation, and another man is building upon it" (1 Cor. 3:9–10). As a steward of God's mysteries to preach the gospel, Paul mediated the gospel of reconciliation as Christ's ambassador: God appealed to the Corinthians through Paul.[326]

We all cooperate with God in our different callings and gifts—to serve; to utter wisdom or knowledge according to the Spirit; to heal, work miracles, prophesy, to discern between spirits; to speak in or interpret tongues, etc. (Rom. 12:3–8, 1 Cor. 12:4–13). As members of Christ's body, the Church, we participate in his mission and work in his vineyard (Matt. 20:1–16), each according to his unique gifts.

We evangelize and pray for unbelievers, and God blesses them through our secondary mediation. This cooperation is essential for their salvation:

For "every one who calls upon the name of the Lord will be saved." But how are men to call upon him in whom they have not believed? And how are they to believe in him of whom they have never heard? And how are they to hear without a preacher? And how can men

205

preach unless they are sent? . . . So faith comes from what is heard, and what is heard comes by the preaching of Christ (Rom. 10:13–17).

We preach so that another may hear God's word; once he hears, he may believe and call upon the name of the Lord and thus be saved. Without the preaching, salvation is thwarted. That doesn't mean that our cooperative work in redemption replaces God's, or that Christ's redemption is somehow incomplete. Not at all. Despite our efforts, only God saves:

> I planted, Apollos watered, but God gave the growth. So neither he who plants nor he who waters is anything, but only God who gives the growth. He who plants and he who waters are equal, and each shall receive his wages according to his labor. For we are God's fellow workers [Greek *syn-ergoi*]; you are God's field, God's building (1 Cor. 3:6–9).

Co-Suffering and Co-Glorification in Christ's Hour

Paul's cooperation in Christ's redemption goes beyond his preaching; he boldly says that he completes Christ's suffering. "Now I rejoice in my sufferings for your sake, and in my flesh I complete what is lacking in Christ's afflictions for the sake of his body, that is, the Church" (Col. 1:24). Paul doesn't say Christ's suffering was inadequate, but that Christ calls him and each one of us to pick up our cross and follow him (Luke 9:23–24).

Christ suffered and calls his body—the Church—to share in his suffering: "For to this you have been called, because Christ also suffered for you, leaving you an example, that you should follow in his steps" (1 Pet. 2:21). All Christ's body shares in his suffering: "If one member suffers, all suffer together" (1

Cor. 12:26), "as we share abundantly in Christ's sufferings" (2 Cor. 1:5). In this way, we offer "spiritual sacrifices acceptable to God through Jesus Christ" (1 Pet. 2:5), winning God's approval by suffering patiently (v. 20). As Paul exhorts, "present your bodies as a living sacrifice, holy and acceptable to God, which is your spiritual worship" (Rom. 12:1). Paul led by his own example: "I have been crucified with Christ; it is no longer I who live, but Christ who lives in me; and the life I now live in the flesh I live by faith in the Son of God, who loved me and gave himself for me" (Gal. 2:20).

In a special way, Mary shared in Christ's sufferings (CCC 969), without detracting from their primacy or adequacy (CCC 970). As John Paul II observes,

> thus Mary is united to her divine Son in this "contradiction," in view of the work of salvation. . . . The primacy of Christ does not rule out but supports and demands the proper, irreplaceable role of woman. By involving his mother in his own sacrifice, Christ wants to reveal its deep human roots and to show us an anticipation of the priestly offering of the cross.[327]

Jesus often referred to his redemptive "hour," beginning at the wedding feast of Cana and ending with the cross,[328] the hour of his glorification (Greek: *doxasthe*) (John 12:23–28), calling Mary *Woman*. Together these two words—*hour* and *Woman*—portray Christ's crucifixion as the wedding feast of his glorification—the complete gift of himself to his bride, the Church, in the *Woman*.

Similarly, Paul connects Christ and the Church in the cross:

> Husbands, love your wives, as Christ loved the church and gave himself up for her, that he might sanctify her,

having cleansed her by the washing of water with the word, that he might present the Church to himself in splendor, without spot or wrinkle or any such thing, that she might be holy and without blemish (Eph. 5:25–27).

As a type of the Church and its first member, Mary represents the bride at the foot of the cross. Christ's manner of self-giving is spousal, emptying himself totally, even unto death. Mary's response is spousal, having the same mind as Christ Jesus (Phil. 2:5–8). Christ's Last Supper words must have meant much to Mary: "When a *woman* is in travail she has sorrow, because her *hour* has come; but when she is delivered of the child, she no longer remembers the anguish, for joy that a child is born into the world" (John 16:21). His hour was her (the *Woman's*) travail.

Mary comes to share in Christ's divine nature (2 Pet. 1:4) as an heir of God and co-heir (Greek: *syn-kleronomos*) with Christ, because she co-suffers (Greek: *syn-paschomen*) with him, being co-glorified (Greek: *syn-doxazo*) with him (Rom. 8:17). This experience applies to all Christians, but especially to Mary, since she did so in his redemptive "hour" on the cross, fulfilling Simeon's prophecy: "Behold, this child is set . . . for a sign that is spoken against (and a sword will pierce through [Mary's] own soul also)" (Luke 2:34–35). As *Woman*, Mary witnesses the unimaginable "hour" (John 19:26–27) of the brutal torture and death of the child she bore. She did so with greater compassion than the women who wept for him beside the road to Calvary (Luke 23:27–31).

Esther's and Judith's *three days* of voluntary fasting, prayer, and physical suffering also prefigured Mary's *three days* of suffering during Christ's passion, death, and time in the tomb (Esther 14:2–15:1, Jth. 9:1–10:4).

Mary's Maternal Role Toward the Church

Like Paul, Mary was Christ's coworker, especially in her maternal relationship with him and with his body, the Church. Mary cooperated in Christ's redemption by nurturing him as a child; she also nurtures his spiritual body, the Church, with all of us in it. We can easily identify Mary's maternal role in Christ's plan of salvation by comparing it to Paul's paternal role of fathering those he evangelized:

> To the present hour we hunger and thirst . . . we labor . . . I do not write this to make you ashamed, but to admonish you as my beloved children. For though you have countless guides in Christ, you do not have many fathers. For I became your father in Christ Jesus through the gospel (1 Cor. 4:11–15).

Paul also felt like a mother giving birth—"my little children, with whom I am again in travail until Christ be formed in you!" (Gal. 4:29)—encouraging his spiritual children to help one another: "So then, as we have opportunity, let us do good to all men, and especially to those who are of the household of faith" (6:10). Don't all mothers do the same, encouraging older children to care for littler ones: "As you did it to one of the least of these my brethren, you did it to me" (Matt. 25:40)? And Jesus directs us: "Again I say to you, if two of you agree on earth about anything they ask, it will be done for them by my Father in heaven . . . [for] there am I in the midst of them" (18:19–20). Wouldn't a spiritual mother do the same, fostering her children to pray together: "All these were persevering with one mind in prayer with the women, and Mary the mother of Jesus, and with his brethren" (Acts 1:14, CCC 726)? God is our true heavenly Father, yet Paul played a paternal role in the salvation of the

Corinthians. Likewise, Catholics view Mary's role alongside Christ as essential as the mother's role in the family.

As Lady Wisdom, Mary builds up the Church, teaching good doctrine and wisdom, instructing our Lord's disciples to obey him. As a good Christian woman, she relieves the afflicted and the poor and frees us from our worries. As our protectrix, Mary also brings us to God, delivering a holy people from sin, guiding and rescuing the righteous, keeping them from sin, and prevailing over evil.[329] She carries out her maternal role by bringing us to Christ (CCC 725) and bringing Christ and his supernatural life to us (CCC 968).

Abraham is the father of many nations, yet God commanded him to respect Sarah's wishes despite his own displeasure: "Whatever Sarah says to you, do as she tells you" (Gen. 21:12). Wouldn't the true Abraham listen to the more blessed Mary? Likewise, Mary is more blessed than Ruth, who supported her mother-in-law even after her husband died. She could have easily returned to her parents' home but became a faithful support for Naomi: "Your daughter-in-law [Ruth] who loves you . . . is more to you than seven sons" (Ruth 4:15). How much Mary supports us, the Church, who are more to her than seven sons!

Proverbs refers to another mode of helping Christ's redemption by presenting Lady Wisdom as a woman who prepares a heavenly banquet (Prov. 9:1–6). At the wedding feast of Cana (John 2:1–12), Mary is the Lord's handmaid in preparing the wedding banquet for his son (Matt. 22:1–14). Through her, God gives us "living bread which has come down from heaven" (John 6:51).

The Evangelical Tim Perry concludes that the Second Vatican Council established Mary's relationship with the Church as the context for Mary's maternal mediation:

It is in this ecclesiological context that the council situates the notion of Mary's mediation. Mary's role as mediatrix or even coredemptrix does not elevate her to the level of Christ and remove her from the church. In these roles she remains with all the redeemed. It is part of the Christian vocation to be coredeemers with Christ; Mary is unique only in the fullness of her response to and participation in it.[330]

As a mother who desires her children to be united to each other and to Jesus, Mary would encourage us. Christ couldn't bear to leave us "desolate" or "orphans" (John 14:18), and it's unimaginable that Mary's maternal heart would, either.

QUESTIONS AND ANSWERS

Q: Defining *intercession* as to witness, evangelize, pray for, and teach is too broad. Wouldn't it be more precise to define *intercession* as *to plead with intensity on behalf of another*?

A: The Bible calls prayer, pleading, and speaking on behalf of others *intercession*: "As for you, do not pray for this people, or lift up cry or prayer for them, and do not *intercede* with me, for I do not hear you" (Jer. 7:16). Jeremiah had been doing this, but now God says it is time for chastisement. In a similar fashion, Paul urges the early Church,

First of all, then . . . that supplications, prayers, intercessions, and thanksgivings be made for all men, for kings and all who are in high positions, that we may lead a quiet and peaceable life, godly and respectful in every way (1 Tim. 2:1–2).

Intercession includes prayer for others, as Mary does at the wedding feast of Cana, making a simple and humble request as her intercessory prayer: "They have no wine" (John 2:3). She doesn't argue with her son; she doesn't use lengthy arguments to convince him; she doesn't put him on a "guilt trip" or manipulate him to get what she wants; she doesn't tell him how to solve the problem. Mary simply places the needs of others before the New Adam, trusting confidently that he will do what is best. In this intercession, she collaborates with him.

Q: The division of *primary* and *secondary* weakens the word *mediation*—we don't find it in the Bible. So how can Mary be *mediatrix* and *coredemptrix* if *mediation* and *redemption* refer only to Christ?

A: If the distinction between *primary* and *secondary* mediation contradicts Scripture, then *mediatrix* and *coredemptrix* make no sense. So you can ignore those titles!

Coredemptrix makes sense only if you acknowledge an assessorial role alongside the primary one. For example, the title *copilot* makes sense only if a person could actually assist the *pilot*. If this role were not possible, then the term *copilot* makes no sense, so you can ignore that one, too.

But Paul acknowledges his secondary role in redemption as "God's coworker," *syn-ergos* (1 Cor. 3:9). If you say that Paul cannot be God's coworker, then you must ignore this passage, but that would alter God's revealed word. The title *coredemptrix* simply summarizes Mary's role alongside Christ, fulfilling Simeon's prophecy—"and a sword will pierce through [Mary's] own soul also" (Luke 2:34–35). Mary's soul was spiritually pierced when the heart in Christ's lifeless body was physically pierced (John 19:34).

Though it is Jesus' passion on the cross that redeemed Paul, he says he has been "co-crucified"—*syn-sustauroo*—with Christ (Gal. 2:20), that he "co-died"—*syn-apothnesko*—(2 Tim. 2:11), was "co-buried"—*syn-thapto*—(Col. 2:12), and ultimately "co-resurrected"—*syn-egeiro* (3:1) with Christ. Mary's *co-passion* at the foot of the cross brings her into intimate union with Christ's crucifixion, death, burial, and resurrection, yet she only *co-redeems* as his helper (Gen. 2:18–20).

Neither Paul's nor Mary's "co-redemption" makes any sense without Christ. As John Paul II notes,

> we pause to reflect on the mother's involvement in her son's redeeming passion, which was completed by her sharing in his suffering. . . . [At] the foot of the cross where the mother endured "with her only-begotten son the intensity of his suffering, associated herself with his sacrifice in her mother's heart, and lovingly consented to the immolation of this victim which was born of her" (*Lumen Gentium* 58). With these words, the [Second Vatican] Council reminds us of "Mary's compassion"; in her heart reverberates all that Jesus suffers in body and soul, emphasizing her willingness to share in her son's redeeming sacrifice and to join her own maternal suffering to his priestly offering.[331]

Q: Doesn't this make Christ's suffering on the cross insufficient?

A: Christians participate in Christ's priesthood (1 Pet. 2:5) with their sacrifices (Heb. 13:15–16). In Colossians 1:24, Paul says his own sufferings "complete what is lacking in Christ's afflictions for the sake of his body, that is, the Church." This doesn't detract from Christ's sufferings or from his priesthood or say that they were incomplete or insufficient, since we are part of our Lord's body; we are called to suffer with our head, Jesus Christ. If all Christians are called to suffer with Christ, then Mary is too, and does, since she is part of his body, the Church.

It is hard to read John 19:25–34 without acknowledging the enormity of Mary's suffering. Still, the Catholic Church reminds us that Mary is only a creature:

> For no creature could ever be counted as equal with the incarnate Word and Redeemer. Just as the priesthood of Christ is shared in various ways both by the ministers and by the faithful, and as the one goodness of God is really communicated in different ways to his creatures, so also the unique mediation of the Redeemer does not exclude but rather gives rise to a manifold cooperation which is but a sharing in this one source (*Lumen Gentium* 62).

Romanos the Melodist (d. 560) called Mary our advocate and mediatrix[332] to express her collaborative suffering with Christ on behalf of the Church.

Q: But this is scandalous, since Scripture never calls Mary advocate or mediatrix!

A: The Jews found Jesus' claim to be God, to be one with the Father (John 10:30–31), scandalous. They couldn't find this in Scripture, so our Lord showed them with his works.

In every aspect of his work, Paul was closely united to our Lord, claiming to be a coworker: not only in Christ's preaching, but also in his crucifixion, death, burial, and resurrection. Paul felt that he was one with Jesus even as Jesus was one with the Father (John 17:20–23), manifested in doing what the Father does (5:19). Scandalous!

Is it so scandalous to believe that Mary is intimately united to her son and savior in his life and work of preaching, crucifixion, death, burial, and resurrection, just as Paul was? Such titles as *mediatrix* or *coredemptrix* express Mary's support and cooperation with Christ in his work of redemption. This should not be scandalous, as it honors her son (John 5:23).

10

A Helper Fit
for the Redeemer

"May he who began a good work in us bring it to completion at the day of Jesus Christ" (Phil. 1:6), uniting us in mind and heart.

Having introduced Mary's cooperation with Christ in Scripture, we must develop the more powerful types that prefigure that cooperation, revealing why the early Christians linked her mission to his so tightly. We will see how sinless Eve, Adam's helper and handmaid, prefigures Mary in relation to Christ, and how sinful Eve—as condemptrix—is antithetical to Mary. Other Old Testament women, such as Jael and Judith, crush the heads of antichrists who enslave God's people, prefiguring Mary. Finally, we will explore parallels between the sacrifices of Jephthah's daughter and of Isaac linking Mary to Christ's sacrifice. With growing clarity, Scripture reveals Mary as a unique "helper" fit for the Redeemer.

Irenaeus of Lyons (d. 202) compares Mary to Eve, who condemned all humanity to death. The Virgin Mary's obedience untied Eve's messy knot of condemnation (Heb. 2:15) and, "by obeying [God], [she] became the *cause of salvation* for herself and for the whole human race."³³³

Irenaeus suggests that Mary is equal to Eve, not to Christ. As Tim Perry explains,

Irenaeus both expands the role of the Virgin Mary in the economy of salvation and subordinates it to the work of Christ. She is called the "cause of salvation" precisely because of her recapitulation of the work of Eve, the "cause of death" . . . [but] he does not mean that she saves alongside and perhaps independently of Christ. Rather, like Eve, she is a thoroughly human vessel.[334]

Amphilochius of Iconium (d. 394) echoes this: "What a grand and most wise strategy against the devil! The world, which had once fallen under the power of sin because of a virgin, is now restored to freedom because of a virgin."[335] Proclus (d. 446) calls Mary the "cause of salvation," "portal of salvation," and, bearing Christ in her womb, "pregnant with salvation," as she "opened paradise" even to Adam.[336] Cyril of Alexandria (d. 444) exclaims: "Through you [Mary], every faithful soul achieves salvation."[337] Caelius Sedulius (d. 445) highlights Mary's cooperation by contrasting her with Eve.[338] The *Catechism* reflects these same ideas (CCC 494). So Pope Benedict XV (d. 1922) will describe Mary's cooperation in her son's redemption:

Mary suffered and, as it were, nearly died with her suffering son; for the salvation of mankind she renounced her mother's rights and, as far as it depended on her, offered her son to placate divine justice; so we may well say that she with Christ redeemed mankind.[339]

Mary: The New Adam's Helper

God's plan for *Man, in the beginning,* was to have *Woman* as a handmaid, helper, and partner in his mission. He made her for this:

> The Lord God caused a deep sleep to fall upon the man, and while he slept took one of his ribs and closed up its place with flesh; and the rib which the Lord God had taken from the man he made into a woman and brought her to the man. Then the man said, "This at last is bone of my bones and flesh of my flesh; she shall be called *Woman*, because she was taken out of *Man*" (Gen. 2:21–23).

It was not good for man to be alone, so God gave Adam *Woman* "as a helper and support. From them the race of mankind has sprung" (Tob. 8:6). Nor should the New Adam be alone in his mission, to be without a *handmaid* (Luke 1:38). So God made the New Eve, an associate in his work (Wis. 8:4), "a helper fit for him and a pillar of support" (Sir. 36:24); from them all Christians have sprung (Rev. 12:1–6, 17). As John Paul II says,

> what is the meaning of Mary's unique cooperation in the plan of salvation? It should be sought in God's particular intention for the mother of the Redeemer, whom on two solemn occasions, that is, at Cana and beneath the cross, Jesus addresses as "Woman" (cf. John 2:4, 19:26). Mary is associated as a woman in the work of salvation. Having created man "male and female" (cf. Gen. 1:27), the Lord also wants to place the New Eve beside the New Adam in the Redemption. Our first parents had chosen the way of sin as a couple; a new pair, the Son of God with his mother's cooperation, would re-establish the human race in its original dignity.[340]

Woman was Adam's helper and partner to accompany him and to help him keep the garden (Gen. 2:15). Mary accompanied Christ in his mission, first as mother, then as a partner and disciple in his work of evangelization, especially as he hung on the cross. The prophets foretold this: "For the Lord has created a new thing on the earth: a woman protects [Hebrew: *cabab*, encompass] a man" (Jer. 31:21–22). God created a "new" thing—New *Woman*—to encompass the New Man in her virginal womb and to support his mission.

Redemption vs. Anti-Redemption

We should compare Mary's role in Christ's redemption to Eve's *"anti-redemptive"* role:

> Now the serpent was more subtle than any other wild creature. . . . He said to the woman, "Did God say, 'You shall not eat of any tree of the garden'?" And the woman said to the serpent, "We may eat of the fruit of the trees of the garden; but God said, 'You shall not eat of the fruit of the tree which is in the midst of the garden, neither shall you touch it, lest you die.'" . . .
>
> The woman saw that the tree was good for food, and that it was a delight to the eyes. . . . She took of its fruit and ate; and she also gave some to her husband, and he ate. Then the eyes of both were opened, and they knew that they were naked. . . .
>
> [God] said, "Who told you that you were naked? Have you eaten of the tree of which I commanded you not to eat?" The man said, "The woman whom thou gavest to be with me, she gave me fruit of the tree, and I ate." Then the Lord God said to the woman, "What is this that you have done?" The woman said, "The serpent beguiled me, and I ate" (Gen. 3:1–13).

Adam, the head of the human family (1 Cor. 11:3–15), caused the condemnation of all: "Sin came into the world through one man . . . one man's trespass led to condemnation for all men" (Rom. 5:12,18). "Much labor was created for every man, and a heavy yoke is upon the sons of Adam" (Sir. 40:1). Adam is the mediator of sin and condemnation, whereas Christ is the mediator of grace and salvation. Now there is "no condemnation for those who are in Christ . . . [who] condemned sin in the flesh" (Rom. 8:1, 3).

Although Adam was the cause of our condemnation, Eve played a prominent role. She succumbed to the serpent's guile, eating the fruit first; Adam followed. Without Eve's contribution, Adam would not have sinned, and we would not have been condemned. Adam even blames her: "The woman whom thou gavest to be with me, she gave me fruit of the tree, and I ate."

Eve's anti-redemptive role occurs on the seventh day of creation, when Adam and Eve are betrothed in the garden. On the seventh day of the new creation, the wedding feast of Cana occurs (John 2:1–11), at the hour of God's new nuptial covenant with man. Now the New Adam and Eve are together. Mary—*Woman*, the banquet's hostess—requests Christ's intervention. He replies, "My hour has not yet come," implying that her request would initiate his "hour," the salvific sacrifice that weds him to his bride. Mary still asks, and Jesus doesn't say no. So begins the hour of the bridegroom, the hour of redemption, Jesus' road of suffering.

As *Woman* of Christ's *hour*, John links Mary's role in Christ's redemption to Eve's role in Adam's anti-redemption. The hour "for the Son of Man to be glorified" is fulfilled on the cross (John 12:23–28), where the New Eve—*Woman*—accompanies the New Adam. This fulfills several Scripture passages: she is the good mother who would die for her child, yet she encourages him to die a martyr.[341] She glories in Christ's suffering, "in the cross of our Lord Jesus Christ" (Gal. 6:14–15), as noted above. First Eve's sin lost access to the fruit of the tree of life that enabled us to "live forever" (Gen. 3:22–24). With Mary, we regain access to the fruit of the tree of life—the risen Jesus, the first fruit of Mary's womb. He who eats this fruit—the true manna—shall live forever.[342] Again, this doesn't mean that Christ's suffering is inadequate—Christ calls all of us to share in his cross. Mary simply answered this call first, making her a special co-heir with him to the grace of life (1 Pet. 3:7).

Besides Eve, the Bible portrays a number of women antithetical to Mary who collaborate with antichrists, leading God's people into sin. The most notorious is Jezebel, who manipulates the power entrusted to her husband Ahab, king of Israel, who "did evil in the sight of the Lord more than all that were before him" (1 Kings 16:30). Jezebel assisted Ahab in his evil, moving Ahab to rebuild Jericho against God's will, erect altars and monuments to Baal and Asherah, and import priests for her idols who would eat at her table (1 Kings 16:31–34, 17:19).

This evil woman is responsible for killing Israel's prophets, and she tries to kill Elijah—a type of Christ. She manipulates her husband's power to kill the holy Naboth, so Ahab could have the vineyard he craves. Ahab recognizes his sin, puts on sackcloth, and fasts to appease God; Jezebel does not, so God curses her for collaborating in evil: "There was none who sold himself to do what was evil in the sight of the Lord like Ahab, whom Jezebel his wife incited" (1 Kings 21:25). God fulfills his curse.[343]

Jezebel reappears in the book of Revelation as the great harlot who induces God's people to sin (Rev. 2:20–23, 17:1–19:3). She lures Christians into forms of idolatry and im-

222

morality. As Jezebel of old killed the prophets, the Jezebel of new is drunk with the blood of the saints and of the "martyrs of Jesus." She is "the great city" (Rev. 17:18), "which is allegorically called Sodom and Egypt, where their Lord was crucified" (Rev. 11:8).

Mary collaborates in Christ's redemption in ways opposite to both Eve and Jezebel.

Crushing Satan's Head

God curses Adam and Eve for their sin, which includes women conceiving and bearing children with pain and blood. Yet while cursing the serpent, God promises us a redeemer: "I will put enmity between you and the woman, and between your seed and her seed; *he* shall bruise your head, and you shall bruise *his* heel" (Gen. 3:15).

The Pentateuch uses the Hebrew pronoun *hw'* for the one crushing the serpent's head. This is an ancient form of Hebrew: *hw'* can be either masculine *hu'* or feminine *hi'*.[344] So, the passage could read either *he* (the *seed*) or *she* (*Woman*) shall bruise your head [Satan], and you shall bruise *his* or *her* heel." The word for *seed* is also ambiguous, as it could refer to one person—the Messiah—or to the collective, that is, to all of the *Woman*'s offspring.

The Jews eliminated these ambiguities when translating Genesis 3:15 in the Greek *Septuagint*. Whereas *seed* is neuter in Greek, the translators identify the subject conquering Satan as the male Messiah by using masculine singular pronouns: "I will put enmity between you and the woman, and between your seed and her seed: *he* shall bruise your head, and you shall bruise *his* heel." They saw how this would fulfill other Old Testament types and prophecies of the male Messiah, such as when Satan bruises the heels of God's people in the desert:

And the people spoke against God and against Moses, "Why have you brought us up out of Egypt to die in the wilderness?" . . . Then the Lord sent fiery serpents among the people, and they bit the people, so that many people of Israel died. And the people came to Moses, and said, "We have sinned, for we have spoken against the Lord and against you; pray to the Lord, that he take away the serpents from us." So Moses prayed (Num. 21:5–7).

To counter Satan, God instructs Moses to make a bronze serpent such that "every one who is bitten" by sin, "when he sees it, shall live" (Num. 21:8). The *Woman*'s seed will fulfill this when he hangs on the cross: "As Moses lifted up the serpent in the wilderness, so must the Son of Man be lifted up, that whoever believes in him may have eternal life" (John 3:14–15). God also prefigures the seed crushing Satan's head when Balak, the Moabite king, asks Balaam to curse Israel; instead, God moves him to say:

The oracle of Balaam the son of Beor . . . who hears the words of God . . . I behold him, but not nigh: a star shall come forth out of Jacob, and a scepter shall rise out of Israel; it shall crush the forehead of Moab, and break down all the sons of Sheth (Num. 24:15–17).

The star, scepter, rises to crush the head of the Antichrist (represented by Moab). David also fulfills this, defeating Goliath by cutting off—crushing—his head (1 Sam. 17:1–51).

Irenaeus of Lyons (d. 202) acknowledges that Christ crushes Satan's head while also acknowledging Mary's role, linking her to Eve:

224

The Lord's . . . obedience on the tree of the cross reversed the disobedience at the tree in Eden; the good news of the truth announced by an angel to Mary, a virgin subject to a husband, undid the evil lie that seduced Eve, a virgin espoused to a husband. . . .

Christ gathered all things into one, by gathering them into himself. He declared war against our enemy, crushed him who at the beginning had taken us captive in Adam, and trampled on his head, in accordance with God's words to the serpent in Genesis: *I will put enmity between you and the woman, and between your seed and her seed; he shall lie in wait for your head, and you shall lie in wait for his heel.*[345]

Yet when the great biblical scholar Jerome (d. 419)—expert in Greek and Hebrew—translated the Bible into the Latin Vulgate, he explicitly rendered this particular passage feminine: "*She* shall crush thy head, and thou shall lie in wait for *her* heel." Why? Did he just make a stupid mistake?*

---

* This was Jon M. Sweeney's conclusion: "Jerome made mistakes in his otherwise groundbreaking translation (the first to translate Scripture into Latin, which was the language of the people in the fourth century). . . . [Since] Jerome's Vulgate became the official version of the Bible used by the Church for many centuries, the mistake led to at least a millennium of doctrinal confusion. . . . For centuries, Jerome's mistake led to confusion about Mary and her powers. For instance, if Mary could perform such salvific heroics as striking down the head of Satan, she must also be without sin. The doctrine of the Immaculate Conception would probably never have arisen if it were not for Jerome's mistake." Sweeney (2006) 34-5.

Sweeney seems to be mistaken, as many Latin Bible translations existed prior to Jerome's. Jaroslav Pelikan explains: "[Jerome] was one of the few scholars in the first several centuries of Christian history to know Hebrew as well as Greek and Latin. . . . But at some point in the transmission of the Latin text of the Vulgate, whether by mistake or by fraud or by pious reflection, that neuter "ipsum" corresponding to the neuter of "semen [seed]" was changed to a feminine. . . . There is clear evidence that this was not how Jerome translated the text; for as a Hebrew scholar, he knew that the pronoun should not be rendered with 'she,' and one of the earliest manuscripts of his translation, as well as an early use of it by Pope Leo I, carried the reading *ipse*, not *ipsa*.

Not likely! Early Christians had a tradition of applying this text to Mary. For example, Ephraim the Syrian (d. 373) testifies, "Because the serpent had struck Eve with his claw, the foot of Mary bruised him."[346] Early Christians concluded this because they saw Mary prefigured in many Old Testament heroines, who crushed the heads of antichrists attempting to destroy God's people.

We first find this in Judges, when God commands Barak—through Deborah—to wage war against Sisera. Fearful, Barak agrees to go only if Deborah accompanies him; she does but prophesies: "I will surely go with you; nevertheless, the Lord will sell Sisera into the hand of a woman" (Judg. 4:9). Indeed, Sisera flees the battlefield and hides in the tent of Jael. While he sleeps, Jael crushes his head with a mallet and tent-peg. Scripture praises her for redeeming Israel, for having "crushed his head" (5:24–27), calls Jael the "most blessed of women." For the early Church, this foreshadowed God delivering his people—the Church—from Satan and his Antichrist by the hand of *Woman*—that is, Mary.

Abimelech was another Antichrist conquered by a woman. He storms the tower of Thebez until a woman throws a millstone from the tower, and it "crushed his skull" (Judg. 9:50–57), saving the city and God's people. Later, when Israel follows Sheba, rebelling against David (prefiguring Christ), his commander, Joab, pursues Sheba to Bethmaacah, where Sheba is holed up. To avoid the town's destruction, a townswoman cuts off Sheba's head and throws it over the wall. Joab then retreats, leaving the city in peace (2 Sam. 20:16–22).

Nevertheless, the reading eventually became *ipsa*, for reasons that are not clear." Pelikan (1996) 26-7, 91.

Similarly, Judith's victory over Holofernes (Jth. 8:1–16:25) prefigures the ultimate battle between Satan and the woman of Revelation 12. Like Jael, Judith kills Holofernes in the tent, cutting off his head. Israel praises Judith just as Christians bless Mary:

> You are the exaltation of Jerusalem, you are the great glory of Israel, you are the great pride of our nation! *You have done all this singlehanded*; you have done great good to Israel, and God is well pleased with it. May the Almighty Lord bless you forever! (15:9–10).

An orphan raised by her uncle Mordecai, Esther is another great heroine who saves God's people from destruction. King Ahasuerus elects her as his queen, but when his prime minister Haman conspires to destroy God's people, Mordecai urges queen Esther to intervene. She does—risking her life—and Haman's head is crushed on the gallows (Esther 2:1–16:11).

As a type for Mary, even the Ark of the Covenant crushes the Antichrist. When the Philistines capture the ark in battle, they take the ark and set it beside their idol Dagon. The next day, the idol is toppled; they upright the statue. The following day, the statue is toppled again, but this time with its head and hands cut off. Now fearful, the Philistines decide to return the ark to the Israelites. Through the ark—a type for Mary—God crushes Satan's head, giving glory to God and moving Israel to repent by purging idolatry from their midst.[347]

He and She Crush Satan's Head

Is the ambiguous Hebrew pronoun masculine or feminine? From what we have just seen, the original ambiguity is

227

probably best, as it includes both masculine seed and *Woman*, the New Adam *and* New Eve. Since Satan conquered the first Adam through the first Eve, it is fitting that the New Adam crush Satan's head with his helper.

The first Adam was the principal mediator for bringing sin and death into the world (Rom. 5:12–21); Christ is the principal mediator for salvation, redeeming us with his blood and reconciling us through his obedience unto death (Rom. 5:6–11, 19). Yet Eve played her part: "From a woman sin had its beginning, and because of her we all die" (Sir. 25:24). The Holy Spirit moves us to seek a woman to undo the ancient catastrophe of woman, with Mary's contribution— antithetical to Eve's.

Of course, the serpent's head is crushed not by human power, but with God's, as the Psalmist says:

Yet God my King is from of old, working salvation in the midst of the earth . . . thou didst break the heads of the dragons on the waters. Thou didst crush the heads of Leviathan (Ps. 74:12–14).

Jesus was "set for the fall and rising of many" (Luke 2:34), bringing about Satan's fall by crushing the head of the "ruler of this world" (John 14:30). Yet Mary cooperates closely united to him, as a sword would pierce her soul, too (Luke 2:35). The Church has always seen this as very scriptural (CCC 2853), especially in her presence at the foot of the cross. She is the first one to "look on him whom they have pierced . . . mourn for him, as one mourns for an only child, and weep bitterly over him, as one weeps over a firstborn" (Zech. 12:12); she gazes upon her son, who is lifted up from the earth in the form of a serpent (Num. 21:8, John 3:14), believing that "he was wounded for our transgressions, he was bruised for our iniquities; upon him was the chastisement that made us whole, and with his stripes we are healed" (Isa. 53:5).

The New Eve's cooperation in crushing Satan becomes definitive in Revelation 12, where *Woman's* Christ child brings about the serpent's definitive defeat. But joining the two is *Woman's* seed, "the rest of her offspring, on those who keep the commandments of God and bear testimony to Jesus" (Rev. 12:17)—i.e., the Church. Thus, the serpent is conquered "by the blood of the Lamb and by the word of their testimony" (v. 11). As Jesus foresaw,

> the seventy returned with joy, saying, "Lord, even the demons are subject to us in your name!" And he said to them, "I saw Satan fall like lightning from heaven. Behold, I have given you authority to tread upon serpents and scorpions, and over all the power of the enemy; and nothing shall hurt you. Nevertheless do not rejoice in this, that the spirits are subject to you; but rejoice that your names are written in heaven (Luke 10:17–20).

So Christ crushes Satan's head by his redemptive suffering on the cross; the Virgin Mary crushes Satan's head by her *fiat*, "yes" to Christ's incarnation, ushering in his hour; and the Church, formed by Christ on the cross, crushes Satan's head by spreading the gospel throughout the world that enables individuals to believe (Rom. 10:14–15). So perhaps the best rendering of Genesis 3:15 is *we*, the woman and her seed, *will crush Satan's head*! This is what Augustine did, applying this text to the Church, the bride of Christ:

> These words [of Genesis] are a great mystery: here is the symbol pointing forward to the Church that is to come:

she is fashioned out of the side of her spouse in the sleep of death. Did not the Apostle say about Adam that "he was a figure of the one to come" (Rom. 5:14)? And is it not also true of the Church? Listen then, understand and realize: it is she that will tread down the serpent's head. O Church, watch for the serpent's head![348]

Sacrificing Isaac and Jephthah's Daughter

Abraham's sacrifice of his son is a great type prefiguring God's sacrifice of his only Son for the expiation of sin. Abraham represents God the Father; his only son, Isaac, represents Christ. Both Jesus and Isaac carry the wood up Mount Moriah (Calvary), upon which each would be sacrificed. This sacrifice manifests a great faith and faithfulness, a model for us all.[349]

Another Bible story of human sacrifice parallels this one in many details: the story of Jephthah's daughter (Judg. 11). This story has baffled scholars because Scripture severely bans human sacrifice as the worst form of idolatry.[350] So when the Ammonites make great incursions into Israel—due to Israel's sinfulness—the latter seek a savior. God's people approach Jephthah—a castaway—to lead them into battle. Before going, Jephthah prays for victory and vows to God—moved by the Spirit (Judg. 11:29)—to offer the first person to greet him from his house as a holocaust for that victory. He is victorious, and the first person to greet him is his only child, his very precious daughter, filling Jephthah with grief.

His daughter courageously offers to fulfill her father's vow: "Do to me according to what has gone forth from your mouth" (11:36), evoking Mary's response to the angel: "Do unto me according to your word" (Luke 1:38). Jephthah's daughter spends a few months in the mountains (Judg. 11:37–39), just as Mary does in the hill country (Luke 1:39–40, 56).

Then Jephthah's daughter dies a virgin, one who "had never known a man" (Judg. 11:39), again evoking Mary's words: "I do not know man" (Luke 1:34, literal). Jephthah and his daughter show great faith in fulfilling their vow to God, pointing to Mary's great act at Calvary. To the heavenly Father, Mary offers her life and love, who is the price of victory for God's people over Satan and his antichrists opposed to the old and new covenants. Just as the deed of Jephthah's daughter continued to be commemorated every year (Judg. 11:39–40), so Mary is to be blessed by all generations (Luke 1:48).

There is a kind of inversion with the sacrifice of Isaac and of Jephthah's daughter. Isaac does not die, though prefiguring Christ who does, whereas Jephthah's daughter does die, though prefiguring Mary, who doesn't physically die at the foot of the cross.

Jephthah's daughter bewailed her virginity, just as Sarah bewailed her inability to bear children (Tob. 3:9–15), as other holy women did their barrenness. By echoing her song of thanksgiving (see page 85ff) in the Magnificat, Mary identifies herself with such women. For Pope John Paul II, Jephthah's daughter was an "example of humble dedication. . . . She agreed to pay for her father's victory over the Ammonites with her own death."[351]

Mary herself must have read Judges 11. Imagine being a mother and hearing words that he had to suffer and die before rising again (Luke 9:22, 17:25, 22:14–16). Identifying herself with Jephthah's daughter, *who knew not man*, Mary could easily have offered to give her life in the place of her son, if that was God's will: *do to me according to what has gone forth from your mouth*. God accepted Mary's offer, not by physically taking her life along with Christ's, but accepting her spiritual sacrifice of a mother who sacrifices her dearest son. How heroic is her willingness to die like Jephthah's daughter to fulfill God the Father's will and to obtain the ultimate victory over the enemies of God's people! It is a model of faith for us (CCC 273).

QUESTIONS AND ANSWERS

Q: Do Catholics trust Mary to save them?

A: Catholics do not trust Mary independently of Christ. If they do, they are not truly Catholic. We have only one Savior and only one mediator in Jesus Christ, for "there is salvation in no one else, for there is no other name under heaven given among men by which we must be saved" (Acts 4:12). The Catholic Church affirms: "Jesus Christ is true God and true man, in the unity of his divine person; for this reason he is the one and only mediator between God and men" (CCC 480).

Like every Christian, Mary also witnesses to Christ, leading others to him, praying to God on their behalf, encouraging them to believe and to walk in the light, and helping them to return to Christ when they stray. Mary does not and cannot detract from Christ's salvific role and mediation (CCC 956, 2674).

As a spiritual mother, Catholics do trust that Mary's maternal love will continue to bring them to Christ.

Q: Doesn't saying that Mary crushes the head of the serpent overemphasize her role, a role principally and exclusively Christ's when he offered his life on the cross?

A: We should not view redemption as either/or: either Christ redeemed the world by himself or Mary did. Christ brings Mary, angels, and saints to collaborate in his redemption.

In describing Satan's ultimate defeat—when his head is finally crushed—Scripture places the Ark of the New Covenant and the *Woman* who mothers the Messiah in the forefront (Rev. 11:19–12:17). The New Covenant ark topples the dragon, destroying his head and hands (1 Sam. 5:1–3). Michael and his angels also participate. Even Christians conquer Satan "by the blood of the Lamb and by the word of their testimony" (Rev. 12:11, 17). How bold it is to say that "they"—*Woman*, the angels, and Christians—conquer Satan; Scripture does so because it occurs through the blood of the Lamb. It is Christ along with Mary, the saints, and the angels who conquer the serpent and crush his head.

Q: God would never approve of human sacrifice, so didn't Jephthah dedicate his daughter to the Lord as a perpetual virgin instead of killing her?

A: That is a possible interpretation,[352] by turning the *and* into an *or*: "Whoever comes forth from the doors of my house to meet me . . . shall be the Lord's, *or* I will offer him up for a burnt offering" (Judg. 11:31). This interpretation reads that, instead of offering his daughter *for a burnt offering*, Jephthah dedicated her to God in her virginity. Nevertheless, all ancient Jewish scholars and early Christian writers read Scripture as saying that Jephthah actually sacrificed his daughter to God.

This episode of Jephthah's daughter has been a great mystery for many Scripture scholars: why would the Holy Spirit inspire Jephthah to make such a vow and have it recorded in the Bible? Even the writer who records this episode seems perplexed at why he is being inspired to write it down, but he does. However, when we apply the principles and keys of Scripture interpretations, God's designs become clear, giving us another piece of the puzzle for understanding Mary.

11

Mary's Rapture

Finding the gospel of Jesus Christ reflected in Mary may help us pursue the unity of spirit and mind that Paul sought:

> Let your manner of life be worthy of the gospel of Christ, so that . . . I may hear of you that you *stand firm in one spirit, with one mind* striving side by side for the faith of the gospel, and not frightened in anything by your opponents (Phil. 1:27–28).

Side by side, of one mind and spirit, let us fight for the Faith against all opposition, testing the spirit of Marian doctrines and beliefs, to discern their worthiness in Christ's gospel:

> Beloved, do not believe every spirit, but test the spirits to see whether they are of God; for many false prophets have gone out into the world. By this you know the Spirit of God: every spirit which confesses that Jesus Christ has come in the flesh is of God. . . . Whoever confesses that Jesus is the Son of God, God abides in him, and he in God (1 John 4:1–3, 15).

Some are surprised that the doctrine of Mary's bodily assumption was not defined until 1950, using little biblical support. The pope decreed that all Catholics must hold and believe as divinely revealed "that the immaculate Mother of God, the Ever-Virgin Mary, having completed the course of her earthly life, was assumed body and soul into heavenly glory" (*Munificentissimus Deus* 44).

Yet this doctrine was no twentieth-century innovation, as Tim Perry explains:

When seeking to understand the bodily assumption of Mary into heaven with any degree of sympathy (this is not to say agreement), two factors need to be kept constantly in mind. The first is the doctrine's ancient roots.[353]

The ancient Church found that it fit Scripture and that it was consistent with other Christian beliefs. By the fourth century, Christians celebrated the feast of Mary's *dormition*, especially in Jerusalem. The *dormition* refers to Mary "falling asleep" before being assumed (taken up bodily) into heaven to be with our Lord. Finding no evidence of Mary's death, Epiphanius (d. 403) suggests that this Marian teaching was true, as "nothing is impossible for God." Several Church Fathers preached about it, such as Germain (d. 733), Andrew of Crete (d. 740), and John Damascene (d. 749). Gregory (d. 594), bishop of Tours, recorded part of a Latin translation of a lost fifth-century Greek book describing Mary's assumption. John of Thessalonica (d. 630) detailed the popular belief regarding Mary's dormition and assumption. Although some details may have been embellished over time, his exposition shows that some truth likely lies behind this commonly held belief.[354]

So why would the Holy Spirit wait for the twentieth century to define this teaching? Perhaps it was to counteract the materialistic and mechanistic view of man propagated by some in the name of science. Mary's assumption reaffirms the Christian hope in bodily resurrection—which science finds absurd—attesting to man having a spiritual dimension that endures unto eternity.[355] Whereas sin naturally produces death and corruption, the teaching of Mary's assumption reinforces the Christian belief in Christ's resurrection (1 Cor. 15:12–19) and in the bodily resurrection of all Christians (CCC 974).

Christian Death and Rapture

To understand the Assumption is to understand Christian belief about death and bodily resurrection. Paul wrote consolingly on death and our hope in bodily resurrection:

> But we would not have you ignorant, brethren, concerning those who are asleep [dormition], that you may not grieve as others do who have no hope. For since we believe that Jesus died and rose again, even so, through Jesus, God will bring with him those who have fallen asleep. . . .
>
> For the Lord himself will descend from heaven with a cry of command, with the archangel's call, and with the sound of the trumpet of God. And the dead in Christ will rise first; then we who are alive, who are left, shall be caught up [raptured] together with them in the clouds to meet the Lord in the air; and so we shall always be with the Lord (1 Thess. 4:13–18).

This description of *rapture* is familiar to most Christians, with many interpretations. One popular belief is that Christians living at Christ's Second Coming will be taken or *caught* up, body and soul, into heaven without dying. So many Bible-believing Christians see Mary's assumption— rapture—into heaven as quite compatible with Scripture.

Another passage from Paul suggests rapture:

Lo! I tell you a mystery. We shall not all sleep [dormition], but we shall all be changed, in a moment. . . . For the trumpet will sound, and the dead will be raised imperishable, and we shall be changed. For this perishable nature must put on the imperishable, and this mortal nature must put on immortality . . . then shall come to pass the saying that is written:
"Death is swallowed up in victory."
"O death, where is thy victory? O death, where is thy sting?"
The sting of death is sin, and the power of sin is the law (1 Cor. 15:51–56).

Not all shall die (sleep), but some shall put on immortality without dying, affirming Christ's victory over sin and death (1 Thess. 4:18). As death is the result of sin, death has no power or sting over a person freed from sin.

Raptured Saints, Missing Tombs, and Relics

Several Old Testament saints were raptured into heaven: "Enoch walked with God . . . three hundred and sixty-five years. Enoch walked with God; and he was not, for God took him" (Gen. 5:22–24). He walked with God, as had Adam and Eve prior to sin.

God also called Elijah to himself after Elijah fulfilled his mission:

[As Elijah and Elisha] went on and talked, behold, a chariot of fire and horses of fire separated the two of them. And Elijah went up [raptured] by a whirlwind into heaven. And Elisha saw it and he cried, "My father, my father!

the chariots of Israel and its horsemen!" And he saw him no more. . . . And he took up the mantle of Elijah that had fallen from him (2 Kings 2:11–13).

Elijah was taken up into heaven in chariots by God's holy angels. Without experiencing death, he was immediately raptured into the next life.

Finally, the Gospel witnesses to the many dead who rose after Christ's crucifixion (Matt. 27:52–53). These souls were raptured from the place of the dead to witness to the divinity of their redeemer, Jesus Christ. After fulfilling their duties, they were taken up bodily.

Would it surprise anyone that Christ would rapture his beloved mother? As Mary is more blessed than any woman, then she would have been more blessed than Jairus's daughter, whom our Lord raised shortly after she had died (Mark 5:35–42). Christians saw Mary's rapture as confirming Christ's divinity and our hope in bodily resurrection on the Last Day.

Moses died without entering the promised land, yet he has no tomb, alluding to the rapture of Moses' body by saying his tomb cannot be found:

So Moses the servant of the Lord died there in the land of Moab . . . and [Joshua] buried him in the valley in the land of Moab opposite Bethpeor; but no man knows the place of his burial to this day. . . . And there has not arisen a prophet since in Israel like Moses, whom the Lord knew face to face, none like him for all the signs and the wonders which the Lord sent him to do in the land of Egypt (Deut. 34:5–6, 10–11).

Jude recounts details of a non-canonical book—*the Assumption of Moses*—that describes the great battle between Satan and the archangel Michael over Moses' body:

Yet in like manner these men in their dreamings defile the flesh, reject authority, and revile the glorious ones. But when the archangel Michael, contending with the devil, disputed about the body of Moses, he did not presume to pronounce a reviling judgment upon him, but said, "The Lord rebuke you." But these men revile whatever they do not understand (Jude 8–10).

Like accounts of Mary's assumption, this non-canonical work may include popular details added to the original story. Yet Jude witnesses to the authenticity of the fact of Moses' rapture.

The empty tomb is the Bible's way of indicating that God took a person to heaven, as with our Lord.[356] Even to this day, Jews maintain the tomb of Abraham and Sarah, of Joseph the patriarch, and of others. This was true for the early Christians who preserved the tombs of Peter and Paul in Rome, Thomas in India, and many of the other apostles and martyrs. They would have dishonored their great saint and leader had they lost sight of Moses' tomb, failing in an important filial duty. But they didn't, because it didn't exist.

After our Lord's ascension into heaven, John took Mary into his care (John 19:26–27). Early Christians tell us that the two lived in Ephesus. Later—yet there is some dispute about this—John brought her back to Jerusalem, where she left this earth. Yet neither city makes any claim to having her remains. In fact, no city does. This is especially surprising since the bones, relics, and artifacts of saints became very important "treasures" to Christians, especially in the Middle Ages; they were jealously guarded and highly prized. Cities even fought over the remains of a saint. Why is there not even one city that claims to have the remains of such a celebrated saint as Mary? Because no bones of Mary could be found. The Christians knew it was futile to search for something that God had raptured, just as the Jews knew that it was futile to search for Moses' bones, or for the Ark of the Covenant.

The Raptured Ark

As a type for Mary, the Ark of the Covenant may also describe her assumption. Psalm 132 prophesies Christ's ascension into heaven: "Arise, O Lord, and go to thy resting place [Christ's ascension], thou and the ark of thy might [Mary]." Why would God want the Ark of the Covenant in his resting place with him, unless it prefigured something or someone extremely dear to him, such as his own mother? This seems to fit with our Lord's promise:

> And when I go and prepare a place for you, I will come again and will take you to myself, that where I am you may be also. . . . The glory which thou hast given me I have given to them. . . . Father, I desire that they also, whom thou hast given me, may be with me where I am (John 14:3, 17:22–24).

Scripture prefigures this when David brings the Ark of the Covenant into Jerusalem (2 Sam. 6:15). David represents our Lord; the ark, Mary; Jerusalem, God's heavenly city. David's joy in bringing the Ark of the Covenant into the earthly Jerusalem prefigures Christ's joy in bringing Mary's body into the heavenly Jerusalem. We don't want to receive Michal's curse by failing to rejoice with Christ as he welcomes his blessed mother into the heavenly Jerusalem (2 Sam. 6:16, 23)!

Finally, Mary's assumption is also prefigured when Jeremiah hides the ark in a cave on the mountain where Moses had been assumed into heaven. Scripture says this ark is never to be found (2 Macc. 2:1–8). Likewise, Mary's body was hidden in a cave, never more to be found on earth because it was taken up. As John Damascene would say, "today the sacred and living ark of the living God, who conceived her Creator himself, takes up her abode in the temple of God, not made by hands."[357]

Revelation 12 also shows the Ark of the New Covenant (Rev. 11:19) in heaven as a woman, clothed with the sun's glory, crowned with twelve stars, and with the moon under her feet (vv. 1-5). The woman—God's New Covenant Ark, the mother of the Messiah—is alive, raptured into heaven.

Why God Raptures Saints

Here is an important question to ask: Why does God rapture only some and not all saints? We turn to Scripture to answer that question. God took Enoch because "he walked with God" and because he "pleased the Lord" (Sir. 44:16), attesting to his faith:

By faith Enoch was taken up so that he should not see death; and he was not found, because God had taken him. Now before he was taken he was attested as having pleased God. And without faith it is impossible to please him. For . . . [God] rewards those who seek him (Heb. 11:5–6).

So God made Enoch's faith and repentance into an example for us: "No one like Enoch has been created on earth, for he was taken up from the earth" (Sir. 49:14). His faith and repentance were so great that he walked with God, recovering what Adam and Eve had lost. His example of holiness was singular, exceptional, and heroic. Mary's example was also outstanding. She is singularly blessed, more than any woman (Luke 1:42); blessed because of her faith (vv. 41-45), walking with God and in his ways (Ps. 119:1–3), as Eve had before the Fall, as had Susanna (Dan. 13:3) and Elizabeth (Luke 1:5–6).

Elijah and Moses are also exceptional examples of faith and holiness. Our Lord speaks to them in the company of three apostles at the Transfiguration. Elijah prefigures John the Baptist, the Messiah's great precursor, and is with God to plea for his people, exemplifying the power of the prayer of a righteous man.[358] "Because of great zeal for the law," Elijah "was taken up into heaven" (1 Macc. 2:58), and "his word burned like a torch" (Sir. 48:1).

Mary is an example of prayer, prefigured in Hannah, Tobit's Sarah, Judith, Esther, and Anna.[359] Mary was more blessed and prayerful than they. She prayed to Jesus to resolve the lack of wine at the wedding feast at Cana—through her prayer, Christ converted water into wine (John 2:1–12). Her zeal for God's law was greater than that of the woman who encouraged her seven sons to die as martyrs for the Law (2 Macc. 7:1–41).

God witnessed to Moses' singular holiness by taking him up into heaven. Moses was God's faithful servant (Isa. 63:11, Dan. 9:11, Mal. 4:4), his "chosen one" (Ps. 106:23)—chosen "out of all mankind" (Sir. 45:4). As God had sanctified him through his faith and fidelity, Moses became beautiful to God; his face glistened with God's glory.[360] Moses received "an everlasting name" (Isa. 63:12) to be blessed by all generations (Sir. 45:1–5); his face would not see corruption.

As he had done with the ark, God chose Zion for his dwelling place and habitation; he chose Mary as the special dwelling place of Immanuel, *God with us*. She too is beautiful before him, as Jerusalem and as many blessed women of old. Like Moses, she was a woman of faith and faithful to God. God sanctified her with his grace and favor, so her name shall be blessed by all generations.[361] Mary spoke to

Jesus face to face from the moment he was born until he ascended into heaven; neither should her face see corruption.

Mary differs from these holy men in sex alone. But would we dare accuse God of prejudice against women? Do only men deserve to be assumed into heaven? Yet Mary was greater—at least "among women." Mary is more blessed than Tabitha—the exemplary widow, full of good works and charity—whom Peter brought back from the dead (Acts 9:36–41). If any woman or man ought to be brought back to life and raptured into heaven it would be Mary, the holy Mother of God, an example of faith for us.

QUESTIONS AND ANSWERS

Q: Scripture mentions how Enoch and Elijah didn't see death and were taken up but says nothing about Mary. Why wouldn't it mention this extraordinary privilege for her?

A: The Bible says nothing *directly* about Mary's assumption, as it says nothing about Mary's life after our Lord's ascension. But Evangelical Scot McKnight notes,

Such things [as assumptions into heaven] can happen.

The question we need to ask about Mary is this: Was she also taken into the presence of God miraculously? As Protestants we go to the Bible first, but we find nothing about Mary's death or her assumption in the Bible. Does that mean Mary wasn't "assumed" into heaven? Obviously not. None of us believes that everything was recorded in the Bible, so we are left to examine the evidence and make up our own minds.[362]

McKnight limits his biblical evidence to literal New Testament testimony, but early Christians didn't. Nor did Martin Luther, who believed in Mary's assumption: "There can be no doubt that the Virgin Mary is in heaven. How it happened we do not know."[363]

But let each of us also examine the abundance of *indirect* biblical evidence about Mary's death and assumption, as presented above, and pray for the Holy Spirit's guidance.

Q: Isn't ascending into heaven like Christ, who is God, a divine perogative?

A: We don't believe that Mary ascended into heaven by her own power, as Christ did forty days after his resurrection, but that God raised Mary from the dead and reunited her soul and body; that God took Mary up to himself in heaven, just as God will do with us on the Last Day. This was all by God's power, not Mary's. Hence, Catholics believe that Mary's assumption never hints of her being divine, just as the assumptions of Enoch, Elijah, and Moses don't hint of their being divine.

Q: All are equal in Christ, as "the same Lord is Lord of all and bestows his riches upon all who call upon him. For 'every one who calls upon the name of the Lord will be saved'" (Rom. 10:12–13), "for you are all one in Christ Jesus" (Gal. 3:27–28), and finally, "Christ is all, and in all" (Col. 3:11). So there are no favorites in heaven.

A: Those passages refer not to heaven, but to our status in the Church, reminding us that being a Jew adds nothing to a Christian before God. Paul wrote a great deal about the differences between Greeks and Jews and why circumcision and other "works of the Law" were no longer required for justification (Col. 2:11–3:11).[364] Through faith and baptism, both Jew and Greek became fully "saved" and members of Christ's body, the Church.

But when Paul does talk about the resurrection from the dead, he also remarks,

> There are celestial bodies and there are terrestrial bodies; but the glory of the celestial is one, and the glory of the terrestrial is another. There is one glory of the sun, and another glory of the moon, and another glory of the stars; for star differs from star in glory. So is it with the resurrection of the dead. What is sown is perishable, what is raised is imperishable (1 Cor. 15:40–42).

With the resurrection of the body, we will all *equally* have imperishable "celestial bodies" in heaven. Yet not all of us will have the glory of the twelve apostles (Rev. 12:1), and Mary's glory "of the moon" will be higher than that of any star (Sir. 43:9–10).

Q: Why did it take so long for Christians to discover this if the Bible truly affirms it?

A: Certainly early Christians heard stories about Mary and Jesus that were not in Scripture—some spurious and some true—Mary's assumption among them. Since death and corruption result from sin, it took the early Church some time (spurred on by some heresies) to develop a more complete understanding of original sin, personal sin, and Mary's immaculate conception. Once these issues were resolved by the likes of Augustine, they could address the issue of Mary's assumption both theologically and scripturally.

What the Church Fathers finally saw was that God had chosen Mary—as he did Enoch, Elijah, and Moses—freeing her from sin at conception, gracing her with perpetual virginity, to be the divine Word's mother, and to share in his salvific work. Since Christ's redemption fully freed her of sin, early Christians found the accounts of the glorification of her soul and body as the most fitting way for her to share in the fruit of that redemption.

Pius XII said of Mary's assumption,

Hence the revered Mother of God, from all eternity joined in a hidden way with Jesus Christ . . . immaculate in her conception, a most perfect virgin in her divine motherhood, the noble associate of the divine redeemer who has won a complete triumph over sin and its consequences . . . [was granted] that she should be preserved free from the corruption of the tomb (*Munificentissimus Deus* 40).

Q: If Mary was conceived without sin, of which death is a consequence, did she die?

A: Although she was wholly innocent and never committed a sin, she died in union with Jesus. Keep in mind that he did not have to die to accomplish our redemption; it would have been sufficient had he just willed it. But he chose to die.

Mary identified herself with his work, cooperating with the divine plan of salvation in her whole life. Certainly she shows us her identification by her response to Gabriel: "Let it be to me according to your word" (Luke 1:38), but it really began at conception. So she would accept death just as Jesus did, and she would suffer (2:34–35) in union with his suffering. Just as she shared in his work, she should share in his glorification. Christ shared his resurrection with her by having her glorified body taken into heaven, the way the glorified bodies of all the saved will be taken into heaven on the Last Day.

Scripture also reminds us, "Precious in the sight of the Lord is the death of his saints" (Ps. 116:15; cf. Sir. 1:13). Mary's death was particularly precious.

Q: Yet the only "hint" of Mary's assumption is typological. Isn't it foolish to rely exclusively on this kind of evidence?

A: Most Old Testament references to our Lord's death and resurrection also were typological, such as how Noah's passage through the waters of death to life represents Christ's death and resurrection. Isaac's sacrifice represents Christ's, as does Joseph's burial in the pit and being raised, and Jonah's being "buried" three days in the fish and then raised, etc.[365]

The typological evidence of Mary's assumption is significant. The main evidence, however, is how this teaching fits in with the whole of what Scripture teaches about Mary in relation to Christ. This is an important key for interpreting Scripture, as we saw earlier. Mary's rapture "fits" in with Mary's being our Lord's virginal mother: her virginal body that remained intact before, during, and after Christ's birth should not see corruption. Also, it fits with Mary's immaculate conception, since death and corruption are the results of sin.

12

Blessing and Praying to Mary in Heaven

Paul says, "For just as the body is one and has many members
. . . so it is with Christ" (1 Cor. 12:12). Paul continues, "The
eye cannot say to the hand, 'I have no need of you,' nor again
the head to the feet, 'I have no need of you'" (1 Cor. 12:21).
So we cannot say, "I have no need of Mary," a member of our
body, because honoring any member honors Christ:

> God has so composed the body, giving the greater honor
> to the inferior part, that there may be no discord in the
> body, but that the members may have the same care for
> one another. . . . If one member is honored, all rejoice
> together (1 Cor. 12:25–26).

Honoring Mary really honors Christ and fosters unity in
his body, the Church. Yet Charles Dickson points out some
concerns over Catholic practices:

> The Reformers wanted to safeguard the true measure of
> honor due to Mary because of the close connection with
> a true understanding of the work of Jesus Christ. But they

did not want to see her elevated to a position they regarded as beyond the intentions of the Scriptures.[366]

We identified the biblical co-mediation of all Christians, how it applies to Mary, and how Scripture prefigures her as the Messiah's handmaid and helper, especially alongside Christ on the cross. But that referred to Mary while she was still on earth. Now we explore her role alongside Christ in heaven, and what Scripture says about praying to and honoring her.

Praying to Angels

Prayer is essential to Christianity. Anyone who doesn't pray isn't Christian: "I appeal to you, brethren, by our Lord Jesus Christ and by the love of the Spirit, to strive together with me in your prayers to God on my behalf" (Rom. 15:30); "Pray at all times in the Spirit . . . for all the saints, and also for me . . . to proclaim the mystery of the gospel . . . as I ought to speak" (Eph. 6:18–20). Our Lord promised: "If you ask anything of the Father, he will give it to you in my name" (John 16:23).

Yet the word *prayer* may mean different things. For non-Catholics, prayer is often restricted to *speaking to God and only to God*, making it forbidden to pray to anyone else, whether to angels, Mary, deceased Christians, or Scripture heroes. For Catholics, *prayer* is not restricted to God alone; for us, *prayer* is broader—it means conversation, as with family or friends, as Mary with Gabriel (Luke 1:26–38) or John with the angel in Revelation. Just as talking with family and friends doesn't compete with our relationship with God, neither does talking to members of our supernatural family: the angels and saints. It pleases our Father God to see his needy children asking their older siblings for help.

Older Bible translations use a broad meaning of *prayer*. For example, the King James Version describes Cornelius beseeching Peter to stay after his baptism: "Then *prayed* they him to tarry certain days" (Acts 10:48). Modern versions read, "Then they *asked* him to remain." The Greek also uses the broader meaning of *prayer*: "In that day you will ask in my name; and I do not say to you that I shall *pray* [Greek: *erotao*] the Father for you; for the Father himself loves you" (John 16:26–27).*

The Bible teaches that angels are God's elect, blameless and wise, with no fear of death, glorious creatures, higher than unredeemed humans. As they enthrone God, bless and praise his name, and contemplate his face, they also serve and worship Jesus Christ.[367] Angels accompany us in our earthly journey, comfort us in our troubles, and lift us up.[368] They are God's emissaries "sent forth to serve, for the sake of those who are to obtain salvation" (Heb. 1:14). Angels begin watching over us while we are children and present our needs before God, as they behold always "the face of [the] Father who is in heaven" (Matt. 18:10). Thus, they intercede similarly to how parents do for their children, preparing us for our life mission, offering our earthly prayers and sacrifices as fragrant incense to God.[369] As the angel Raphael describes it,

> when you and your daughter-in-law Sarah prayed, I brought a reminder of your prayer before the Holy One. . . . I am Raphael, one of the seven holy angels who present the prayers of the saints and enter into the presence of the glory of the Holy One (Tob. 12:12–15).

---

* The same word *erotao* is used when the Levites *ask* John the Baptist, "Who are you?" (John 1:19); when the Jews *prayed* (*erotao*) to the paralyzed man (5:12) and to the man born blind (9:15); and when the Greeks *prayed* to Philip to be able to see Jesus (12:21).

When God gives Moses and the Israelites the Ten Commandments (Exod. 20:1–17), instead of forbidding prayer to angels, God commands them to listen and follow his angelic representatives:

Behold, I send an angel before you, to guard you on the way and to bring you to the place which I have prepared. Give heed to him and hearken to his voice, do not rebel against him, for he will not pardon your transgression; for my name is in him. But if you hearken attentively to his voice and do all that I say, then I will be an enemy to your enemies and an adversary to your adversaries.

When my angel goes before you, and brings you in to the Amorites, and the Hittites . . . you shall not bow down to their gods, nor serve them. . . . You shall serve the Lord your God, and I will bless your bread and your water; and I will take sickness away from the midst of you. . . . Little by little I will drive them out from before you, until you are increased and possess the land. . . . You shall make no covenant with them or with their gods . . . for if you serve their gods, it will surely be a snare to you (Exod. 23:20–33).

God's angels mediate and intercede for his people: to guard and guide, to help us conquer our enemies so as to possess the promised land, granting us food, water, and long life. By listening to and obeying angels, we serve God; by rebelling against them, we rebel against God. So God expects us to listen and to respond to them, as Zechariah and Mary responded to God's call through Gabriel, and as did Abraham and Moses.[370]

Scripture shows them fighting Satan, discerning good and evil, and executing God's justice, especially upon evildoers. They lead, protect, rescue, watch over, and redeem us from evil. We can pray and obey them, receiving them as we would Jesus Christ,[371] as Abraham entertains three angels and *prays* so that they would not destroy Sodom (Gen. 18:1–33).

Angels also rescue, as when God sends an angel to rescue Shadrach, Meshach, and Abednego from the fiery furnace, having refused to worship the king's idol (Dan. 3:12–28). Nebuchadnezzar recognizes the angel's mediation: "Blessed be the God of Shadrach, Meshach, and Abednego, who has sent his angel and delivered his servant." But it is God—not the angel—who saves these three young men; this particular angel, like all angels, is an intermediary. So Nebuchadnezzar decreed,

> Any people, nation, or language that speaks anything against the God of Shadrach, Meshach, and Abednego shall be torn limb from limb . . . for there is no other god who is able to deliver in this way (Dan. 3:29).

Jacob also asks "the angel who has redeemed me from all evil" (Gen. 48:15–16) to intercede for his two grandsons. This shows how God redeems through angels, who exercise a true, *secondary* mediation.

Praying to Saints and to Mary

A *saint* is one who is *holy*. In most languages, the two terms are synonymous (*sanctus* in Latin, *santo* in Spanish, etc.). The New Testament refers to all living Christians as saints. That is so because the Spirit *sanctifies* every Christian at baptism in Christ's blood, becoming sanctified after yielding his body to righteousness, by abstaining from unchastity and sin, fulfilling God's call to be holy and blameless.[372] So every Christian is a *saint*, due to his relationship with Christ, yet typically we apply it to those who have died and who are now united to

Christ in heaven, since after dying in the Lord, their relationship is now deeper, more intimate, and fully spiritual.

A Christian's prayer has great power: "If you have faith and never doubt . . . even if you say to this mountain, 'Be taken up and cast into the sea,' it will be done. And whatever you ask in prayer, you will receive, if you have faith" (Matt. 21:21–22). Our Lord promises: "If two of you agree on earth about anything they ask, it will be done for them by my Father in heaven. For where two or three are gathered in my name, there am I in the midst of them" (18:19–20). Prayer is powerful because Jesus joins himself to the prayer of those of faith and holiness: "The prayer of a righteous man has great power in its effects" (James 5:16). The righteous man's prayer should gain power—not lose it—as he becomes fully united with Christ in heaven. Likewise, if our prayer is united to the saints' in heaven, it should be even more powerful, as they are more united to Christ.

Whereas praying to God acknowledges him as our Creator and Lord, with a complete dependence on him,* praying to angels and saints acknowledges our fellowship with them (Phil. 4:6) and our mutual "partnership in the gospel" (1:3–6). Early Christians prayed to saints—especially martyrs who, like Christ, offered their lives to God. Praying to the saints reflects our belief in the resurrection of the dead, that those who die in Christ are really alive in him, as

---

* As Pope John Paul II explains, "the veneration of the faithful for Mary is . . . inferior to the cult of adoration reserved to God, from which it essentially differs. The term 'adoration' indicates the form of worship that man offers to God, acknowledging him as Creator and Lord of the universe. Enlightened by divine Revelation, the Christian adores the Father 'in spirit and truth' (John 4:23). With the Father, he adores Christ, the incarnate Word, exclaiming with the apostle Thomas: 'My Lord and my God!' (John 20:28). Lastly, in this same act of adoration he includes the Holy Spirit, who 'with the Father and the Son is worshiped and glorified' (DS 150), as the Nicene Constantinopolitan Creed recalls" (Pope John Paul II [2000] 248).

they "have washed their robes . . . in the blood of the Lamb [and stand] before the throne of God, and serve him day and night within his temple; and he who sits upon the throne will shelter them with his presence" (Rev. 7:9–17). All who die in Christ offer prayers to the Father, just as the martyrs and elders do.[373]

Christ taught that saints "are accounted worthy to attain to that age and to the resurrection from the dead . . . [and] are equal to angels and are sons of God, being sons of the resurrection" (Luke 20:36); so we treat Mary and saints in heaven as we do angels (Rev. 22:8–9), not as we do God. Christ also exemplifies prayer to the saints when he conversed—*prayed* in the broad sense—with Old Testament saints awaiting redemption: Moses and Elijah (Luke 9:30–31). He taught that saints are living, not dead (Matt. 22:32). He also taught us the parable of a rich man beseeching Abraham to intercede for his brothers, which would make little sense if saints couldn't intercede for others (Luke 16:19–31).

Like angels, saints serve as God's emissaries, looking over their fellow human beings as they had before they went to heaven. They intercede for others as parents, friends, pastors, and prayer partners had before dying. Like the angels, the "great cloud of witnesses" (Heb. 12:1–2) continue their Christian prayer in heaven. So it is fitting to call on them, as on the angels—and among the saints, Mary is the most favored.

So prayer to angels and saints is based in Scripture. We can and should pray to Mary, invoking her by name, as did Gabriel (Luke 1:30), joining all nations (Jth. 14:7) and all generations in blessing her (Luke 1:48). She is mother of the Church and our spiritual mother. As a spiritual mother, Mary prayerfully intercedes for her children, as she did for the couple and their guests at the wedding feast of Cana

(John 2:1–12, CCC 2618). Imagine having the wine run out at your wedding celebration, perhaps because too many guests showed up to celebrate. Wouldn't you appreciate having Christ around to work a miracle? Wouldn't you appreciate having his mother around to notice your needs and to ask her son to intervene?

The Syrophoenician woman prayed for our Lord to cure her possessed daughter (Mark 7:25–30). Mary is more blessed and virtuous; we picture Mary as constantly pleading to God and to our Lord for us children, whom she sees as her own. So, as we approach Mary as the Ark of the New Covenant—with its Mercy Seat—we can "with confidence draw near to the throne of grace, that we may receive mercy and find grace to help in time of need" (Heb. 4:16).

Devotion to Mary was also common among Christians in those early years of the Church. They saw her as their mother (Rev. 12:17) and relied on her maternal protection. The prayer *sub tuum praesidium—we fly to thy patronage*—was found on a third-century Christian papyrus in Egypt, showing us that Marian devotion began very early. It expresses deep confidence in her. Gregory Nazianzen (d. 390) also encouraged us to pray, "imploring the Virgin Mary to bring her assistance."[374] Similarly, Severus of Antioch (d. 538) entreated, "We implore her who is the birthgiver of God and pray her to intercede for us, she who is honored by all the saints."[375]

Honoring Saints

Although Scripture portrays godly people bowing to and making images of angels,[376] they never worship them as gods (Col. 2:18–19), which would be idolatry. Early Christians sought to remember the saints' heroic sacrifice and generous response to grace. They realized that the example of heroic love for Christ could inspire others to the same. Archeologists have uncovered evidence of how early Christians created and visited the catacombs—a series of underground tunnels where Christians were buried. Christians gathered in these catacombs not to hide, but to worship, especially near the remains of those martyred for their faith in Christ.

God may testify to their sanctity by working miracles through their intercession, as God did to Elijah's holiness by working miracles through his mantle (2 Kings 2:1–15). God also raised a dead man when his body came into contact with Elisha's bones (2 Kings 13:20–21). In both cases, the power to work these miracles comes from God, not the saint. God does such miracles to motivate us to imitate the saints' example and to take their words seriously.

Early Christians did the same. For example, when Polycarp was martyred in A.D. 156, the Christians of Smyrna petitioned the Roman official for the martyr's remains. The Jews attempted to block that request, fearing that the Christians "should forsake the crucified one and take to worship this man instead." But the official granted their request:

> We gathered up his bones—more precious to us than jewels, and finer than pure gold—and we laid them to rest in a spot suitable for the purpose. There we shall assemble, as occasion allows, with glad rejoicings; and with the Lord's permission we shall celebrate the birthday of his martyrdom.[377]

Scripture indicates that we should honor "those who fear the Lord" (Ps. 15:4; Sir. 10:19):

> Let us now praise famous men, and our fathers. . . . The Lord apportioned to them great glory, his majesty from

the beginning . . . all these were honored in their generations, and were the glory of their times.

There are some of them who have left a name, so that
men declare their praise. . . . These were men of mercy,
whose righteous deeds have not been forgotten. . . . Their
posterity will continue forever, and their glory will not
be blotted out . . . and their name lives to all generations.
Peoples will declare their wisdom, and the congregation
proclaims their praise (Sir. 44:1–15).

God called these saints to greatness—as he does us—in
a variety of ways: leadership, wisdom, writing, music. God
calls us to proclaim their praise and to remember their example so it can have a positive influence (1 Macc. 2:51–64).
In honoring Elijah and the miracles God performed after
his death, Scripture shows us how to honor Christian saints:

Then the prophet Elijah arose like a fire, and his word
burned like a torch. . . . By the word of the Lord he shut up
the heavens, and also three times brought down fire. How
glorious you were, O Elijah, in your wondrous deeds! And
who has the right to boast which you have? You who raised
a corpse from death and from Hades, by the word of the
Most High. . . . You who were taken up by a whirlwind of
fire, in a chariot with horses of fire; you who are ready at
the appointed time, it is written, to calm the wrath of God
before it breaks out in fury, to turn the heart of the father to
the son, and to restore the tribes of Jacob. Blessed are those
who saw you. . . . Nothing was too hard for him, and when
he was dead his body prophesied. As in his life he did wonders, so in death his deeds were marvelous (Sir. 48:1–14).

Glorifying the saints—including Abraham, Isaac, Jacob,

Moses, David, Isaiah—glorifies God (Sir. 44:1–50:29). Hebrews 10 and 11 finishes with confident words of reassurance:

Therefore, since we are surrounded by so great a cloud of witnesses, let us also lay aside every weight, and sin which clings so closely, and let us run with perseverance the race that is set before us, looking to Jesus the pioneer and perfecter of our faith (Heb. 12:1–2).

If New Testament saints are greater than those of the Old, then Christian saints deserve honor even more, imitating what is good in their godly example.[378] Naturally, Mary would be among those honored as godly and worthy of imitation, as Evangelical Timothy George says:

No friend of the divine Son can dethrone him by honoring her aright: indeed, as he himself did. It was of him she spoke when exclaiming, "My soul doth rejoice in God my Savior!" Can one truly honor him and despise and ignore the woman who gave him human birth? Can one have his mind and forget her for whom love was uppermost to him in his supreme last hours? Can one honor her aright and yet dethrone the son whom she enthroned? She bore him, then lived for him. She honored herself in bearing him, and was his mother, his teacher, and his disciple. He revered her, she worshiped him.[379]

Mary's Unique Honor: Queen

The Holy Spirit foretold that all generations would bless Mary above women, because she "believed that there would be a fulfillment of what was spoken to her from the Lord." God calls us to join those generations in recognizing the "great things" he has done in her;[380] she is the greatest miracle and marvel of his creation (Ps. 136:4). "God's mighty works (including Mary) witness to his authority, so that we praise and believe in him (Deut. 6:4–5, Ps. 66:1–7, Acts 4:29–30). So Mary is uniquely blessed among women (Luke 1:42), and among all other human beings.

Prefiguring Mary, God did "great things" in Eve before the Fall, making her the first Adam's pure, holy, and immaculate helper, mother of all the living according to the flesh. He did "great things" in other Old Testament women, such as Sarah, Rebecca, Rahab, and Judith: "blessed by the Most High God above all women" prior to Mary.[381] Recognizing the great things in them disposes us to recognize what God did in Mary.

David set aside great riches to build God's dwelling with us (1 Chron. 22:11, 14)—prefiguring what God would do for Mary. This inspired early Christians to take the praises for the Temple and redirect them to the creature they prefigured:

How lovely is [Mary] thy dwelling place, O Lord of hosts! My soul longs, yea, faints for the courts of the Lord; my heart and flesh sing for joy to the living God [dwelling in Mary's pure body]. Even the sparrow finds a home, and the swallow a nest for herself, where she may lay her young, at thy altars, O Lord of hosts, my King and my God. Blessed are those who dwell in thy house, ever singing thy praise! (Ps. 84:1–4).

Ambrose (d. 397) says that no one is nobler than she.[382] Ephraim the Syrian (d. 373) ushers in similar praises in a hymn titled "Marvelous Mother."[383] Epiphanius (d. 403) warns that those who honor Jesus must honor the vessel that brought him into the world and that those who dishonor Mary dishonor Jesus.[384] Yet the Church severely condemns every attempt to worship Mary as divine (CCC 971), such as offering sacrifices to her.[385]

The Spirit moves us to honor Mary's queenship through a wonderful, messianic Psalm:

> My heart overflows with a goodly theme; I address my verses to the king. . . . Your divine throne endures forever and ever. Your royal scepter is a scepter of equity. . . . Daughters of kings are among your ladies of honor; at your right hand stands the queen in gold of Ophir.
>
> Hear, O daughter, consider, and incline your ear; forget your people and your father's house; and the king will desire your beauty. Since he is your lord, bow to him. . . . The princess is decked in her chamber with gold-woven robes; in many-colored robes she is led to the king, with her virgin companions, her escort, in her train. . . . I will cause *your name to be celebrated in all generations; therefore the peoples will praise you forever and ever* (Ps. 45).

The Holy Spirit links this Psalm to the mother of the Redeemer by moving her to prophesy that *all generations will call her blessed* (Luke 1:48).

As Bathsheba—who is a type for Mary—was Solomon's queen mother (1 Kings 1:1–2:46), Mary was for Christ. When David lay dying, Adonijah had himself crowned king, yet Bathsheba interceded to guarantee David's promise for Solomon to succeed him. So Solomon had her enthroned at his honored right hand (1 Kings 2:19), establishing the office of queen mother (Hebrew: *gebirah*). Her power flowed from her son's: "Make your request, my mother; for I will not refuse you" (v. 20); Jesus did the same with Mary (John 2:3).

As king, Solomon was above his mother, yet he continued to honor her, even bowing to her.

Scripture typically described kings and their queen-mothers as good or evil together (1 Kings 22:51–52). If they did evil, both the king and queen mother were deposed (Jer. 13:18). One good king even deposed his own queen mother for committing idolatrous abominations, as did Maccah (1 Kings 15:13). Athaliah, an evil queen mother, caused her son to walk "in the ways of the house of Ahab"; she was "his counselor in doing wickedly" (2 Chron. 22:1–3). This antithetical type implies that Mary counseled Jesus in doing good, in walking in God's ways. As God, Jesus needed no help or counsels, yet as man he learned the Father's will through his mother; he was obedient and subject to her as he grew in wisdom and stature (Luke 2:51–52).

Queen Esther is another type for Mary, interceding for her people before King Ahasuerus, who threatens to destroy Israel. She risks her life, and his love for her moves him to grant her every request (Esther 5:3–8), which would bring mercy on Israel (7:1–10).

As Paul saw the Thessalonians as his crown, in Revelation we see *Woman* enthroned in heaven as the Messiah's queen mother and crowned with the twelve apostles who surround her as at Pentecost. As the queen mother for the new people of God, alongside her son in his heavenly kingdom, Mary uses her real and powerful intercession to obtain mercy for her people. And as Mary gives birth to the physical body of Christ—whose spiritual counterpart we are in the Church—so she is the mother of the Church and continues in her intermediary role in heaven. Yet also, as a member of the Church, she too is Christ's bride and queen[386]—in fact, the queen of heaven and earth.

Apparitions

Adam's and Eve's sin lost the privilege of conversing with God face to face. Instead, God began sending us angelic messengers, who appear when we are fully awake or in our dreams. They transmit God's revealed word in Scripture, proclaim the gospel, prophesy, exhort, and work miracles to encourage us to carry out God's will.[387] They *share* with us what they have received, just as we *share* with others the gospel we have received. This pleases God, just as it pleases parents to see a child *share* his gifts with a sibling.

Apparitions are nothing new to Christianity, as angelic visions and visitations were common to the Old and New Testaments. Angels appear to Abraham and Moses; to Daniel; and to Peter, Paul, and John. Scripture also describes apparitions of saints, such as when Moses and Elijah appear to Christ, Peter, James, and John at the Transfiguration. Jeremiah appears to the high priest Onias, to strengthen Israel's faith for battle.[388] The possibility of more apparitions was foretold by Joel and by the apostle Peter (Acts 2:16–18, quoting Joel 2:28–29).

So God may use Mary and other saints to bring his people to Christ as he used angels.[389]

Although most people focus on apparitions occurring in the nineteenth and twentieth centuries—such as in Lourdes, France (1858), and Fátima, Portugal (1917)—Marian apparitions have a long history, including in early Christianity. Around A.D. 44, tradition has that Mary appeared to the apostle James as he evangelized Spain, on top of a pillar carried by angels. This purported pillar is preserved in the cathedral of Saragossa.

Then, in the year 358, a wealthy and childless Roman couple asked God to show them what to do with their wealth. Mary appeared simultaneously to them and Pope

Liberius, urging the couple to build a church to honor her divine maternity on the hill covered with snow. It was early August, the hottest time of the year in Rome. Nevertheless, snow fell miraculously on one of its hills, where the couple then built the basilica of Mary Major.

Gregory of Tours (d. 594) wrote *Libri Miraculorum—The Book of Miracles*—which contains a large collection of apparitions and miracles attributed to Mary.[390] This book offers compelling testimony that Marian apparitions and miracles were quite common in the early Church.

What makes Scripture credible, worthy of belief? The Holy Spirit, inspiring it with divine authority and manifesting "works of the Spirit" (Gal. 3:5) such as prophetic predictions that come to pass and miracles performed by its writers. These motivate us to believe. A writer's holiness and how his writings inspire others to be holy are also motives of belief. All these things together give us a picture of its credibility. Likewise, what makes apparitions credible—and the only thing that would do so—would be God's will and his discernible power behind it.

The Catholic Church does not require anyone to believe in apparitions. But, in carrying out her mission "to test the spirits" (1 John 4:1–3), the Church studies alleged apparitions to prevent any false or evil spirit from misleading the faithful. The bishops interview witnesses to discern the credibility of their testimony and to make sure alleged messages do not contradict Scripture or Church teaching. After the investigation, which includes even consultation with non-Catholic experts and scientists, they may issue a declaration, stating that nothing in the alleged apparition opposes Christian faith and morals (so it is safe to believe in it), or that serious concerns merit caution regarding the alleged apparition, or that we should avoid it as deceptive and false.

No Christian—Catholic or not—needs to believe in any apparitions. We are free in this and must let God speak to us in our heart to discern what he asks of us.

Images of Saints

Does it offend God to keep a photograph (an image graven on silver film) of a spouse, friend, son, or daughter in your bedroom, office, or wallet? No. On the contrary, a mother would be moved to find a daughter with a picture of her father in her bedroom or school locker. To hold a picture of a loved one to our heart, to kiss it, or to put fresh flowers beside it is not idolatry, but an act of love. This is how the Church regards religious images:

Christian veneration of images is not contrary to the First Commandment, which proscribes idols. Indeed, "the honor rendered to an image passes to its prototype," and "whoever venerates an image venerates the person portrayed in it" (CCC 2132).

The Decalogue condemns real idol worship, such as polytheism and believing in or venerating "other divinities than the one true God" (CCC 2112). "An idolater is someone who 'transfers his indestructible notion of God to anything other than God'" (CCC 2114).[391] Although it is possible to worship Mary as a goddess, no true Catholic would ever do so. The real modern threat of idolatry consists in worshiping money, fame, or pleasure, or even our own spouses or children by placing them over God: "If any one . . . does not hate his own father and mother and wife and children and brothers and sisters, yes, and even his own life, he cannot be my disciple" (Luke 14:26).

Idolatry consists in divinizing what is not God. Man commits idolatry whenever he honors and reveres a creature in place of God, whether this be gods or demons (for example, satanism), power, pleasure, race, ancestors, the state, money, etc. Jesus says, "You cannot serve God and mammon" (Matt. 6:24) . . . Idolatry rejects the unique Lordship of God (CCC 2113; cf. CCC 1723).

QUESTIONS AND ANSWERS

Q: Jesus says: "I am the way, and the truth, and the life; no one comes to the Father, but through me" (John 14:6). Doesn't God want us to go to him only through Christ, not Mary?

A: We never go to the Father through Mary independently of Christ. In the wedding feast, the servants go to Christ through Mary to work his first miracle (John 2:1–12). When we go to Mary, she directs us to Christ, and through Christ, we go to the Father. There is no contradiction of Scripture here.

The dream of Jacob's ladder (Gen. 28:10–22) was a sign reassuring him that God's promise to his father Abraham and Isaac would be fulfilled in him. Jacob's ladder is a type for Mary. Mary too is seen as a sign of assurance, as a ladder set upon the earth that reaches heaven by which the Son of God descended. When Jacob awakes from his dream, he says, "How awesome is this place! This is none other than the house of God, and this is the gate of heaven" (Gen. 28:17), as is Christ's mother.

Similarly, when Israel wants to enter into the promised land, prefiguring heaven, the river Jordan is overflowing its banks, keeping the Israelites out of paradise. Yet Joshua sends the Ark of the Covenant, prefiguring Mary, into the river, parting the waters, and Israel crosses over on dry land (Josh. 3:1–4:18). The ark creates a gateway into the promised land.

A creature alone has no power to part the waters, but only as an instrument of God's power. Mary's role is similar.

Q: In Revelation 22:8–9, the angel tells John not to bow or worship him. Doesn't this tell us that we should not give angels and Mary any special reverence?

A: It reveals that angels and the saints—those sanctified in the blood of the Lamb—have essentially the same relationship with God. Prior to Christ's passion and death, and our sanctification, the angels are above us, as they are sanctified and behold God face to face (Matt. 18:10), and we show angels proper respect by bowing to them (Gen. 18:1–3). But having entered into an intimate friendship with God in Christ (John 15:13–15), we now have the same dignity as the angels. Therefore, we are like brothers and sisters of the angels in Christ, instead of creatures of lower dignity.

As Mary is the mother of Christ and the mother of all Christ's sisters and brothers, we are equal to her as redeemed by Christ, but we show her special respect as our mother— just as children are of equal dignity to their mothers and fathers as human beings but show special respect to parents as parents.

Q: You say that the Catholic Church condemns sacrifices to Mary. Why, then, do Catholics light candles before her statues? Isn't this offering sacrifices to idols?

A: Just as the smoke from the incense represents the prayers of the saints (Rev. 5:8), the candles represent the prayers and intercessory requests we make through the hands of Mary. Also, at Easter and at Christian baptism, we are given candles lit from the Easter candle that represent the light of grace that has come to us from Christ. The Catholic Church never views those candles as sacrifices.

Q: Yet Catholics go overboard by praying to Mary as if she were divine. Scripture just doesn't let us go there. Wouldn't it be easier for Christians to bless Mary and to acknowledge her response of faith without such exaggerated "devotions"?

A: The Bible has God blessing man and man blessing God, which is a form of prayer and devotion. Certainly blessing Mary as divine—or other exaggerated devotion—goes against official Church teaching, as the Second Vatican Council states:

> This most holy synod deliberately teaches this Catholic doctrine and at the same time . . . exhorts theologians and preachers of the divine word to abstain zealously both from all gross exaggerations as well as from petty narrow-mindedness in considering the singular dignity of the mother of God. . . . Let the faithful remember moreover that true devotion consists neither in sterile or transitory affection, nor in a certain vain credulity, but proceeds from true faith, by which we are led to know the excellence of the mother of God, and we are moved to a filial love toward our mother and to the imitation of her virtues (*Lumen Gentium* 67).

So the Church agrees that overly pious "devotions" marginalizing Christ are not truly Catholic or Christian. But Roberts also recognizes Mary's singular dignity:

> Here is an astounding truth: Mary carried in her womb the divine Son of God. . . . What happened within Mary is one of, perhaps even the greatest mystery of all time

and history: the Word of God became flesh. . . . Thus Mary has been given a leading role in the drama of human history. As she said in the Magnificat, indeed "all generations will call me blessed." There is strong biblical support for singling out Mary as profoundly blessed, even the most blessed of all people. Nevertheless, in saying this we must remember that "blessed" speaks of God's gracious action more than the worthiness of the individual.[392]

It may seem that Catholics exalt Mary too much; perhaps that seems to be so because Christians (whether Protestant or Catholic) don't exalt Christ's dignity enough.

Q: Is Mary really necessary in the life of a true Christian?

A: It would be better to ask: Was Mary necessary in Christ's life? In an absolute sense, no, as Christ is God. He did not need Mary or anyone. Yet, when the Word took flesh, becoming the Son of Man, he chose to be needy, to need a woman to be his mother and to be dependent on her. He chose Mary, and she replied with the generous gift of herself to him.

Do we need Mary? In an absolute sense, we could equally say no, since redemption comes from Christ and his sole mediation. However, for us to become fully Christian, we must also become fully Christlike. The only way for that to happen is to have the same Father and same mother, and to love Christ's mother as he did. In this sense, Christ made Mary necessary for us to be true Christians. Even Martin Luther understood this:

Mary is the mother of Jesus and the mother of us all. If Christ is ours, we must be where he is, and where he is, we must be also, and all that he has must be ours, and his mother therefore also is ours.[393]

269

Conclusions

God calls us to believe in the gospel of Jesus Christ, to entrust our lives to him, and to witness to that gospel in our words and deeds. Love is a powerful way to do this, as Jesus prayed: *"By this all men will know that you are my disciples, if you have love for one another . . .* that we may all be one *. . . that the world may believe that thou hast sent me"* (John 13:25, 17:21). As Christ's disciples, let's not grieve him or the Spirit by dissension and disunity:

> And do not grieve the Holy Spirit of God, in whom you were sealed for the day of redemption. Let all bitterness and wrath and anger and clamor and slander be put away from you, with all malice, and be kind to one another, tenderhearted, forgiving one another, as God in Christ forgave you. Therefore be imitators of God, as beloved children. And walk in love, as Christ loved us and gave himself up for us, a fragrant offering and sacrifice to God (Eph. 4:30–5:2).

We have seen how Scripture can be applied to derive various Marian teachings, and we have also seen the relationship of those teachings with essential Christian teachings.

Scriptural and Dogmatic Insights

The book's objective was to uncover as many passages of Scripture as possible referring to the Virgin Mary, either directly or indirectly, and then to put them together so as to see Scripture's portrait. We began by exploring modern Christian insights, which helped us identify many Marian passages. It also helped us develop greater sensitivity to Protestant concerns and issues regarding Mary in the Bible.

Yet when we explored early Christians' insights, we found passages that neither Protestants nor modern Catholics would ever dare apply to Mary. So we sought out keys and principles underlying their reading of the Bible, which led us to many prophecies that referred to her in relation to Christ. We also were able to uncover countless positive and antithetical types and figures for Mary, especially of Old Testament women.

One of the most effective keys that we found came from Mary's being blessed among women. That meant that any time a woman is mentioned in Scripture, it says something about Mary. If it says something positive about a particular woman or women in general, then it says something positive about Mary as more blessed. If it says something negative, then it describes something antithetical to Mary. Some women express both, such as Eve: before the Fall, she typifies Mary in a positive way; in succumbing to Satan, Eve is antithetical to Mary.

Early Christians saw the various dwellings of God among his people—especially the Ark of the Covenant and the Temple—as prefiguring the time Jesus dwelt in Mary's womb and then in her home. These dwellings were so sacred that violating them was a sacrilege meriting death. Yet these were just "patterns" of God's great sign to us: a virgin conceiving and becoming the Immanuel's dwelling. Early Christians linked this miraculous sign to women who miraculously conceive a Messiah-like son as prefiguring the mother of the Word incarnate.

Using poetic license, early Christians also applied to Mary feminizations, such as Israel and Lady Wisdom. They did so quite naturally because she is the most blessed of women, even if these realities are depicted as such only poetically in Scripture. We then compared the early Christian canon of Scripture with the Palestinian canon. Holy women depicted exclusively in the Septuagint—Judith, Susanna, Tobit's Sarah, etc., and Lady Wisdom—gave a scriptural picture of Mary consistent with what was found in canonical books common to Catholics and Protestants.

Finding these Marian passages helped us to piece together a wonderful mosaic of biblical teachings. In her Magnificat, for example, Mary identifies herself with barren women, especially by echoing Hannah's song of joy for having miraculously borne the prophet Samuel, knowing that it was impossible. This helped us to identify other scriptural evidence for Mary's virginity.

We did the same for Mary's divine maternity, sinlessness, assumption, and co-mediation with Christ, using Scripture to address many of the common Protestant objections. For example, we not only found evidence of Mary's sinlessness based on being "full of grace," having found "favor with God," but also based on her virginity as a sign of that sinlessness. A number of biblical types reaffirmed Mary's sinlessness, such as the sinless Eve before the Fall.

Considering Paul's cooperation in Christ's redemptive mission, we gained insights into Mary's. We saw how our secondary mediation of prayer, witness, and sharing of gifts depends radically on Christ's, including suffering with him. Yet Mary's co-mediating role was unique. Called to be the Redeemer's helper, the Virgin Mary is foreshadowed in Eve, Adam's helper, and in the many women (along with the Ark of the Covenant) who crushed the heads of Old Testament antichrists. This also gave new light to the sacrifice of Jephthah's daughter.

We gave Mary's assumption into heaven a biblical context, looking at the rapture of other Old and New Testament saints, biblical typology, and scriptural reasons for God rapturing the dead. We then applied all this to Mary and her ongoing role in heaven alongside Christ. We also explored what equality with angels means for the saints in heaven: intercession, apparitions, communicating God's will to individuals, etc. This led us to discover Mary's unique greatness as queen mother.

Crushing the Head of Disunity

Pride divides Christians (Rom. 12:3–8, 16; Jude 4:19–21), destroying the united front needed to fight the corrupting forces of modern, anti-religious secularism. Christians need unity to fulfill our mission. At the Amsterdam 2000 Conference, Evangelical leaders suggested,

> Jesus prayed to the heavenly Father that his disciples would be one so that the world might believe. One of the great hindrances to evangelism worldwide is the lack of unity among Christ's people, a condition made worse when Christians compete and fight with one another rather than seeking together the mind of Christ.

Pope John Paul II expressed similar sentiments:

> We must recognize that the division among Christians damages the holy work of preaching the gospel to every creature and is a barrier for many in their approach to the faith. . . . It is thus urgent to work for the unity of Christians, so that the missionary activity can be more effective.[394]

Will each person fight his battle alone, or will Christians come together to fight? Christ prayed: *Sanctify them in the truth; thy word is truth* (John 17:17), *that they may be one* (vv. 11,21). We don't pursue unity by negotiating agreements and ignoring differences, but by discerning the truth that Christ taught and that the Spirit inspires. As Tim Perry notes,

> ecumenism is not about negotiating a series of treaties among divided churches, but about those churches learning to accept what God has accomplished and discerning together what unity-in-the-truth means and implies.[395]

For Christ's prayer for unity to be truly effective, let us grow in faith, prayer, and mutual service. Finding a scriptural consensus on Mary—discovering the *Bible Mary*—should aid the Church in this. Only together and as one will the seed of the woman crush the head of disunity and evil.

For John Macquarrie, Mary may be the key to our unity:

> Can Mary really be a center for reconciliation and unity among Christians of different traditions, as the Ecumenical Society of the Blessed Virgin Mary has hoped? Or must she be an embarrassment who will perpetually remind Christians of some deep divisions that may never be fully healed?[396]

Jason Byassee also sees Mary as a potential source of Christian unity:

> But recently there has been a flurry of publications by Protestants on Mary, works that suggest she could be an ecumenical bridge—or at least that the Protestant aversion to Marian devotion is eroding.[397]

Humility allows the Holy Spirit to enter our hearts, so that God's inspired words may form us into an organic, fruitful union in Christ, like branches on the vine (John 15:1–7). Entering into God's mind and heart regarding Mary should unite us to the vine and thus to one another.

Cyril (d. 444) knew that Mary could unite, in orthodox teaching, those gathered for the Council of Ephesus to resolve Nestorius's claim that there are two persons in Christ. Their love and affection for Christ's mother motivated the council fathers to put aside partisan differences, so as to seek the good of the whole people of God. He made them realize that they were assembled in the city where Mary had lived with the apostle John, as if she had called them together to resolve this controversy: "I see here a joyful company of Christian men meeting together in ready response to the call of Mary, the holy and ever-virgin mother of God."[398] Their resulting unity was decisive for the Church.

Scripture's Model of Femininity

By calling his mother *Woman* (John 2:4, 19:26), our Lord made Mary the model of femininity, replacing Eve as the archetype for women just as Christ replaced Adam as the archetype for men. Also, being more blessed than any woman (Luke 1:42), Mary becomes the model for "blessed" Christian women.

Many Protestants are intuitively rediscovering this. Kathleen Norris sees it as a way to recover mystery and femininity, overcoming the stale, masculine approach to the Bible sometimes found among Protestants.[399] Lutheran Charles Dickson also describes this tendency:

Protestantism, in general, has produced a religious experience with harsh masculine emphasis. Such harshness has been tempered in Catholic experience by the presence of feminine qualities associated with Mary. For Protestants, part of the future of dialogue lies in the attention given to the tenderness element of faith represented by Mary.[400]

For John Macquarie, Mary models Christ's humility and *kenosis* of love for all Christians,[401] as does Pope John Paul II:

The Church sees in Mary the highest expression of the "feminine genius," and it finds in her a source of constant inspiration. Mary called herself the "handmaid of the Lord" (Luke 1:38). Through obedience to the word of God she accepted her lofty yet not easy vocation as wife and mother in the family of Nazareth. Putting herself at God's service, she also put herself at the service of others: a service of love. . . . For her, "to reign" is to serve! Her service is "to reign"![402]

For the pope, Mary's response to God's invitation to be the mother of his only-begotten Son was an exercise of her feminine "I," a wonderful example of what it means to be a woman:

The particular union of the *Theotokos* with God . . . is a pure grace and, as such, a gift of the Spirit. At the same time, however, through her response of faith Mary exercises her free will and thus fully shares her personal and feminine "I" in the event of the Incarnation. With her "fiat," Mary becomes the authentic subject of that union with God which was realized in the mystery of the Incarnation of the Word, who is of one substance with the Father. All of God's action in human history at all times respects the free will of the human "I." And such was the case with the Annunciation at Nazareth.[403]

He concludes that the "'prophetic' character of women in their femininity finds its highest expression in the virgin mother of God,"[404] teaching all of us to love and to correspond to the Holy Spirit.

A Personal Relationship With Mary

Christ repeatedly prophesied the importance of humility: "Every one who exalts himself will be humbled, but he who humbles himself will be exalted" (Matt. 11:23).[405] Mary fully embraces the gospel by humbling and emptying herself, following Christ's example, yet doing so in a feminine way by entrusting her life to God, believing in his word, and abandoning herself to his providential plans. She brings the needs of others to Christ, as at the wedding feast of Cana, trusting that Christ would find a way to resolve those needs despite his apparent indifference.

Mary, then, is an example for all Christians—not just for women—"a model of the fundamental Christian . . . virtue of humility,"[406] which leads to the heights of intimate cooperation with Christ's redemption.

Behind everything in this work has been an effort to introduce the reader to a real person through Scripture. Yet to truly get to know Mary, we must take some initiative to speak to her, to understand her so as to enter into a relationship with her. The person who doubts God's existence but sincerely seeks to resolve that doubt needs to humble himself and approach God as a person—because God is a person (in fact, three persons!). The prideful effort to prove to himself that God does or does not exist would do little good. He still wouldn't have a relationship with God. How much better off he would be if he would only pray with humility—perhaps something like "God, if you are really there, help me to get to know you. Tell me about yourself . . . reveal yourself to me . . . perhaps through your

278

Scripture." This is the way to get to know God, to begin a relationship with him, as with any *personal* being. Likewise, this is what is needed to get to know Mary.

Few people think that spousal, maternal, paternal, or fraternal love somehow detracts from their love for God. There is no reason why it should. In fact, such human love strengthens our love for God. That is how my love for Mary affects me. I try to be like John, Christ's "beloved disciple," by taking Mary into my home (John 19:26–27). I think this makes me more a man and more a Christian.

As my spiritual mother, Mary has meant a lot to me, just as the feminine presence of a mother or wife has made many a man. I ask myself: Would I have remained Catholic or even Christian had it not been for Mary's special feminine presence in my life? When younger, I was very rational, heady, and even self-righteous, often having an overly critical eye. I still have a long way to go, but I can honestly say that Mary has helped me progress against these defects to become more understanding, with a deeper concern for others.

Mary's feminine way is more humble and teaches us to have more heart, compassion, and understanding. In other words, she teaches us to love and forgive, while developing and deepening our personal relationship with Jesus Christ. Without Mary, likely I would have been a heartless priest, had I become one at all. Mary still encourages me.

God's original plan for man (Adam) was for him to have a helper to assist him (Gen. 2:18–25). Adam needed Eve, and the New Adam needs the New Eve. As a Christian, we must be Christlike and have the New Eve as our helper, too. I hope my reader can discover his own relationship with Mary. Christ offers her to us through Scripture. In discovering the *Bible Mary*, may you go deeper in your understanding of the "*Bible Christ*" and of his "*Bible Body*," the Church.

QUESTIONS AND ANSWERS

Q: Don't Catholics overdo it with Mary's role?

A: Perhaps some do; certainly, Christ is the primary focus of our faith. But that doesn't mean we should ignore Mary, her relationship with Christ, or her role in a Christian life. This study focused on Mary in Scripture, letting the Holy Spirit inspire us to discover what he wanted us to know and believe about Mary, especially in her relationship with Christ.

Q: Is not all this speculation about Mary and Old Testament types a way of "adding" to Scripture, contrary to God's commands?

A: Certainly God forbade adding to Scripture (Deut. 4:2; Prov. 30:5–6; Rev. 22:18–19), yet he also forbade subtracting from his Word. Jesus came to fulfill the whole Old Testament Law and the prophets, such that not one "iota," not a single "dot," will pass without it being fulfilled in him and his kingdom (Matt. 5:17–19). So every passage of the Old Testament must have some fulfillment in the New. To ignore certain passages—"one of the least commandments" or teachings—because they don't find immediate literal fulfillment in the New Covenant, would be "relaxing" or subtracting from Scripture. This study attempted to do as our Lord did, seeking what fulfilled Solomon, Jonah, etc.—seeking what fulfills the other Old Testament types.

Q: Bible Christians don't subtract from Scripture or remove anything from the Bible!

A: Somebody is not a "Bible Christian" if he implicitly takes away from the Bible, by ignoring a passage or declaring it irrelevant to modern Christian life (Rev. 2:9). For example, if references to circumcision were removed from the Bible, would it affect the "Bible Christian's" teaching on baptism? Does he find a New Testament fulfillment in the ark and its being captured by the Philistines? What about the sacrifice of Jephthah's daughter? If such passages were eliminated from the Bible, would it affect his teaching?

Q: Why would God hide these doctrines about Mary if he really wanted us to believe them? Wouldn't the Bible make them more explicit?

A: The Bible makes a number of explicit references to Mary. These form the foundation upon which we find links to the other Marian passages. Jesus tells us that God chose to do it this way to hide them from the "wise" and "know-it-alls":

> In that same hour he rejoiced in the Holy Spirit and said, "I thank thee, Father, Lord of heaven and earth, that thou hast hidden these things from the wise and understanding and revealed them to babes; yea, Father, for such was thy gracious will" (Luke 10:21).

Let's be humble, simple as babes, so as to understand how God wants us to read Scripture. Perhaps what the Holy Spirit really wants us to learn is how to complement the masculine way of reading Scripture, of logical literalism and legal wisdom, with a more feminine way, with the logic of love, and the fuller meaning the Holy Spirit intends.

Q: Aren't you basing all these Marian dogmas on some new theoretical method of reading Scripture that is accepted by very few Christians?

A: This way is not theoretical or new at all, but one used by the early Christians and by the Jews of our Lord's time. It is how the New Testament, inspired by the Holy Spirit, approached the Old. Early Christians did so quite naturally, without developing a theory or method. We, "wise and knowledgeable" modern Christians, have simply failed to grasp it.

Justin Martyr (d. 165) is a great example of early Christian typology. In his dialogue with Rabbi Trypho, Justin tries to convince Jews that Jesus Christ fulfilled numerous Old Testament prophecies. Unconvinced, Trypho saw fulfillments of those prophecies in the Old Testament. Then Justin extensively developed the biblical types for Christ (such as Melchizedek, Isaac, Joshua, David's royal offspring, Jonah, etc.) and for John the Baptist (e.g., Elijah), for the Church as the new people of God, for the sacraments, etc. He used the whole Old Testament to paint a portrait of Christ as the incarnate Word of God.[407] In a similar way, Augustine approached the blessed Trinity. Now we try to do the same with Mary, systematizing what early Christians did quite naturally.

Modern hermeneutical approaches try to analyze Scripture using "scientific" methods developed in the scientific revolution—a recent phenomenon. These (masculine) methods try to treat Scripture as an object of modern science, with its legalistic positivism, ignoring the meaning of God's interpersonal dialogue with man intended by the Holy Spirit.

Fr. Farkasfalvy considers the example of the Mary/Eve parallel and notes:

For many [moderns] the parallel seemed an interesting but ultimately arbitrary comparison between two biblical figures. However, a more recent and still growing knowledge of early Christian reading of the Old Testament and the role it played for Christian beginnings brought new insights. . . .

The custom of reading the Old Testament through Christological "lenses" pervades theology from apostolic times. What Justin Martyr says about Mary and Eve extends what Paul said about Adam and Christ.[408]

We have tried to learn from these insights as well.

Q: But we don't see the New Testament writers using your techniques.

A: Yes we do. Paul insists on interpreting Scripture this way so that God's word would not fail:

> But it is not as though the word of God had failed. For not all who are descended from Israel belong to Israel, and not all are children of Abraham because they are his descendants; but "through Isaac shall your descendants be named." This means that it is not the children of the flesh who are the children of God, but the children of the promise are reckoned as descendants (Rom. 9:6–8).

God's word would fail if we take Scripture too literally in reference to *Israel*. Israel does not refer to those who are born of the flesh—the literal interpretation of the Old Testament, such as Genesis 21:12. Those born of the flesh are "those who say that they are Jews and are not, but are a synagogue of Satan" (Rev. 2:9). It is the Christian who is the true Israelite.

Throughout this work, we have tried to use Paul's way of interpreting Scripture.

Q: Can these techniques really be used to resolve other issues dividing Christians?

A: These techniques could be used to address other key issues that divide us, such as justification, the nature of the Church, and of its authority. A more expanded approach to these topics would be to identify all the scriptural passages that may pertain to a topic and then to classify and draw out the necessary conclusions.

About the Author

Fr. John Waiss is a priest of Prelature of Opus Dei and currently pastor of St. Mary of the Angels parish in Chicago. He has preached numerous retreats and days of recollection and holds a Ph.D. in ecclesiastical philosophy from Rome's Pontifical University of Santa Croce, as well as a B.S. and M.S. from Notre Dame and Stanford. His books include *Letters Between a Catholic and an Evangelical, Born to Love, and What Happens When You Die?*

Ancient Keys to Understanding Mary in Scripture

KEY 1: Literal references to Mary take priority.

KEY 2: Christ, our true model, fulfills all Scripture. We identify prophecies, laws, customs, and dogmas describing Mary based on prophecies, laws, customs, and dogmas describing Christ.

KEY 3: God graced (favored) Mary by loving, electing, and choosing her for a special vocation. This links her to others so graced.

KEY 4: Mary is blessed in Christ as more blessed than any woman. Thus, when any woman or feminine attribute is praised, Mary is, too.

KEY 5: Mary, Christ's first disciple, is blessed for her faith. Persons of faith may prefigure her.

KEY 6: Persons of charity or service may reflect Mary's faith-filled response of love.

KEY 7: Mary magnifies God through Old Testament Scripture, which she knew and pondered, as she did Christ. Her faith-filled pondering links her to other Old Testament figures and anticipates losing Christ at the cross.

KEY 8: Prophecies and types may have multiple fulfillments.

KEY 9: Old Testament types of women supporting men may apply to Mary in relation to Christ, such as Eve alongside

Adam: Christ became the New Adam and archetype for all men as Mary becomes the New Eve and *Woman*, the archetype and courageous model for women.

KEY 10: Women in Scripture are types of Mary, especially other "handmaids" and "servants of the Lord" who cooperated with God with their feminine generosity. Women who miraculously conceive prefigure Mary's virginal conception of Jesus.

KEY 11: As coherent and consistent with the rest of Scripture, poetic texts extolling feminine virtues, such as personifications of Wisdom, may portray Mary.

KEY 12: Persons, objects, or places where God dwells may be types for God dwelling in Mary. Those that God abandons may be types antithetical to Mary.

KEY 13: The fruit of a tree (vine, stalk, etc.) may prefigure Christ in relation to Mary.

KEY 14: Signs and miraculous works that elicit faith may prefigure Mary.

KEY 15: Collective persons portrayed as feminine may be types for Mary.

KEY 16: Objects may be types for Mary by reflecting her perfections.

KEY 17: Evil and cursed women may be antithetical types for Mary.

KEY 18: Texts in the Septuagint canon follow the same keys and principles as the rest of Scripture.

KEY 19: Early Marian teaching always resulted from scriptural reflections.

Cited References

Thomas Aquinas, *Summa Theologica* (Cambridge University Press, 2006).

Jason Byassee, "What about Mary? Protestants and Marian devotion" in *Christian Century* (December 14, 2004).

E.W. Bullinger, *Great Cloud of Witnesses in Hebrew 11* (1911).

Heinrich Bullinger, "Die Marienpredigt," in Perry (2006).

Catholic Encyclopedia, (Robert Appleton Company, 1912; Online Edition: Kevin Knight, 2003) http://www.newadvent.org/cathen/.

Catechism of the Catholic Church, 2nd ed. (revised in accordance with the official Latin text promulgated by Pope John Paul II), United States Catholic Conference, Inc. and Libreria Editrice Vaticana (1997).

John Calvin, *Calvini Opera*, 45:35, in *Corpus Reformatorum* (Braunshweig-Berlin, 1863-1900).

Jean Danielou, S.J., *From shadows to Reality; studies in the typology of the Fathers*, Wulstan Hibbert, trans. (Westminster, MD: Newman Press, 1960).

Richard M. Davidson, *Typology in Scripture. A Study of Hermeneutical Tupos Structure*, Andrews University Seminary Doctoral Dissertation Series (Berrien Springs, MI: Andrews University Press, 1981).

Henry Denzinger, Roy J. Deferrari, trans., *The Sources of Catholic Dogma* (Powers Lake, ND: Marian House, 1957).

Charles Dickson, *A Protestant Pastor Looks at Mary* (Huntington, IN: Our Sunday Visitor, 1996).

Nancy J. Duff, "Mary, Servant of the Lord: Christian Vocation at the Manger and the Cross" in Gaventa-Rigby (2002).

Easton's Bible Dictionary (1897).

R.J. Foster, "The Formation and History of the Canon (OT and NT)" in Dom Bernard Orchard, M.A., *A Catholic Commentary on Holy Scripture* (New York: Thomas Nelson & Son, 1953) 11a-18f, pp. 13-21.

Clarence William Friedman, *Prefigurations in Meistergesang: types from the Bible and nature* (Washington: The Catholic University of America Press, 1943).

Luigi Gambero, *Mary and the Fathers of the Church: the Blessed Virgin Mary in Patristic Thought*; trans. Thomas Buffer (San Francisco: Ignatius Press, 1999).

Beverly Roberts Gaventa, *Mary: Glimpses of the Mother of Jesus* (Columbia, SC: University of South Carolina Press, 1995).

"Standing Near the Cross" in Gaventa-Rigby (2002).

and Cynthia L. Rigby, ed., *Blessed One: Protestant Perspective on Mary* (Louisville, KY: Westminster John Knox Press, 2002).

Timothy George, "The Blessed Evangelical Mary: Why we shouldn't ignore her any longer" *Christianity Today* (December 2003), Vol. 47, No. 12.

"Recovering a Protestant Mary: A conversation with Timothy George" in *Christian History & Biography* Issue 83, Vol. XXIV, No. 3 (Fall 2004).

H.F.W. Gesenius, et.al., *Hebrew Grammar*, Oxford University Press (1922).

Brunero Gherardini, *Dignitas terrae: Note di mariologia aostiniana* (Casale Monferrato: Piemme, 1992).

Leonard Goppelt, *Typos: The Typological Interpretation of the Old Testament in the New Testament*, Donald H. Madvig, trans. (Grand Rapids: Eerdmans, 1982).

Robert M. Grant, *A Short History of the Interpretation of the Bible* (New York: Macmillan, 1963).

Kilian J. Healy, *The Assumption of Mary* (Wilmington, DE: Michael Glazier, Inc., 1982).

Francis Johnston, *The Wonder of Guadalupe* (Rockford, IL: Tan Books, 1981).

David Lyle Jeffrey, "Hail Mary: Her moment of obedience triggered two millennia of reverence" *Christian History & Biography,* Issue 83, Vol. XXIV, No. 3 (Fall 2004).

William A. Jurgens, *The Faith of the Early Fathers*, (Collegeville, MN: The Liturgical Press, 1970-1979).

Shannon Kubiak, *God Called a Girl: How Mary Changed Her World and You Can Too* (Minneapolis, MN: Bethany House Publishers (April 1, 2005).

Bernard Leeming, "Protestants and Our Lady," *Marian Library Studies* (January 1967).

The Liturgy of the Hours: According to the Roman Rite (New York: Catholic Book Publishing Co., 1975).

Marin Luther, *Luther's Works*, Weimar edition, Jaroslav Pelikan and William J. Cole, eds. (St. Louis: Concordia).

John Macquarrie, *Mary for all Christians* (London: T & T Clark, 1990).

Lois Malcolm, "What Mary Has to Say about God's Bare Goodness" in Gaventa-Rigby (2002).

Dick McClain, "Mary's devoted heart" in *Christian History & Biography*, Issue 83, Vol. XXIV, No. 3 (Fall 2004).

Lee Martin McDonald and James A. Sanders, *The Canon Debate* (Peabody, MA: Hendrickson Publishers, Inc., 2002).

Scot McKnight, *The Real Mary: Why Evangelical Christians Can Embrace the Mother of Jesus* (Brewster, Massachusetts: Paraclete Press, 2007).

Daniel L. Migliore, "Woman of Faith: Toward a Reformed Understanding of Mary" in Gaventa -Rigby (2002).

Bonnie J. Miller-McLemore, "Pondering All These Things" in Gaventa-Rigby (2002), 99.

The Navarra Bible: Joshuah – Kings (New York : Scepter Publishers, 2002a).

   Chronicles – Maccabees (New York : Scepter Publishers, 2002b).

John Henry Newman, *The Mystical Rose* (New York: Scepter, 1996).

Kathleen Norris, *Meditations on Mary* (New York: Penguin Putnam, 1999) in Gaventa-Rigby (2002).

Jaroslav Pelikan, *Mary Through the Centuries: Her Place in the History of Culture* (Yale University Press, 1996).

   Development of Christian Doctrine: Some Historical Prolegomena (New Haven: Yale University Press, 1969).

Tim Perry, *Mary for Evangelicals: Toward an Understanding of the Mother of Our Lord* (Downers Grove, IL: InterVarsity Press, 2006).

Pope Benedict XV, *Inter Sodalicia* (1918).

Pope Benedict XVI, *General Audience*, March 14, 2012.

Pope John Paul II,

General Audience, March 17, 1928.

Redemptoris Mater—Encyclical *On the Blessed Virgin Mary in the Life of the Pilgrim Church* (March 25, 1987).

Mulieris Dignitatem—Apostolic Letter *On the Dignity and Vocation of Women on the Occasion of the Marian Year* (August 15, 1988).

Letter to Women, June 29, 1995.

General Audience, September 6, 1995.

Theotókos: Woman, Mother, Disciple. A Catechesis on Mary, Mother of God (Boston: Pauline Books & Media, 2000).

Pope Pius X, *Ad diem illum* (February 2, 1904).

Pope Pius XII, *Munificentissimus Deus* (November 1, 1950).

Ignace de la Potterie, S.J., *Mary in the Mystery of the Covenant* (New York: Alba House, 1992).

Denis Farkasfalvy, O.Cist. (Staten Island, NY: St. Pauls, 2014).

Johannes Quasten, *Patrology* (Westminster, MD: The Newman Press, 1962).

Cynthia L. Rigby, "Mary and the Artistry of God" in Gaventa-Rigby (2002).

Patrick Henry Reardon, "Mary at the Cross: From three little verses in John has come a rich tradition of song and art" in *Christian History & Biography,* Issue 83, Vol. XXIV, No. 3 (Fall 2004).

Mark D. Roberts, "The Protestant Mary? Reflections on the TIME Cover Story," (March 20, 2005) http://www.mark-droberts.com/htmfiles/resources/protestantmary.htm.

Second Vatican Council (documents available at http://www.vatican.va/archive/hist_councils/ii_vatican_council/index.htm).

   Lumen Gentium: Dogmatic Constitution on the Church (November 21, 1964).

   Dei Verbum: Dogmatic Constitution on Divine Revelation (November 18, 1965).

Mark Shea, "Five Myths About Seven Books," http://www.mark-shea.com/archives.html.

Fulton J. Sheen, *The World's First Love: Mary, Mother of God* (San Francisco: Ignatius, 1996).

Maxwell Stanmforth, trans., *Early Christian Writings: The Apostolic Father* (London: Penguin Books, 1968).

Jeanne Stevenson-Moessner, "The Hidden Years: What did Mary do during the youth and ministry of her son?" in *Christian History & Biography,* Issue 83, Vol. XXIV, No. 3 (Fall 2004).

Jon M. Sweeney, *Strange Heaven: The Virgin Mary as Woman, Mother, Disciple, and Advocate* (Brewster, MA: Paraclete Press, 2006).

F. Adeney Walpole, *Women of the New Testament* (London: James Nisbet, 1901).

Marina Warner, *Alone of all her sex: the myth and the cult of the Virgin Mary* (New York: Alred A. Knopf / Random House, 1976).

Abraham Wasserstein and David J. Wasserstein, *The Legend of the Septuagint: From Classical Antiquity to Today* (Cambridge: Cambridge University Press, 2006).

Sarah Hinlicky Wilson, "Temple & Sword: At the temple, long before the cross, her son's cruel death pierced Mary" in *Christian History & Biography,* Issue 83 (Fall 2004) Vol. XXIV, No. 3.

George Earnst Wright, *God Who Acts: Biblical Theology as Recital,* Studies in Biblical Theology, 8 (London SCM Press, 1952).

Ulrich Zwingli, *Opera Completa* (Zurich, 1828-42).

Index to the
Catechism of the Catholic Church

53   God's revelation culminates in the Word, Christ 121

64   Mary shines among the holy women in Scripture 48

81   Scripture: God's speech 121

102 God speaks one Word, 121

128-130 Scripture uses typology 74

144 Abraham (Mary): models of faith 55

148 Mary freely assents to God's plan with faith 55;
     to conceive & bear a son without loss of virginity 52

149 Mary: remains faithful to Christ on the cross 53

165 Mary's dark night of faith: God could raise her son 55

273 Mary: a model of faith 232

411 Mary (New Eve) graced to be conceived without sin 174;
     needs a savior 194

452 *Yahweh-saves*-has special fulfillment in Jesus 94

456 the Creeds link Mary's divine maternity with Christ's
     humanity 158

466 Mary's divine maternity & Christ's humanity reaf-
     firmed against Nestorius 159

480 Catholics believe: only one mediator: Jesus Christ 232

484 *Mother of God* affirms Christ's fullness of deity dwells bodily 170

487 Marian dogmas: based on Christological dogmas 38

488, 490 Mary freely assented to God's plan with faith 55

489 Mary shines among the holy women in Scripture 48

491-92 Mary still needs a savior 194; with Jesus, full of grace 199

493 conceived without sin 174

494 Mary's, New Eve's role in salvation is similar to Eve's 218

495 *Mother of the Lord* means *Mother of God* 168

496 Mary's virginity: sign of Christ's divinity 123

497 the fulfillment of Isaiah's prophecy 126-127

499 Mary: ever-virgin 123

500 Jesus' "siblings" are not Mary's children 147

501 Jesus: Mary's only son 151

503 her virginity shows God's absolute initiative 141

504 Jesus: truly the New Adam in a new creation 141

505 Mary's virginity shows how God's children are born again through faith 141

506 Mary's a faith "unadulterated by any doubt" 141

507 Mary's faith points to the Church's 141

508 Immaculate Conception: a great grace from God 182

509   Mary mother of the God made man 182

510   Augustine witnesses to her perpetual virginity 126

532   Christ obeys Mary as he does the Father 63

697   God overshadows Mary (Ark of the Covenant) 101

721   Tradition applies *Lady Wisdom* to Mary 491

722   *Mother of God*-affirms Christ's fullness of deity dwells bodily 170

724   burning bush: Mary 152

725   she mothers us by bringing us to Christ 210

726   Mary gets her children to pray together 209

744   Mary: chosen to be the special dwelling place of Emmanuel: *God with us* 100

773   Mary: Christ's bride 57

829, 867 type of the Church: both are holy, virgin & mother 165

956   her secondary mediation doesn't detract from Christ's salvific role 232

964   Christ gives us to her 162

967   Mary: type of the Church 166

968   Mary brings Christ & his supernatural life to us 210

969   Mary shares in Christ's sufferings as co-mediatrix 207

970   Mary doesn't diminish this 207

971   honor Mary without worshiping her 261

974   the Assumption reaffirms belief in Christ's resurrection and that of all Christians 237

1723 idol worship includes seeking power, money, etc. 266

2097 we ought to recognize the great things God does in her 259–260

2112 idolatry: polytheistic 265

2113 includes seeking power, money, etc. 266

2114 turns creature into a god 265

2132 Catholics do not idolize religious images 265

2618 Mary intercedes for us with prayer 256

2674 her secondary mediation doesn't detract from Christ's salvific role 232

2675, 2682 prayer includes magnifying the great things God has done in Mary 259–260

2853 crushing Satan's head with Christ: very scriptural 228

Scripture Index

This book contains hundreds of Scripture references that pertain to the Blessed Mother and her place in God's plan of salvation history. For a full annotated index of all these references, visit https://cdn.catholic.com/wp-content/uploads/bible-mary-scripture-index.pdf or scan the code below.

Endnotes

1 Farkfasfalvy (2014) 48. (Full references are given in the *Cited References* at the
   end of the book.)
2 Cf. *On the Birth of Christ* PG 46.1133D-1136B, in Gambero (1999) 155.
3 *Contra Palagianos* 2.4 and *Tractatus de Psalmo* 96.1, in Gambero (1999) 211-212.
4 Perry (2006).
5 Migliore in Gaventa-Rigby (2002) 129.
6 Quotations from the *Catechism of the Catholic Church* (1997) will be referenced
   with CCC and paragraph number. For example, (CCC 112) refers to paragraph
   112 of the *Catechism*.
7 McKnight (2007) 5.
8 Dickson (1996) 22.
9 *Time* March 21, 2005, Vol. 165, No. 12 (New York) 60-69.
10 *Christianity Today* December 2003, Vol. 47, No. 12.
11 *Christian History & Biography* Issue 83, Fall 2004, Vol. XXIV, No. 3.
12 See *Protestant Mary* Episode no. 816, December 17, 2004.
13 Cf. Pelikan (1996). Jaroslav Pelikan left being a Lutheran minister to become an
   Orthodox layman in 1998.
14 Cf. Macquarrie (1990).
15 Cf. Gaventa (1995). Gaventa has also compiled a book of essays by various
   scholars on the subject, cf. Gaventa-Rigby (2002).
16 Pelikan (1996) 216.
17 Perry (2006) 15.
18 Migliore in Gaventa (2006) 117-118. William J. Abraham considers this an
   oversight in an honest reading of the Bible: "This was recently brought home
   to me dramatically when one of my students noted how odd it was to preach
   about all the leading figures in the Gospel materials (John the Baptist, the
   disciples, the rich young ruler, Herod and the like) and ignore Mary" (William
   J. Abraham's Foreword to Perry (2006) 9-10).
19 Gaventa in Gaventa-Rigby (2002) 47.
20 Lozano-Diaz in Gaventa-Rigby (2002) 87.
21 Stevenson-Moessner (2004).
22 Cf. McClain (2004).
23 Cf. McKnight (2007) 143. He also points out the negative approach to Mary:
   "Many of us Protestants have reacted against Mary . . . Mary has been pushed
   entirely off the stage. Most of us know far more about what we don't believe
   about Mary—that she wasn't immaculately conceived, that she . . . wasn't
   perpetually virgin, etc.—than what we do believe about Mary" (5).
24 George (2003).

25   Luther, "Sermon Preached at Erfurt on the Journey to Worms, John 20:19-
     20, April 7, 1521," in *Luther's Works* 35:275. Heinrich Bullinger, "Die
     Marienpredigt," in Perry (2006) 218. In summary, Reformers saw Mary as "the
     model of salvation by faith alone through grace alone" (214).

26   Gaventa in Gaventa-Rigby (2002) 1: "The time has come for Protestants to
     join in the blessing of Mary. . . . Filled with the Holy Spirit, Elizabeth twice
     proclaims that Mary is blessed (1:42, 45). . . . Mary herself declares that "from
     now on all generations will call me blessed" (1:48). This rich blessing of Mary
     has scarcely extended to Protestant faith and life. . . . Although we Protestants
     identify Scripture as authoritative, the Lukan blessing of Mary has rarely
     inspired Protestants to act accordingly."

27   Miller-McLemore in Gaventa-Rigby (2002) 99.

28   Gaventa (1995) ix.

29   Gaventa in Gaventa-Rigby (2002) 47.

30   Miller-McLemore in Gaventa-Rigby (2002) 97-98.

31   George (2003).

32   Sweeney (2006) 193-4.

33   Norris in Gaventa-Rigby (2002) ix.

34   Kubiak (2005) 12.

35   Byassee (2004).

36   Stevenson-Moessner (2004)

37   Cf. Kubiak (2005) 66.

38   Migliore in Gaventa (2006) 122.

39   Roberts (2005).

40   Sweeney (2006) 33-34.

41   *Dialogue with Trypho the Jew*, 100, in Gambero (1999) 47.

42   Wilson (2004).

43   Pope John Paul II (2000) 153.

44   Perry (2006) 39.

45   Gaventa in Gaventa-Rigby (2002) 43, 46.

46   Byassee (2004).

47   Macquarrie (1990) 64.

48   Perry (2006) 29-31.

49   Perry includes Phil. 2:5–11 and Rom. 1:3–4. While neither text mentions Mary
     directly, they do show an undeveloped "idea of Christ's preincarnate existence"
     while affirming his human descent from David's seed; cf. id. 22-7.

50   Jeffrey (2004).

51   Migliore in Gaventa (2006) 123.

52   Kubiak (2005) 29.

53   *Id*. 26-27 and Byassee (2004).

54   Praise God for the good things he does in Mary (Luke 1:49); as in his marvels (Ps.
     136:3–4, 7–9; 145:5); remember leaders (Heb. 13:7); honor all men (1 Pet. 2:17).

55   Sweeney (2006) 35-6.

56   Beauty (1 Sam. 25:2–3), gracefulness (Prov. 5:18–19), and temperance (1 Tim.
     3:11–13). A more complete list of feminine qualities is found in Appendix IV.

57   Wise (2 Sam. 20:16), kind (Ruth 1:9), trustworthy (Prov. 31:10–11), reverent
     (Titus 2:1–5), respectful (Eph. 5:33), and full of good works (1 Tim. 2:8–10).

Modest (1 Tim. 2:15), pure and undefiled (Eph. 5:25–27; Rev. 14:1–5), preserved from violation (Gen. 12:10–20; 20:1–18; 26:7–11). Purity and virginity: highly honored (Deut. 22:13–21; Isa. 62:5), virgin daughter (2 Kings 19:20–21), pure bride (2 Cor. 11:2–3), freed of worldly pursuits (1 Cor. 7:32–35) to follow the Lamb (Rev. 14:1–5) and serve his kingdom (Matt. 19:10–12).

58   Holy (Ps. 87:1–5; 1 Pet. 3:1–6), good (Prov. 12:4), humble, lowly (Luke 1:48), putting hope in God (1 Tim. 5:3–10).

59   Jeffrey (2004).

60   George (2004).

61   Roberts (2005) part 6.

62   Dick McClain explains how Mary believed this—McClain (2004).

63   "Mary was a disciple of Christ before she was his mother, for had she not believed, she would not have conceived. Mary's faith too is not the achievement of merit, but the gift of divine grace. This means that when we praise and love Mary, it is God whom we praise for his gracious favor to his chosen handmaid" —George (2003).

64   Sweeney (2006) 46-7.

65   Pelikan (1996) 20; cf. 160-1.

66   Kubiak (2005) 148-149.

67   Abraham—a model of faith (Rom. 4:12); with deeds of faith (John 8:39–40, James 2:18–24); hope, patient endurance (Heb. 6:11–20); and obedience (Heb. 11:8–10). Through faith Abraham is the father of Jews (John 8:33–53, etc.); of Jesus (Heb. 2:16, etc.); of us (Gal. 3:6–29, etc.); puts us in relationship with (John 8:33–58) the *God of Abraham* (Acts 3:13, etc.); Abraham's blessing (Gal. 3:13–14); he is among the living (Matt. 8:11; 22:32, etc.) destined to be with the saints (Luke 16:19–31), etc.

68   Augustine, *Sermo,* 25.7–8.

69   Pope John Paul II (1987) n. 12–21.

70   McKnight (2007) 13; cf. 9, 19-20, 27.

71   Cf. Byassee (2004).

72   Gaventa (1995) 72-73; see also p. 56.

73   Jeffrey (2004).

74   McKnight (2007) 4, 151-5.

75   Perry (2006) 77-8.

76   Jeffrey (2004).

77   Sweeney (2006) 40-2.

78   Kubiak (2005) 80, 89.

79   Byassee (2004) citing Luke 2:19, 51.

80   Miller-McLemore in Gaventa, Rigby (2002) 105-106.

81   Perry (2006) 84.

82   Macquarrie (1990) 14-15.

83   Sweeney (2006) 4.

84   Miller-McLemore in Gaventa-Rigby (2002) 105, 110.

85   Gaventa (1995) 63-66.

86   Perry (2006) 86-7.

87   McClain (2004).

88   Wilson (2004).

89   Kubiak (2005) 132.

90   Byassee (2004), citing Luke 2:34–35.

91   Kubiak (2005) 146-7.

92   Byassee (2004).

93   Migliore in Gaventa (2006) 128

94   "The presence of the Mother of God with the Eleven after the Ascension is not a mere historical annotation of something of the past but acquires a significance of great value for she shares what is most precious to them: the living memory of Jesus in prayer; and she shares this mission of Jesus: to preserve the memory of Jesus and thereby to preserve his presence" —Pope Benedict XVI, *General Audience*, March 14, 2012.

95   "Luke explicitly describes Mary as "Mother of Jesus" (Acts 1:14), almost as if he wished to suggest that something of the presence of the Son who had ascended into heaven has remained in the presence of the mother. She reminded his disciples of Jesus' face, and with her presence in the community she was the symbol of the Church's fidelity to Christ the Lord" —Pope John Paul II (2000) 19.

96   Kubiak (2005) 48-49.

97   Migliore in Gaventa (2006) 123-124.

98   Miller-McLemore in Gaventa-Rigby (2002) 107.

99   Kubiak (2005) 105.

100 William J. Abraham's Foreword to Perry (2006) 10.

101 Pelikan (1996) 23-4.

102 Sweeney (2006) 84-85. Cf. *id.*, 14-15.

103 Id. 15, 42-3. Pelikan (1996) 25-6, 67, 78.

104 Sweeney (2006) 86-7.

105 Limited space prevents us from developing a complete exposition of the rules for biblical typology. We simply present this brief summary. Two Catholic books on biblical typology are Friedman (1943) and Danielou (1960). The *Catechism of the Catholic Church* also summarizes this teaching (CCC 128-130). Several Protestants also deal extensively with this: Wright (1952), Grant (1963), Davidson (1981), Goppelt (1982).

106 *Shadow* or *copies* of the Sabbath and festivals (Col. 2:16–17); of high priesthood, etc. (Heb. 8:1–5; 9:18–10:2).

107 Jonah in the fish (Matt. 12:38–42); the flood (1 Pet. 3:18–22) and circumcision (Col. 2:11–15).

108 John injects the symbolism of creation, sequencing the days leading up to Cana: counting "in the beginning" (John 1:1) as day one, "the next day" (1:29) as day two, "the next day" (1:35 and 1:43) as days three and four; then "On the third day" (2:1) becomes day seven, the Sabbath day of God's New Covenant with his people, the Church or Christ's Bride. Cf. Scott Hahn and Michal Elizabeth Hunt, http://www.agapebiblestudy.com/John_Gospel/Chapter%202.htm.

109 Roberts (2005), part 5.

110 Byassee (2004).

111 *Woman* at the cross (John 19:18–34); doing God's will (Phil. 2:8; Luke 11:27–28); spiritual "birthing" (Matt. 12:46–50)

112 George (2004) 13.

113 Byassee (2004).

114 "Mary is among the *witnesses* of Jesus. The Johannine mother of Jesus who stands at the cross does so without a single word. She stands to watch what takes place, she hears the words of Jesus, and she goes from that place with the Beloved Disciple, given her as a son . . . In a sense, Mary remains a model for all Christians" (Gaventa-Rigby [2002] 30).

115 Byassee (2004).

116 Migliore in Gaventa (2006) 127.

117 Kubiak (2005) 157, 163, quoting Deut. 31:6 and Heb. 13:5.

118 Id. 155-156.

119 Migliore in Gaventa (2006) 128.

120 *De carne Christi,* 17.5, in Gambero (1999) 66.

121 *De virginibus velandis,* 6.1, in Gambero (1999) 68.

122 Pelikan (1996) 15, 20, 39-53, 69, 73, 87, 141-2. George (2003).

123 *Adversus haereses,* 3.22.4, in Jurgens (1970-1979) 1:93.224; cf. Tertullian (d. 250), *De carne Christi* 17.4-5, in Gambero (1999) 67.

124 *Dialogue with Trypho the Jew,* 100, in Gambero (1999) 47.

125 *Adversus haereses,* 3.22.4, in Gambero (1999) 54.

126 Farkasfalvy (2014).

127 We'll cover Mary's virgin birth of our Lord and whether Mary suffered birthing pangs in Chapter 6.

128 Gaventa (1995) 4: "The woman gives birth to a son who is clearly a messianic figure, and then she flees to the wilderness under God's protection. To the extent that the child represents Jesus, the woman may be understood as Mary. Given the highly symbolic nature of this vision, however, even that assertion remains tentative."

129 Macquarrie (1990) 47: "The apocalypse of John portrays the sufferings of the Church under the Roman Empire. The woman described in our quotation above may stand for the Church or for the Virgin Mary or, more likely, for both of them. But I doubt if anything of theological importance is to be learned from an attempt to interpret this obscure symbolism, and I do not intend to become involved in it. We already have enough material derived from more secure sources."

130 Perry (2006) 112-3.

131 Macquarrie (1990) 44.

132 McClain (2004): "Her answer to the angel was a model of submission. 'I am the Lord's servant. May it be to me as you have said' (Luke 1:38). Why was she so ready to submit? Because she understood herself to be God's servant. Maybe the reason we are so prone to resist God is that we see him as our servant . . . [as a] spiritual genie that we hope will magically fulfill our every whim."

133 Pelikan (1996) 81-94. *Handmaid of the Lord* (Luke 1:38,48); the *son of the handmaid* (Ps. 86:16).

134 Perry (2006) 71-3. Abraham (Ps. 105:42), Moses (Neh. 9:14; Mal. 4:4), Joshua (Josh. 24:29; Judg. 2:8), David (Ps. 89:3), Daniel (Dan. 6:20), the Messiah (Ezek. 34:23), Shiphrah and Puah (Exod. 1:15–21), Deborah (Judg. 4–5), Jael (Judg. 5:24–27), and Esther (Esther 2–16); New Testament *doulos* texts (Acts 2:18, 4:29, 16:17; Rom. 1:1, 18; 1 Cor. 7:21–24).

135 Favored or graced (Esther 2:17; Luke 1:28–30), with his Spirit (Joel 2:26–29) and prophecy (Exod. 15:20–21; Acts 2:14–21). God clothed her (Gen. 3:21)

with strength, dignity (Prov. 31:25), and righteousness (Luke 1:5–6). God's handmaid, as Abigail (1 Sam. 25:24), the Messiah's mother (Ps. 86:14–16).

136 Bride (Isa. 54:5–6; Eph. 5:25–26); faithful to Christ (1 Tim. 3:11–13) as to her love (Titus 2:4). Virgin fit for priests (Lev. 21:7, 13–15; Ezek. 44:21–22); obedient wife (1 Pet. 3:1–6); treasure (Prov. 3:13–15; Song of Sol. 4:9–10), and worthy of honor (1 Pet. 3:7).

137 Good mother (Ps. 131:2); fruitful womb (Ps. 127:3); loves (Titus 2:4), nurses her child (Exod. 2:9; 1 Sam. 1:22–5); ready to die for her child (1 Kings 3:16–27). Christ honored (1 Kings 2:19; Esther 2:15–18), refused her nothing (1 Kings 2:20; Esther 5:1–8); obeyed (Luke 2:51), fulfilled commandments (Deut. 5:16); respected, listened to her and her counsels (2 Chron. 22:1–3).

138 Give good things to children (Luke 21:1–4), in teaching (Titus 2:1–5); being charitable and hospitable (Acts 16:11–15), to the poor (Prov. 31:20; 1 Tim. 5:3–10), in their needs (John 2:1–12); accompanying (Rev. 12:17), as Rahab (Josh. 2:1–21).

139 Cf. Matt. 26:6–13; bless other women (Judg. 5:24, etc.) for good works (Prov. 31:31), which shine (Matt. 5:14–16); *all generations* (Luke 1:48).

140 *Homily on Genesis,* 49.2, in Gambero (1999) 176. Cf. Perry (2006) 153-154 and note 24.

141 Sarah waits with faith (Heb. 11:11–12); preserved from violation (Gen. 12:10–20; 20:1–18); mother of believers (Gen. 17:15–16; Rom. 9:6–9; Gal. 4:19–31). Angels appear to Abraham (Gen. 18:1–15), Zachariah (Luke 1:5–24), and Joseph (Matt. 1:18–25).

142 Sweeney (2006) 16-7, 31-2, 39.

143 Conceive miraculously: Rebekah (Gen. 24:3–25:26); Rachel (Gen. 30:1–2, 22–24), associated with Messiah's birthplace (Gen. 35:16–20; 48:7; Matt. 2:13–18).

144 Pope John Paul II (2000) 71.

145 Adam (Rom. 5:12–21; 1 Cor. 15:20–50); Melchizedek (Heb. 5–7); Isaac (Rom. 9:6–9; Gal. 4:22–29; Heb. 11:17–19); Jacob (Rom. 9:10–13).

146 Sweeney (2006) 32, 39.

147 Pelikan (1996) 97, quoting Augustine *Expositions on the Book of Psalms* 67.26; cf. 28.

148 Perry (2006) 290.

149 Id.144-5, quoting Pelikan (1969), 101-2.

150 *On the Song of Songs* 13, in Gambero (1999) 158.

151 *De institutione virginis* 49, in Gambero (1999) 198.

152 Beautiful and graceful (Prov. 5:18–9), precious and pleasant (3:15–7); righteous and just (2:6–10); feeds her children (1:20–33; 9:1–6) with right knowledge, understanding, and prudence, truth and righteousness (2:10–11; 8:6–12); is discreet (2:11) sister and intimate friend (7:4–5).

153 Loves her (Ps. 87:1–6); a tree or fountain of life (Prov. 3:18; 16:22), involved in creation (3:19–20; 8:22–31); a protectrix (2:1–22) of her children (4:6) from sin (7:5); they seek, listen to (1:20–33), and love her (4:6); she crowns them with holiness (4:8–9, 8:17–21, 14:24).

154 Pelikan (1996) 25.

155 Macquarrie (1990) 63.

156 "We are not wrong in believing that long ages before she was conceived in the womb of Anna, Mary was ontologically conceived and sanctified in the divine

purpose, so that could also apply to her the word of the Lord which came to Jeremiah: 'before I formed you in the womb, I knew you and before you were born, I consecrated you' (Jer. 1:5). So the first step in unpacking the idea of an Immaculate Conception is to go back to the original conception in the mind and purpose of the Eternal"—Macquarrie (1990) 65.

157 *Jesus:* son of Nun (Deut. 34:9), of Bethshemesh (1 Sam. 6:14), governor (2 Kings 23:8), high priest (Hag. 1:1; Zech. 6:11), son of Sirach (Sir. 50:27).

158 *General Audience,* May 29, 1996.

159 Justin Martyr, *Dialogue with Trypho,* 62, in *Writings of Saint Justin Martyr,* translated by Thomas B. Falls, D.D., Ph.D. (Washington: Catholic University of America, 1948).

160 *The Trinity,* Stephen McKenna, C.SS.R. (Washington: Catholic University of America, 1963) 6:1; 7:3; 14:1, 12; 15:2–3.

161 *In Hebr. Frag.,* 24,359 cited in Quasten (1962) v. 2, 78.

162 *Oratio* 2.78, in *The Liturgy of the Hours* for Thursday of the Thirtieth Week of Ordinary Time.

163 *Id.* 2.81–82, in *The Liturgy of the Hours* for Tuesday of the Sixth Week of Ordinary Time.

164 Sweeney (2006) 16.

165 Holy mount (Ps. 74:1–7), temple-house (84:1–4), chosen city (Ezra 7:11–16, Ps. 46:4).

166 Sweeney (2006) 38-9: "Mary is also imagined in the New Testament as one who is protected by God and who, in turn, protects God. Just as the cherubim and the cloud were made to protect the ark of the (first) covenant, Mary was the ark of Jesus, the new covenant. She was able to do this only by divine assistance. God said to Moses on Mount Sinai: 'You shall make two cherubim of gold. . . . The cherubim shall spread out their wings above, overshadowing the mercy seat with their wings' (Exod. 25:18, 20). And 'the cloud of the Lord was on the tabernacle by day, and fire was in the cloud by night, before the eyes of all the house of Israel' (40:38). So, too, does the Holy Spirit 'overshadow' Mary. 'The angel said to her, "The Holy Spirit will come upon you, and the power of the Most High will overshadow you; therefore the child to be born will be holy; he will be called Son of God"'" (Luke 1:35).

167 Overshadowed Mary (Luke 1:35), the Ark (Lev. 16:1–2; 1 Kings 8:10–11; CCC 697); the ark: God's resting place (2 Chron. 6:41); the ark of the New Covenant is the Mother of the Redeemer (Rev. 11:19–12:6).

168 Oration "The Lord is my Shepherd," in Theodoret, *Dialogue* 1. This fragment may be interpreted as applying the Ark of the Covenant to Christ's body.

169 "O [ark of the New] Covenant, clothed with purity instead of gold! You are the ark in which is found the golden vessel containing the true manna, that is, the flesh in which divinity resides" (*Homily of the Papyrus of Turin* in Gambero [1999] 106).

170 "The prophet [David] dances before the ark; but what is the ark if not holy Mary? The ark contained the tablets of the testament, Mary held in her body the heir to the testament; the ark carried the Law, Mary the gospel; the ark held the voice of God, Mary the Word; inside and out, the ark shone with gold, the light of Mary's virginity shines inside and out; the ark was decorated with earthly gold, Mary with the gold of heaven" (*Sermons,* 42.5, in *The Navarra Bible* [2002a] 333). Ark traveling to Jerusalem (2 Sam. 6:1–23; 1 Chron. 15:1–24); Mary's journey (Luke 1:39–45,56).

171 *Poems about Others* 7.180-194, in Gambero (1999) 163-164.

172 Temple: of God's special presence (Exod. 15:13–18); a holy (Ezek. 45:1–5) and beautiful bride (Isa. 62:3–5), a glorious throne (Jer. 17:12) and seat of power (Ps. 68:5, 15–18, 24–25, 34–35); where we contemplate (63:1–2), praise (150:1), and pray; where God listens (28:2, 6–7), speaks (60:5–6), and makes promises (108:7); a sign of eternal covenant (Ezek. 37:26–28), support (Ps. 20:2), and emanating waters (Ezek. 47:1–12); must be reverenced (Lev. 19:30; 26:2).

173 McKnight (2007) 36.

174 *De carne Christi* 21.5; PL 2, 833, in Gambero (1999) 71.

175 *Christ and Antichrist* 8 PG 10, 733-36, in Gambero (1999) 90.

176 Contradicted *sign* (Luke 2:34–35) of Jonah (Luke 11:29–30; Matt. 12:38–40), the cross (John 2:18–22; 3:14–15, etc.).

177 Peter Chrysologus (d. 450), *Sermo* 148: PL 52.596

178 Cf. *Homily 67,* cited in Gambero (1999) 314.

179 *On the Birth of Christ* in Gambero (1999) 155.

180 Jerusalem, the *mother in Israel* (2 Sam. 20:16–22) as Deborah (Judg. 5:7). Jeremiah *a fortified city* (Jer. 1:18–19).

181 God dwells in Israel (Exod. 29:45–46); in Jerusalem (Ps. 132:13–17); holy city and mount (48:1–2); foreshadowed in the desert (Deut. 12:5–14); a barren widow conceives many children (Isa. 54:1–6); the heavenly city (Rev. 14:1).

182 Jerusalem: exalted maternity (Isa. 66:6–13; Gal. 4:26), physical radiance (Rev. 21:9–27), and beauty (Ps. 48:1–2); gives joy as God's delight (Isa. 62:4). God loves (Ps. 87:1–6) her faithfulness (Zech. 8:3) and holiness (Joel 3:17); a virgin daughter (Isa. 37:21–25; Jer. 31:1–4) and Christ's virgin bride (Rev. 21:1–3); a mother who teaches all nations (Mic. 4:2), glorious and blessed for all generations (Ps. 48:13).

183 Sweeney (2006) 32, 36-7.

184 George (2003). He goes on to say, "But it is not an easy redemption. In the Old Testament, the Daughter of Zion is depicted as being in the labor of childbirth: "Writhe and groan, O Daughter of Zion, like a woman in travail" (Mic. 4:10). "For I heard a cry as of a woman in travail, anguish as of one bringing forth her first child, the cry of the Daughter of Zion gasping for breath" (Jer. 4:31).

185 *Paedagogus,* 1.6, in Gambero (1999) 71.

186 *Sermo ad noct. Resurr.*, 1.534; *Diatessaron* 12.5; *Hymns on the Crucifixion* 4.17, in Gambero (1999) 115.

187 *Expositio in Lucam* 2.7, 24, in Gambero (1999) 198-199.

188 Sweeney (2006) 24-5.

189 Of Num. 24:17 and Sir. 50:6; in Pelikan (1996) 93-4.

190 Sweeney (2006) 37-8.

191 Sun: Christ (Mal. 4:2; Rev. 1:12–16, 21:23, 22:5); the moon: lesser glory (1 Cor. 15:40–42); clothed with the sun (Rev. 12:1); lights and lamps: John (John 5:35) and Christians (Matt. 5:14–16). So early Christians applied other scriptural texts to Mary, such as "and God made the two great lights, the greater light to rule the day, and the lesser light to rule the night; he made the stars also. . . . God saw that it was good" (Gen. 1:16–18).

192 Harlots (Lev. 19:29); violated (Gen. 34:1–31), discharging blood (Lev. 15:19–33), deceitful (Acts 5:1–11) and idolatrous women (Exod. 34:11–16); drunks (Titus

2:3), immoral (Rev. 2:20), tempt to curse God (Job 2:9–10).

193 Jezebel manipulates power (1 Kings 21:5–16, 23–25), kills God's prophets (1 Kings 18:3–4, 13–19; 19:1–2); refuses God (Rev. 2:21). *Folly* (Prov. 9:13–18; 14:1) and *Wickedness* (Zech. 5:9).

194 Jerusalem: faithless daughter (Jer. 31:21–22), repulsed by husband (Job 19:17), a whore (Jer. 2:1–3, 20–25, 32–33); rebellious (Ezek. 5:1–10), blasphemous (Rev. 17:3), idolatrous (Isa. 10:10–32), defiles sanctuary (Ezek. 5:11; 8:1–18), kills prophets (Matt. 23:37–39); contemptuous (Nah. 3:6), abominations (Rev. 17:4–5), false sister (Jer. 3:1–10, 15–24), and a widow (Lam. 1:1).

195 Virgin Babylon, Chaldea (Ps. 137:4–9; Isa. 47:1–5; Jer. 50:1–46; 51:1–64; Zech. 2:7); Damascaus (Jer. 49:23–27); Edom (49:7–22; Lam. 4:21–22); virgin Egypt (Jer. 46:2–28; Nah. 3:8–9); Gallim (Isa. 10:30); Libya and Put (Nah. 3:8–9); Moab and its cities (Jer. 48:1–47); Nineveh (Nah. 3:1–7); Ophrah (Judg. 8:24–35); Rabbah of the Ammonites (Jer. 49:1–6); Samariah, "Oholah" (Ezek. 16:46–61, 23:2–44); Sidon (Isa. 23:4); Sodom (Ezek. 16:46–61); Tarshish (Isa. 23:10); Tyre, who honors the great mother City, Mary (Ps. 45:12, Isa. 23:15–18, Ezek. 26:1–21).

196 One could easily go into more detail, but we must leave that to the experts. I found the following resources useful in preparing this chapter: Foster (1953) 11a-18f, pp. 13-21; Mark Shea, "Five Myths About Seven Books," and other Jewish, Protestant, and Catholic sources. A recent work edited by McDonald-Sanders (2002) includes several Protestants arguing for the *Septuagint* canon.

197 An example of this is Luke 3:23–38, which gives us the genealogy of Christ that follows 1 Chronicles 1:1–4; 24–28; 2:1–15: Luke mentions Cainan between Arphaxad and Shelah, which concurs with the Septuagint version of 1 Chronicles but not with the Hebrew version.

198 Cf. Irenaeus, *Against Heresies, 3.21.* Wasserstein (2006) also shows how even Jews considered the *Septuagint* translation divinely inspired. The Septuagint canon of the Old Testament included the books of Genesis, Exodus, Leviticus, Numbers, Deuteronomy, Joshua, Judges, Ruth, 1 and 2 Samuel, 1 and 2 Kings, 1 and 2 Chronicles, Ezra, Nehemiah, Tobit, Judith, Esther, Job, Psalms, Proverbs, Qohelet (Ecclesiastes), Song of Songs (Song of Solomon), Wisdom, Sirach (Ecclesiasticus), Isaiah, Jeremiah, Lamentations, Baruch, Ezekiel, Daniel, Hosea, Joel, Amos, Obadiah, Jonah, Micah, Nahum, Habakkuk, Zephaniah, Haggai, Zechariah, Malachi, and 1 and 2 Maccabees.

199 Pelikan (1996) 28-30.

200 Id. 33, 189-200.

201 Id. 33-6, 201-13. Early Christians used Genesis 5:24 and 2 Kings 2:11–12 as scriptural rationale for the tradition that Mary too was taken up.

202 Sweeney (2006) 188-9, quoting Martin Luther, "The Magnificat," 322-23.

203 Id., 158-9.

204 Pelikan (1996) 222.

205 1 Cor. 11:25; Matt. 26:28; Mark 14:24; Luke 22:20. Heb. 9:18–22, 10:19–29, 12:22–24, 13:20–21 point out how the early Christians made this typological connection.

206 Elisha: double spirit (2 Kings 2:9); raises son (4:8–37), feeds crowd (vv. 42–44), heals leprosy (5:1–19). Particular aspects of Elijah's life appear to correspond more to Jesus than to John. For example, Elijah gathers the people of Israel

on Mount Carmel, challenging the priests of Baal; Christ does so on Calvary, challenging the Levitical priests. Elijah's sacrifice is consumed by fire (1 Kings 18:20–40); Christ sacrificed himself completely. Elijah travels through the desert for forty days without food or drink (19:8), and our Lord fasts in the desert for forty days. Elijah ascends into heaven in a fiery chariot (2 Kings 2:11–13); our Lord ascends under his own power (Acts 1:9–11).. These facts link Elijah to Christ, not to John the Baptist.

207 McKnight (2007) 109-10.
208 Justin Martyr (d. 165), *First Apology,* 33, in Jurgens (1970-1979) 1:53.122a.
209 Aristides of Athens (d. 145), *Apology,* 15, in Jurgens (1970-1979) 1:49.112.
210 *The Ascension of Isaiah,* 11 [A.D. 70].
211 *The Odes of Solomon,* 19 [A.D. 80].
212 *Letter to the Smyrnaeans,* 1.1, in Jurgens (1970-1979) 1:24.63; cf. *Letter to the Ephesians* 19.1.
213 Clement of Alexandria, *Stromata* 7.16, paraphrasing Isaiah 66:6–13.
214 *De carne Christi* 23.1-5; *Monogamy* 8.2, in Jurgens (1970-1979) 1:147.359, 158.380.
215 *Discourses Against the Arians* 2.70, in Jurgens (1970-1979) 1:330.767a.
216 *Sermo* 117.3; 148.1, in Gambero (1999) 294-295.
217 The Fifth Ecumenical Council, the Second of Constantinople, A.D. 553, *The Capitula of the Council,* in Denzinger (1957) 86, 87, 89.
218 *On the Mysteries,* 53.
219 Cf. also cf. CCC 497.
220 According to Perry (2006) 159, Ambrose championed this interpretation, later used by Thomas Aquinas (*S.Th.* III.28.2) and Luther ("Lecture on Isaiah" in *Luther's Works* 16:84).
221 *De carne Christi* 19:1–2. A complete exposition of this issue is found in Potterie (1992) 96-122 and Farkasfalvy (2014) 40–42. Protestant Mariologist, Marina Warner (1976) 15-16, also explains the history of this reading in both Catholic and Protestant theologians. Pope John Paul II also mentions this, saying that the truth of Mary's virginal conception, "according to a recent exegetical discovery, would be explicitly contained in verse 13 of the Prologue of John's Gospel, which some ancient authoritative authors (for example, Irenaeus and Tertullian) present, not in the usual plural form, but in the singular: "He, who was born not of blood nor of the will of the flesh nor of the will of man, but of God." This version in the singular would make the Johannine Prologue one of the major attestations of Jesus' virginal conception, placed in the context of the mystery of the Incarnation" (Pope John Paul II [2000] 113).
222 Ambrose, *Commentary on Psalm 37*:5, in Pelikan (1996) 191.
223 Cf. John Calvin, *Commentary on Matthew, Mark, Luke* on Luke 1:34 (http://www.ccel.org/ccel/calvin/calcom31.ix.vii.html#ix.vii-p6.1).
224 Farkasfalvy (2014) 28.
225 *Sermo* 225.2 and 291.5.
226 Pope John Paul II (2000) 123.
227 Jerome in Gambero (1999) 211.
228 See also Wisdom 7:22–24; Eph. 5:25–27; Rev. 14:1–5.
229 Harlotry is antithetical to Mary's virginity, filling the land with wickedness (Lev. 19:29). Called to be a virgin, Jerusalem becomes an idolatrous harlot

(Jer. 18:12–17), moving God to curse her as a widow (Lam. 1:1), forsake her (Jer. 12:7–9), expose her nakedness and shame (Ezek. 16:36–37), letting other nations conquer (Isa. 22:1–4), violate, and enslave her into captivity (Lam. 1:5). God still loves Jerusalem and calls her to be holy, as a virgin daughter (2:13), yet she prefers to be the whore of Babylon (Rev. 17:1–19:3), earning the name *Oholibah—my tabernacle* (or *sanctuary*) *is in her*—instead of the name *Jerusalem— the city of peace* (Ezek. 23:2–48).

Individual women are also antithetical types of Mary, since anyone who loosens "the girdle of a virgin" defiles her, puts her to shame, pollutes her womb and disgraces her (Jth. 9:1–2), as is Dinah (Gen. 34:1–31), whereas the undefiled barren woman who avoids sinful unions will be blessed and fruitful (Wis. 3:13), like Mary.

After sinning, Eve is antithetical to Mary as Adam is antithetical of Christ. Before the Fall, they were naked and had no shame; afterward, both are without this virginal innocence (Gen. 2:25, 3:7–12). *Woman*'s name then changes to *Eve*, "the mother of all the living" (3:20), when Adam and Eve came "to know" each other (4:1).

230 John Paul II (1982) 5.
231 Honors modesty and purity (Isa. 62:5; 1 Tim. 2:15), virginity (1 Cor. 7:32–35) to follow the Lamb (Rev. 14:1–5) and to serve the kingdom (Matt. 19:10–12); God's people: a pure bride (2 Cor. 11:2–3; Eph. 5:25–27).
232 *De virginitate perpetua,* 19, in Gambero (1999) 208.
233 Perry (2006) 162, citing Jerome, *Against Jovinian* 1.32 (*NPNF²* 6:370).
234 Travail in Micah 5:1–4: Jerusalem's destruction (Jer. 6:1–9, 22–26), world's end (Isa. 13:4–8), and its redemption (Isa. 45:9–14), slaughter of the innocents (Matt. 2:16–18), disciples at the crucifixion (Isa. 53:10–11; John 16:20–22; Gal. 4:19); and longing for the Messiah (Romans 8:18–23).
235 Pope John Paul II (2000) 128.
236 Also Matt. 12:46; 13:55–56; Mark 6:3; Luke 8:19–20; John 2:12; 7:3, 10; Acts 1:14; 1 Cor. 9:5.
237 Perry (2006) 27-8.
238 *Homily on Matthew,* 5.2, in Gambero (1999) 178. Earlier, Athanasius of Alexandria (d. 373) argued that Jesus would not have given Mary to John as his mother in John 19:27 had she had other children, *De virginitate*, 42.242-244, in Gambero (1999) 104.
239 Perry (2006) 40.
240 *Homily on Matthew,* 5.3, in Gambero (1999) 177; earlier Basil of Caesarea (d. 379) argued the same, in *On the Holy Generation of Christ,* 5, in Gambero (1999) 146; Jerome (d. 419) concurs, *De virginitate perpetua* 5, in Gambero (1999) 206.
241 Perry (2006) 57n.68.
242 Cf. Jerome (d. 419) *De virginitate perpetua,* 7, in Gambero (1999) 207.
243 Cf. also Col. 1:15; Rom. 8:29.
244 Cf. also John 1:18; 3:16–18; 1 John 4:9.
245 Perry (2006) 82n.71, quoting Nolland, *Luke,* p. 105.
246 *On the Birth of Christ* PG 46.1133D-1136B, in Gambero (1999) 155.
247 *Homilia in Joannem,* 1.1-14, in Gambero (1999) 209; cf. John 20:19.
248 Sweeney (2006) defends this position 18-23, 30.
249 Id. 25-6, 65-7.

250 *Luther's Works* 6:510 and 11:319-320.

251 In Leeming (1967) 9.

252 *Opera*, 1:424.

253 *Letter to the Ephesians*, 18.2, in Jurgens (1970-1979) 1:18.42.

254 *Against Heresies,* 5.19.1, in Jurgen, I:101.256a.

255 Socrates, *History of the Church* 7.32, in Gambero (1999) 73-74.

256 *On Virginity* 3, in Gambero (1999) 101.

257 *Songs of praise,* 1.12, 1.20, in Jurgens (1970-1979) 1:312.711.

258 *Letter 101*PG 37.177C-180A, in Gambero (1999) 162.

259 Cf. Gambero (1999) 193-196.

260 Council of Ephesus, *The Anathemas of the Chapter of Cyril,* in Denzinger (1957) n. 113. Cf. also CCC 466.

261 *Mother of Jesus Christ* (Matt. 1:16,18); *of Jesus* (Acts 1:14; Luke 1:31; John 2:1, 3, 6:42); *his mother* (Matt. 2:11, 13, 14, 20, 21; 12:46; 13:55; Luke 2:33, 48; John 2:5, 12; 19:25–27); *Son of God* (Luke 1:35); *Son of the Most High* (v. 32); *the son of Mary* (Mark 6:3; Luke 2:7,48).

262 Conceived of the Holy Spirit (Matt. 1:20); bore the *Immanuel* (Isa. 7:14; 8:8; Matt. 1:23).

263 God's handmaid (Luke 1:38,48) linked to mothering (Ps. 86:14–16); she loved (Titus 2:4), nursed (Exod. 2:9), and fed him (Sir. 6:19); sacrificed everything (1 Kings 3:16–27), interceding (Mark 7:25–30), for his inheritance (Gen. 27:1–46) and kingship (1 Kings 1:5, 11–31); encouraging him to die (2 Macc. 7:1–41), that God could raise him (Heb. 11:17–19; 1 Kings 17:10–24; Luke 7:11–15).

264 Fulfilled Law (Matt. 5:17–19); way to eternal life (Luke 18:18–20); honored (Exod. 20:12; Deut. 5:16; Eph. 6:1–3), revered (Lev. 19:3), glorified her (Sir. 3:4) spiritual mother (Matt. 12:50) with rights over him (Sir. 3:2).

265 Wise conduct (Prov. 23:24–25), listening (Prov. 1:20–33), to her wise counsels (2 Chron. 22:1–3) and good doctrine (Titus 2:1–5), obeying her voice (Eph. 6:1–3; Luke 2:5).

266 The thought of Jesus ever backtalking, cursing, dishonoring, being unruly, angering or striking his mother is unthinkable (Exod. 21:15–17; Lev. 20:9; Deut. 21:18–21; 27:16; 33:9; Prov. 19:26; 20:20; Sir. 3:16), as is Jesus rejecting his mother's teachings (Prov. 1:8–9), disobeying (Prov. 30:17), or saddening and despising her by foolishness (Prov. 10:1; 15:20; 17:25), as an undisciplined child (Prov. 29:15,17); disgracing (Sir. 3:11), treating her with contempt (Ezek. 22:7); failing to bless her (Prov. 30:11) or stealing from her (Prov. 28:24).

267 *Commentary on John* 1:6, in Gambero (1999) 80.

268 Pope John Paul II (2000) 234.

269 Eve: mother of the living (Gen. 3:20). Mary: *mother of many children* (Ps. 113:5–9; Isa. 54:1); *mother of all Christians* (Rev. 12:17; Isa. 44:1–3, 24–28); *mother in Israel* (Judg. 5:7; Samuel 20:19).

270 Sarah; mother of all nations (Gen. 17:15–16) and of his people (Isa. 51:2–3); according to the promise (Rom. 9:6–9; Gal. 4:19–31). Mount Moriah is Calvary (2 Chron. 3:1).

271 Son of Abraham (Matt. 1:1; Luke 3:34); human form (Phil. 2:5–8); first fruit of the dead (1 Cor. 15:20); fruit of Mary's womb (Luke 1:41); belong to Christ (1 Cor. 15:23), born again of water and the spirit (John 3:1–6).

272 *Wisdom:* mother of all good things (Wis. 7:11–12) and of all (Sir. 40:1); fills us with an abundance (1:16–17); protects us (6:29), shelters us (14:26–27), and gives us rest (6:26–28) to serve God (4:11–15).

273 Rebekah: mother of Jacob (Gen. 25:21–26); of Israel (Gen. 32:28); of a company of nations (Gen. 35:9–12).

274 Mother of children (Isa. 54:1), all nations are of her (Ps. 87:1–6), our mother (Gal. 4:26); of a nation (Isa. 66:8).

275 *Expositio in Lucam* 2.7, in Gambero (1999) 198.

276 Sermo 192.2, in Gambero (1999) 223; *De sancta virginitate*, 2, in Gambero (1999) 224.

277 *Sermo Denis* 25.8, in Gambero (1999) 223.

278 *Id.* 25.7, in Gambero (1999) 222.

279 *De sancta virginitate,* 6, in Gambero (1999) 223.

280 *Of the Lord: House* (such as Josh. 6:24)*; Mountain* (such as Zech. 8:3)*; City* (such as Ps. 101:8). *Of God: House* (Gen. 28:17); *Mountain* (Ezek. 28:14–16), and *City* (Ps. 87:3).

281 Pope John Paul II (2000) 149-50.

282 *Luther's Works* 22:492-493.

283 *Id.* 24:107.

284 *Calvini Opera*, 45:35, in *Corpus Reformatorum* (Braunshweig-Berlin, 1863-1900).

285 *In Evang. Luc.*, 1:639, in *Opera Completa* (Zurich, 1828-42), Volume 6.

286 *On the Holy Spirit* 3.11.80.

287 *Catholic Encyclopedia* (1912) "Pelagius and Pelagianism."

288 *De natura et gratia* 36.42, in Gambero (1999) 226. Jaroslav Pelikan also writes: "This doctrine of original sin was established in Western teaching through the thought of Augustine of Hippo, which in turn made necessary a special treatment of the place of Mary in the schema of sin and salvation," in Pelikan (2006) 191. On this point Pelikan references Gherardini (1992).

289 Cf. Giamberardini, *Culto mariano,* 1:126, n. 192 cited in Gambero (1999) 77.

290 *The Trinity,* 3.4, in Jurgens (1970-1979) 2:162.1073.

291 *Carmina Nisibena* 27.8 in Gambero (1999) 109.

292 *Expositio in Lucam* 2.8, in Gambero (1999) 197.

293 *On Psalm 118* 22.30, in Jurgens (1970-1979) 2:1314.166. Perry (2006) 155-6, gives other Ambrosian citations to support the Immaculate Conception.

294 Gregory of Nazianzus *On the Theophany* 13, cited in Perry (2006) 153, and *Sermon* 38.13, in Gambero (1999) 162-3.

295 *Commentary on the Song of Songs* (trans. Casimir McCambley [brookline: Hellenic College Press, 1987] cited in Perry (2006) 151.

296 Perry (2006) 153, citing Gregory of Nyssa *To Eustathia, Ambrosia, and Basilissa.*

297 Theoteknos of Livias, *Panegyric for the Feast of the Assumption,* 5-6, in Pope John Paul II (2000) 91.

298 *Sermon I on the Dormition of Mary* in Pope John Paul II (2000) 92.

299 Theodotus of Ancyra, *Homily,* 4.3 and 6.11, in Gambero (1999) 267 and 268. Romanos the Melodist, *On the Birth of Mary* 1 and *On the Annunciation* 1.1, in Gambero (1999) 328 and 329. Andrew of Crete, *Great Canon,* ode 4 and 5, in Jurgens (1970-1979) 3:326.2336b; *Homily 1 on Mary's Nativity* in Gambero (1999) 394-5; *Homily 4 on Mary's Nativity* in Gambero (1999) 393. Germain I of Constantinople, *Second Sermon on the Dormition of the Blessed Virgin Mary,*

in Jurgens (1970-1979) 3:327.2336c. John Damascene, *Second Homily on the Dormition of the Blessed Virgin Mary*, in Jurgens (1970-1979) 3:349.2389.

300 Clothed with sun (Rev. 12:1); sharing Christ's glory (Matt. 17:2); pour out Spirit (Joel 2:29; Acts 2:14–21); *handmaid of the Lord* (Luke 1:38, 48).

301 *Sermo* 38.13, in Gambero (1999) 163.

302 Preserve from defilement (Gen. 12:10–20, 20:1–18, 26:7–11).

303 *Dialogue with Trypho the Jew*, 100, quoted on page 35.

304 No shame (Gen. 2:25); reflect God's image and likeness (Gen. 1:26–27, 5:1–2); experiencing shame (Gen. 3:7–12).

305 Pope John Paul II (2000) 94.

306 Overshadowed: Mary (Luke 1:35); Ark (Lev. 16:1–2); Immanuel (Isa. 7:14; 8:8; Matt. 1:23). The Ark contained . . . (Heb. 9:1–5); Mary: God's Word (John 1:14), his bread (John 6:32–35, 48–51), high priest (Heb. 2:17–3:1).

307 Holy: God alone (Rev. 15:4); nothing unclean can enter (Rev. 21:27). Immaculate (Eph. 1:3–4); perfect (Song of Sol. 5:2).

308 Similarly, Romans 3:14 paraphrases Psalm 10:7, where *they* refers to the *wicked* man, *greedy for gain,* who *does not seek* but *curses the Lord.* Such are God's *foes—evildoers, filled with cursing, deceit, and oppression*—who *murder the innocent, seize the poor,* and crush *the hapless,* thinking: "God will never see it." The *they* doesn't include the *poor, afflicted, hapless, fatherless, meek, oppressed,* or he who *commits himself to* God.

Romans 3:15–17 paraphrases Isaiah 59:7–8, where *they* refers to those whose *iniquities* separate them from God, whose *hands are defiled with blood,* whose *lips have spoken lies* and *wickedness,* who *conceive mischief and bring forth iniquity* with *deeds of violence,* whose *feet run to evil,* shedding *innocent blood,* who do not know *the way of peace* or *justice* but who *walk in gloom* along *crooked roads, groping for the wall like the blind . . . who have no eyes, like dead men.*

Romans 3:18 paraphrases Psalm 36:1, where the *they* refers to every *wicked man,* who *fears not God,* who *flatters himself in his own eyes that his iniquity cannot be found out and hated,* with *words of mischief and deceit,* who ceases *to act wisely and do good,* an *evildoer* who *plots mischief* and *spurns not evil. They* does not refer to those who *take refuge in the shadow of God's wings to feast* in God's house, *the upright of heart* who *know God* and *his salvation.*

309 *De natura et gratia* 4.4, in Jurgens (1970-1979) 3:110,1791.

310 Id. 36.42, in Jurgens (1970-1979) 3:111.1794. Cf. 4.4, in Jurgens (1970-1979) 3:110,1791.

311 Cf. also 1 John 3:5.

312 Perry (2006) 297.

313 Newman (1996) 54.

314 *Luther's Works*, 4:694.

315 Deliverance from: barrenness (2 Sam. 1:1–2,6); captivity (Exod. 14:13; Exod. 15:2; Deut. 32:15, etc.); evildoers (Ps. 14:7); enemies (Ps. 3:2,8).

316 Chosen: *at birth* (Ps. 71:6–7; Song of Sol. 8:5–6); *in mothers' wombs* (Ps. 139:1, 13; Isa. 49:1–18); *Jerusalem* (Isa. 44:1–3, 24–28; 46:3–4); *consecrating* in the womb (Jer. 1:5; Sir. 49:7).

317 Jesus: without sin (2 Cor. 5:21) and darkness (1 John 1:5), for he was the light (John 1:4–5), grace, and truth (John 1:14). Mary; clothed with the sun (Rev. 12:1) to shine before men (Matt. 5:14–16) with a lamp that does not go out

(Prov. 31:18).

318 See Macquarrie (1990) 70-71: "What then would be a more definitely personal (and therefore more adequate) way of understanding sin? I think this is to be found in such imagery for sin as 'separation' and 'alienation.'"

319 *Luther's Works* 43:40.

320 Ignatius: *Letter to the Ephesians,* 18.2. Athanasius: *Against the Arians,* 3.29, in Gambero (1999) 102. Ambrose: *De fide,* 3.46, in Gambero (1999) 195. Leo the Great: *Sermo* 22.1, in Gambero (1999) 307.

321 *De Sancta Virginitate,* 6, as mentioned in Pope John Paul II (2000) 185.

322 Gregory Nazianzen, *Sermon* 24.11, in Gambero (1999) 167. Gregory of Tours, *Libri Miraculorum* in Gambero (1999) 354-8.

323 *Homily for the Liberation of Constantinople* 23, in Gambero (1999) 385. Modern Catholic authorities continue this tradition, as Pope Pius X (d. 1914) writes: "Now from this common sharing of will and suffering between Christ and Mary, she 'merited to become most worthily the *Reparatrix* of the lost world and therefore *Dispensatrix* of all the gifts which Jesus gained for us by his death and by his blood. . . . But Mary, as St. Bernard [of Siena (d. 1444)] fittingly remarks, is the 'channel' or, even, the neck, through which the body is joined to the head, and likewise through which the head exerts its power and strength on the body. 'For she is the neck of our Head, by which all spiritual gifts are communicated to His Mystical Body'" (*Ad Diem Illum* 13).

324 Pope John Paul II (2000) 241.

325 Perry (2006) 305: "The distinction between 'created mediation' and 'uncreated mediation'—or at least one like it—made by scholars such as Jaroslav Pelikan is key. Pelikan uses the distinction carefully to circumscribe the mediation offered by Mary and the saints from the singular mediation in salvation provided by the incarnate God. Although obviously related, both in terms of kind and degree they are fundamentally different."

326 Urged to preach (1 Cor. 9:15–18), steward of God (1 Cor. 4:1), Christ's ambassador (2 Cor. 5:18–6:1).

327 Pope John Paul II (2000) 162.

328 Cf. John 2:4, 5:25–29, 7:30, 8:20, 13:1, 16:1–4.

329 Builds up the Church (Prov. 14:1), teaches good doctrine (Titus 2:1–5) and wisdom (Sir. 15:3), instructing Our Lord's disciples to obey him (John 2:5). As a good Christian woman, she relieves the afflicted (1 Tim. 5:3–10), cares for the poor (Prov. 31:20), and frees us from our worries (Wis. 6:15), protectrix (Prov. 2:1–22; Sir. 6:29, etc.), brings to God (Wis. 6:19), delivers, guides and rescues (10:1–21), from sin (Sir. 24:22), prevails over evil (Wis. 7:30).

330 Perry (2006) 248.

331 Pope John Paul II (2000) 183.

332 *On Christmas,* 2.11 and *On the Birth of Mary,* 10, in Gambero (1999) 327 and 329 respectively.

333 *Adversus haereses,* 3.22.

334 Perry (2006) 132-3.

335 *On Christmas* 4, in Gambero (1999) 170.

336 *Homily* 8, in Gambero (1999) 253; *Homily* 1.3, in Gambero (1999) 254; *Homily* 1.2, in Gambero (1999) 254; *Homily 3 on the Incarnation,* in Gambero (1999) 258.

337 *Homily* 11, in Gambero (1999) 170.

338 *Elegia* 5-8; *Carmen* 4.265-269, in Gambero (1999) 285.

339 Apostolic Letter, *Inter Sodalicia,* 1918.

340 Pope John Paul II (2000) 186.

341 Mary: at the cross: (John 19:25–27); rather die for her child (1 Kings 3:16–27); encourages martyrdom (2 Macc. 7:1–41).

342 Christ, the first fruit of her womb (Luke 1:42; Rom. 7:4); true manna (John 6:48–51); live forever (John 6:58)

343 Killing prophets (1 Kings 17:4,13), attempting to kill Elijah (19:1–3), killing Naboth (21:1–25); put on sackcloth (vv. 27-28). God curses Jezebel (v. 23; 2 Kings 9:6–10) and fulfilled his curse (2 Kings 9:30–37).

344 Cf. Gesenius (1922) 107. In Genesis 3:20, *hw'* refers to Eve: "The man called his wife's name Eve, because *she* was the mother of all living."

345 *Adversus haereses,* 5.19.1-20.2, in *The Liturgy of the Hours* for Friday of the 2nd week of Advent.

346 *Diatessaron* 10.13, in Gambero (1999) 117.

347 Head and hands cut off (1 Sam. 5:1–5); return Ark (1 Sam. 5:11–12); bringing glory (1 Sam. 6:5); moving to repent (1 Sam. 7:3–6).

348 *Enarrationes in Psalmos* 103.6, quoted in Farkasfalvy (2014) 280.

349 Sacrificing son (Gen. 22:1–19); great faith and faithfulness (Sir. 44:19–21), that is a model for us all (James 2:18–24).

350 Bans human sacrifice (Exod. 23:7); idolatry (Lev. 18:21; 20:1–5; Deut. 12:29–31; 18:9–10; 2 Kings 3:26–27; 16:1–4; Mic. 6:7).

351 Pope John Paul II (2000) 77.

352 Cf. Bullinger (1911) 328-30 and *Easton's Bible Dictionary* (1897).

353 Perry (2006) 239-40.

354 Epiphanius, *Panárion* 78.11, in Gambero (1999) 126. Gregory of Tours, *Libri Miraculorum,* 1, *De gloria deatorum martyrum 4;* in Gambero (1999) 353. Germain, *Homilies 1-3 on the Dormition,* in Gambero (1999) 383-387.Andrew of Crete, *Homilies 1-4 on the Dormition,* in Gambero (1999) 395-397. John Damascene, *Homilies 1-3 on the Dormition,* in Gambero (1999) 403-409. More on Mary's Assumption in the Fathers of the Church can be found in Healy (1982).

355 Cf. Sheen (1996) 130-141 and Dickson (1996) 55-59.

356 Cf. Matt. 28:1–8; Mark 16:1–8; Luke 24:1–9, 23–24; John 20:1–18.

357 *In Assumptionem,* 2, in *On holy images, followed by three sermons on the Assumption.* Trans. Mary H. Allies (London: Thomas Baker, 1898).

358 Transfiguration (Matt. 17:1–4). Elijah: John the Baptist (Mal. 4:5; Matt. 11:12–15; Luke 1:17, etc.); pleas for people (Rom. 11:1–4); prayer of righteous man (James 5:16–17).

359 Hannah (1 Sam. 1:10–21), Sarah (Tob. 3:11–15, 8:4–8, 12:11–21), Judith (Jth. 8:8, 31; 9:1–10:4; 12:5–8; 13:3–10), Esther (Esther 14:1–15:1), and Anna (Luke 2:36–37).

360 Moses: sanctified through faith (Heb. 11:23–29); fidelity (3:1–6); beautiful to God (Acts 7:20); glistening face (Exod. 34:1–2, 29–35, 2 Cor. 3:7–13).

361 Zion: God's dwelling (Ps. 132:13–17); beautiful (48:1–2) as blessed women (Gen. 12:11, etc.). Mary: woman of faith (Luke 1:41–45); faithful (1 Tim. 3:11–13); graced (Luke 1:28,30); name forever blessed (v. 48).

362 McKnight (2007) 133.

363 *Luther's Works* 10:268.

364 Cf. also Rom. 2:1–5:1; 1 Cor. 7:18–19; Gal. 2:1–21, 5:1–14, 6:12–15; Phil. 3:2–11.

365 Noah (Gen. 6:1–9:29; Matt. 24:37–39); Isaac's sacrifice (Gen. 22:1–19; Heb. 11:17–19; James 2:21); Joseph (Gen. 37:1–36; Acts 7:9–16); Jonah (Jon. 1:1–2:10; Matt. 12:38–42).

366 Dickson (1996) 21.

367 God's elect (1 Tim. 5:21), glorious (Ezek. 10:4), higher than humans (Heb. 2:7), blameless (1 Sam. 29:9), celibate (Matt. 22:23–33), wise (2 Sam. 14:20), don't fear of death (Luke 20:36), enthrone (2 Sam. 6:2), bless his name (Ps. 103:20), contemplate his face (1 Pet. 1:12), serve (1 Pet. 3:22), worship Christ (Rev. 5:8–14).

368 Angels accompany us (Ps. 34:7), comfort (Gen. 16:1–13), and lift up (2 Sam. 19:24–31).

369 Mediators (Job 33:23–28), intercede (Acts 5:17–21), between heaven and earth (Gen. 28:10–16), offering the saints' prayers (Rev. 8:3–5).

370 Zechariah and Mary responded to angels (Luke 1:26–38); Abraham (Heb. 13:2) and Moses (Exod. 3:1–6) did too.

371 Fight Satan (Rev. 12:7–8), good and evil (2 Sam. 14:17), executing justice (2 Sam. 24:15–17), protect (Ps. 91:11–12), rescue (Acts 12:1–17), watch over (1 Cor. 4:9), and redeem from evil (Ps. 35:4–6; Isa. 63:9). We pray (Judg. 6:11–24) and obey them (Matt. 2:13–22) as Christ (Gal. 4:12–14).

372 The Spirit *sanctifies* us (2 Thess. 2:13) at baptism (1 Cor. 6:9–11; Eph. 5:25–27) in Christ's blood (Heb. 13:12); fully (1 Thess. 5:23) after yielding to righteousness (Rom. 6:19), abstaining from unchastity (1 Thess. 4:2–7) and sin (1 Cor. 6:9–11), being holy and blameless (Eph. 1:3–4)

373 Elders offer prayers to God (Rev. 5:8–10; 8:3–5); martyrs plead for Church (Rev. 6:9–11).

374 *Sermo* 24.11, in Gambero (1999), 167.

375 *Ottoeco,* 14.18, in Gambero (1999), 315.

376 Bowing to angels (Num. 22:31); making images of them (1 Kings 6:23–36; Heb. 9:1–5).

377 Evarestus, "*The Martyrdom of Polycarp*," 17-18, in Stanmforth (1968) 130-131.

378 Christian saints greater (Matt. 11:11); imitating what is good (3 John 11) in them (2 Thess. 3:7–8; Heb. 13:7).

379 George (2003).

380 Luke 1:42–49. Cf. also CCC 2675, 2682, and 2097.

381 In Eve (Gen. 2:18–25; 3:20), Sarah (Heb. 11:11–12; 1 Pet. 3:1–6), Rebecca (Rom. 9:10–16), Rahab (Heb. 11:31; James 2:25), Judith (Jth. 13:15–20).

382 *De virginibus,* 2.7, in Gambero (1999) 191.

383 *Hymns on the Nativity* in Gambero (1999) 118-119.

384 Cf. *Adversus haereses,* 78.21, in Gambero (1999) 127.

385 Cf. id. 79.4, in Gambero (1999) 127.

386 Thessalonians, Paul's crown (1 Thess. 2:19–20); twelve apostles surround Mary (Acts 1:14), her crown (Rev. 12:1); queen-mother of God's people (Rev. 12:17); in heavenly kingdom (John 18:36); Christ's bride and queen (Song of Sol. 7:1).

387 Sent to us (Rev. 1:1) appearing (Judg. 2:1–5; Matt. 28:1–8), in dreams (Matt. 1:18–25), proclaim gospel (Rev. 14:6–7), prophesy (Zech. 1:7–21), exhort (Zech. 3:6–9), reveal Scripture (Acts 7:20–53; Heb. 2:1–3, etc.), miracles (Dan.

6:19–22), to do God's will (Rev. 7:1–2).

388 Moses and Elijah (Matt. 17:1–4), Jer. (2 Macc. 15:12–16).

389 Pelikan (1996) 30-33, 177-87. Sweeney (2006) 97-113 also mentions Marian apparitions, but does not connect them with Christian reflections on Scripture, as Pelikan does, but focuses on how *strange* such apparitions seem to a Protestant.

390 Cf. Gambero (1999) 354-358.

391 Quoting Origen, *Contra Celsum* 2.40.

392 Roberts (2005) part 6.

393 *Luther's Works* 29:655-656.

394 *The Mission of the Redeemer,* 50.

395 Perry (2006) 15-16.

396 Macquarrie (1990) 101.

397 Byassee (2004).

398 Cyril, *Homily delivered at the Council of Ephesus.*

399 Norris (2002) xii, quoting Nancy Mairs.

400 Dickson (1996) 23. Cf. also his description of evangelizing "fatherless" innercity youth, on page 80; Pelikan (1996) 3,219, quoting Walpole (1901) 835.

401 Macquarrie (1990) 8. He repeats this idea on page 124.

402 John Paul II (1995) 10.

403 John Paul II (1987) 4.

404 *Id.* 29.

405 Also Matt. 23:12; Luke 10:15, 14:11, 16:15, 18:14; Phil. 2:8–9; James 1:9–10, 4:10; 1 Pet. 5:5–6.

406 Pelikan (1996) 221 quoting Augustine *Expositions on the Book of Psalms* XCII.3.

407 Justin Martyr, *Dialogue with Trypho.*

408 Farkasfalvy (2014) 106, 155.